Haskell 98 Language and Libraries

The Revised Report

edited by
Simon Peyton Jones

CAMBRIDGE
UNIVERSITY PRESS

Published by the Press Syndicate of the University of Cambridge
The Pitt Building, Trumpington Street, Cambridge CB2 1RP
40 West 20th Street, New York, NY 10011-4211, USA
10 Stamford Road, Oakleigh, Melbourne 3166, Australia

© Simon Peyton Jones 2003

First published 2003

Printed in Great Britain at the University Press, Cambridge

Library of Congress cataloguing in publication data available

A catalogue record for this book is available from the British Library

ISBN 0-521 826144 hardback
ISSN 0956-7968

Copyright Notice

A special issue of the *Journal of Functional Programming*

Contents

Preface

"Some half dozen persons have written technically on combinatory logic, and most of these, including ourselves, have published something erroneous. Since some of our fellow sinners are among the most careful and competent logicians on the contemporary scene, we regard this as evidence that the subject is refractory. Thus fullness of exposition is necessary for accuracy; and excessive condensation would be false economy here, even more than it is ordinarily."

Haskell B. Curry and Robert Feys
in the Preface to *Combinatory Logic* [4], May 31 1956

In September of 1987 a meeting was held at the conference on Functional Programming Languages and Computer Architecture (FPCA '87) in Portland, Oregon, to discuss an unfortunate situation in the functional programming community: there had come into being more than a dozen non-strict, purely functional programming languages, all similar in expressive power and semantic underpinnings. There was a strong consensus at this meeting that more widespread use of this class of functional languages was being hampered by the lack of a common language. It was decided that a committee should be formed to design such a language, providing faster communication of new ideas, a stable foundation for real applications development, and a vehicle through which others would be encouraged to use functional languages. This book describes the result of that committee's efforts: a purely functional programming language called Haskell, named after the logician Haskell B. Curry whose work provides the logical basis for much of ours.

Goals

The committee's primary goal was to design a language that satisfied these constraints:

1. It should be suitable for teaching, research, and applications, including building large systems.

2. It should be completely described via the publication of a formal syntax and semantics.

3. It should be freely available. Anyone should be permitted to implement the language and distribute it to whomever they please.

4. It should be based on ideas that enjoy a wide consensus.

5. It should reduce unnecessary diversity in functional programming languages.

Haskell 98: language and libraries

The committee intended that Haskell would serve as a basis for future research in language design, and hoped that extensions or variants of the language would appear, incorporating experimental features. Haskell has indeed evolved continuously since its original publication. By the middle of 1997, there had been four iterations of the language design (the latest at that point being Haskell 1.4). At the 1997 Haskell Workshop in Amsterdam, it was decided that a stable variant of Haskell was needed; this stable language is the subject of this book, and is called _Haskell 98_.

Haskell 98 was conceived as a relatively minor tidy-up of Haskell 1.4, making some simplifications, and removing some pitfalls for the unwary. It is intended to be a "stable" language in sense the _implementors are committed to supporting Haskell 98 exactly as specified, for the foreseeable future_.

The original Haskell Report covered only the language, together with a standard library called the `Prelude`. By the time Haskell 98 was stabilised, it had become clear that many programs need access to a larger set of library functions (notably concerning input/output and simple interaction with the operating system). If these program were to be portable, a set of libraries would have to be standardised too. A separate effort was therefore begun by a distinct (but overlapping) committee to fix the Haskell 98 Libraries.

The Haskell 98 Language and Library Reports were published in February 1999.

Revising the Haskell 98 Reports

After a year or two, many typographical errors and infelicities had been spotted. I took on the role of gathering and acting on these corrections, with the following goals:

- Correct typographical errors.

- Clarify obscure passages.

- Resolve ambiguities.

- With reluctance, make small changes to make the overall language more consistent.

This task turned out to be much, much larger than I had anticipated. As Haskell becomes more widely used, the Report has been scrutinised by more and more people, and I have adopted hundreds of (mostly small) changes as a result of their feedback. The original committees ceased to exist when the original Haskell 98 Reports were published, so every change was instead proposed to the entire Haskell mailing list.

This book is the outcome of this process of refinement. It includes both the Haskell 98 Language Report and the Libraries Report, and constitutes the official specification of both. It is *not* a tutorial on programming in Haskell such as the "Gentle Introduction" [9], and some familiarity with functional languages is assumed.

The entire text of both Reports is available online (see 'Haskell Resources' on p. x).

Extensions to Haskell 98

Haskell continues to evolve, going well beyond Haskell 98. For example, at the time of writing there are Haskell implementations that support:

- **Syntactic sugar**, including:
    - pattern guards;
    - recursive do-notation;
    - lexically scoped type variables;
    - meta-programming facilities;

- **Type system innovations**, including:
    - multi-parameter type classes;
    - functional dependencies;
    - existential types;
    - local universal polymorphism and arbitrary rank-types;

- **Control extensions**, including:
    - monadic state;
    - exceptions;

— concurrency.

There is more besides. Haskell 98 does not impede these developments. Instead, it provides a stable point of reference, so that those who wish to write text books, or use Haskell for teaching, can do so in the knowledge that Haskell 98 will continue to exist.

Haskell Resources

The Haskell web site

```
http://haskell.org
```

gives access to many useful resources, including:

- Online versions of the language and library definitions, including a complete list of all the differences between Haskell 98 as published in February 1999 and this revised version.

- Tutorial material on Haskell.

- Details of the Haskell mailing list.

- Implementations of Haskell.

- Contributed Haskell tools and libraries.

- Applications of Haskell.

We welcome your comments, suggestions, and criticisms on the language or its presentation in the report, via the Haskell mailing list.

Building the language

Haskell was created, and continues to be sustained, by an active community of researchers and application programmers. Those who served on the Language and Library committees, in particular, devoted a huge amount of time and energy to the language. Here they are, with their affiliation(s).

Arvind (MIT)
Lennart Augustsson (Chalmers University)
Dave Barton (Mitre Corp)
Brian Boutel (Victoria University of Wellington)
Warren Burton (Simon Fraser University)
Jon Fairbairn (University of Cambridge)
Joseph Fasel (Los Alamos National Laboratory)
Andy Gordon (University of Cambridge)

Maria Guzman (Yale University)
Kevin Hammond (Uniiversity of Glasgow)
Ralf Hinze University of Bonn)
Paul Hudak [editor] (Yale University)
John Hughes [editor] (University of Glasgow; Chalmers University)
Thomas Johnsson (Chalmers University)
Mark Jones (Nottingham University)
Dick Kieburtz (Oregon Graduate Institute)
John Launchbury (University of Glasgow; Oregon Graduate Institute)
Erik Meijer (Utrecht University)
Rishiyur Nikhil (MIT)
John Peterson (Yale University)
Simon Peyton Jones [editor] (University of Glasgow; Microsoft Research Ltd)
Mike Reeve (Imperial College)
Alastair Reid (University of Glasgow)
Colin Runciman (University of York)
Philip Wadler [editor] (University of Glasgow)
David Wise (Indiana University)
Jonathan Young (Yale University)

Those marked [editor] served as the co-ordinating editor for one or more revisions of the language.

In addition, dozens of other people made helpful contributions, some small but many substantial. They are as follows: Kris Aerts, Hans Aberg, Sten Anderson, Richard Bird, Stephen Blott, Tom Blenko, Duke Briscoe, Paul Callaghan, Magnus Carlsson, Mark Carroll, Manuel Chakravarty, Franklin Chen, Olaf Chitil, Chris Clack, Guy Cousineau, Tony Davie, Craig Dickson, Chris Dornan, Laura Dutton, Chris Fasel, Pat Fasel, Sigbjorn Finne, Michael Fryers, Andy Gill, Mike Gunter, Cordy Hall, Mark Hall, Thomas Hallgren, Matt Harden, Klemens Hemm, Fergus Henderson, Dean Herington, Ralf Hinze, Bob Hiromoto, Nic Holt, Ian Holyer, Randy Hudson, Alexander Jacobson, Patrick Jansson, Robert Jeschofnik, Orjan Johansen, Simon B. Jones, Stef Joosten, Mike Joy, Stefan Kahrs, Antti-Juhani Kaijanaho, Jerzy Karczmarczuk, Wolfram Karl, Kent Karlsson, Richard Kelsey, Siau-Cheng Khoo, Amir Kishon, Feliks Kluzniak, Jan Kort, Marcin Kowalczyk, Jose Labra, Jeff Lewis, Mark Lillibridge, Bjorn Lisper, Sandra Loosemore, Pablo Lopez, Olaf Lubeck, Ian Lynagh, Christian Maeder, Ketil Malde, Simon Marlow, Michael Marte, Jim Mattson, John Meacham, Sergey Mechveliani, Erik Meijer, Gary Memovich, Randy Michelsen, Rick Mohr, Andy Moran, Graeme Moss, Arthur Norman, Nick North, Chris Okasaki, Bjarte M. Østvold, Paul Otto, Sven Panne, Dave Parrott, Ross Patterson, Larne Pekowsky, Rinus Plasmeijer, Ian Poole, Stephen Price, John Robson, Andreas Rossberg, George Russell, Patrick Sansom, Felix Schroeter, Julian Seward, Nimish Shah, Christian Sievers, Libor Skarvada, Jan Skibinski, Lauren Smith, Raman Sundaresh, Ken Takusagawa, Satish Thatte, Simon Thompson, Tom Thomson, Tommy Thorn, Dylan Thurston, Mike Thyer, Mark Tullsen, David Tweed, Pradeep Varma, Malcolm Wallace, Keith Wansbrough, Tony Warnock, Michael Webber, Carl Witty, Stuart Wray, and Bonnie Yantis.

Finally, aside from the important foundational work laid by Church, Rosser, Curry, and others on the lambda calculus, we wish to acknowledge the influence of many noteworthy programming languages developed over the years. Although it is difficult to pinpoint the origin of many ideas, we particularly wish to acknowledge the influence of Lisp (and its modern-day incarnations Common Lisp and Scheme); Landin's ISWIM; APL; Backus's FP [1]; ML and Standard ML; Hope and Hope$^+$; Clean; Id; Gofer; Sisal; and Turner's series of languages culminating in Miranda.[1] Without these forerunners Haskell would not have been possible.

Simon Peyton Jones
Cambridge, November 2002

---

[1]Miranda is a trademark of Research Software Ltd.

Part I

The Haskell 98 Language

JFP **13** (1): i–xii, 1–6, January 2003. © 2003 Cambridge University Press
DOI: 10.1017/S0956796803000315   Printed in the United Kingdom

Chapter 1

Introduction

Haskell is a general purpose, purely functional programming language incorporating many recent innovations in programming language design. Haskell provides higher-order functions, non-strict semantics, static polymorphic typing, user-defined algebraic datatypes, pattern-matching, list comprehensions, a module system, a monadic I/O system, and a rich set of primitive datatypes, including lists, arrays, arbitrary and fixed precision integers, and floating-point numbers. Haskell is both the culmination and solidification of many years of research on non-strict functional languages.

This book defines the syntax for Haskell programs and an informal abstract semantics for the meaning of such programs. We leave as implementation dependent the ways in which Haskell programs are to be manipulated, interpreted, compiled, etc. This includes such issues as the nature of programming environments and the error messages returned for undefined programs (i.e. programs that formally evaluate to ⊥).

1.1   Program Structure

In this section, we describe the abstract syntactic and semantic structure of Haskell, as well as how it relates to the organization of the rest of the report.

1. At the topmost level a Haskell program is a set of *modules*, described in Chapter 5. Modules provide a way to control namespaces and to re-use software in large programs.

2. The top level of a module consists of a collection of *declarations*, of which there are several kinds, all described in Chapter 4. Declarations define things such as ordinary values, datatypes, type classes, and fixity information.

3

3. At the next lower level are *expressions*, described in Chapter 3. An expression denotes a *value* and has a *static type*; expressions are at the heart of Haskell programming "in the small."

4. At the bottom level is Haskell's *lexical structure*, defined in Chapter 2. The lexical structure captures the concrete representation of Haskell programs in text files.

This book proceeds bottom-up with respect to Haskell's syntactic structure.

The chapters not mentioned above are Chapter 6, which describes the standard built-in datatypes and classes in Haskell, and Chapter 7, which discusses the I/O facility in Haskell (i.e. how Haskell programs communicate with the outside world). Also, there are several chapters describing the Prelude, the concrete syntax, literate programming, the specification of derived instances, and pragmas supported by most Haskell compilers.

Examples of Haskell program fragments in running text are given in typewriter font:

```
let x = 1
    z = x+y
in  z+1
```

"Holes" in program fragments representing arbitrary pieces of Haskell code are written in italics, as in if e_1 then e_2 else e_3. Generally, the italicized names are mnemonic, such as e for expressions, d for declarations, t for types, etc.

1.2   The Haskell Kernel

Haskell has adopted many of the convenient syntactic structures that have become popular in functional programming. In this Report, the meaning of such syntactic sugar is given by translation into simpler constructs. If these translations are applied exhaustively, the result is a program written in a small subset of Haskell that we call the Haskell *kernel*.

Although the kernel is not formally specified, it is essentially a slightly sugared variant of the lambda calculus with a straightforward denotational semantics. The translation of each syntactic structure into the kernel is given as the syntax is introduced. This modular design facilitates reasoning about Haskell programs and provides useful guidelines for implementors of the language.

1.3   Values and Types

An expression evaluates to a *value* and has a static *type*. Values and types are not mixed in Haskell. However, the type system allows user-defined datatypes of various sorts, and permits not only parametric polymorphism (using a traditional Hindley-Milner type structure) but also *ad hoc* polymorphism, or *overloading* (using *type classes*).

Errors in Haskell are semantically equivalent to $\perp$. Technically, they are not distinguishable from nontermination, so the language includes no mechanism for detecting or acting upon errors. However, implementations will probably try to provide useful information about errors (see Section 3.1).

1.4 Namespaces

There are six kinds of names in Haskell: those for *variables* and *constructors* denote values; those for *type variables*, *type constructors*, and *type classes* refer to entities related to the type system; and *module names* refer to modules. There are two constraints on naming:

1. Names for variables and type variables are identifiers beginning with lowercase letters or underscore; the other four kinds of names are identifiers beginning with uppercase letters.

2. An identifier must not be used as the name of a type constructor and a class in the same scope.

These are the only constraints; for example, `Int` may simultaneously be the name of a module, class, and constructor within a single scope.

JFP **13** (1): 7–16, January 2003. © 2003 Cambridge University Press
DOI: 10.1017/S0956796803000418 Printed in the United Kingdom

Chapter 2

Lexical Structure

In this chapter, we describe the low-level lexical structure of Haskell. Most of the details may be skipped in a first reading.

2.1 Notational Conventions

These notational conventions are used for presenting syntax:

$[pattern]$	optional
$\{pattern\}$	zero or more repetitions
$(pattern)$	grouping
$pat_1 \mid pat_2$	choice
$pat_{\langle pat' \rangle}$	difference – elements generated by pat except those generated by pat'
`fibonacci`	terminal syntax in typewriter font

Because the syntax in this section describes *lexical* syntax, all whitespace is expressed explicitly; there is no implicit space between juxtaposed symbols. BNF-like syntax is used throughout, with productions having the form:

$$nonterm \quad \rightarrow \quad alt_1 \mid alt_2 \mid \ldots \mid alt_n$$

Care must be taken in distinguishing metalogical syntax such as | and [. . .] from concrete terminal syntax (given in typewriter font) such as | and [...], although usually the context makes the distinction clear.

Haskell uses the Unicode [15] character set. However, source programs are currently biased toward the ASCII character set used in earlier versions of Haskell.

This syntax depends upon properties of the Unicode characters as defined by the Unicode consortium. Haskell compilers are expected to make use of new versions of Unicode as they are made available.

2.2   Lexical Program Structure

$$
\begin{array}{rcl}
program & \rightarrow & \{\ lexeme\ |\ whitespace\ \} \\
lexeme & \rightarrow & qvarid\ |\ qconid\ |\ qvarsym\ |\ qconsym \\
 & | & literal\ |\ special\ |\ reservedop\ |\ reservedid \\
literal & \rightarrow & integer\ |\ float\ |\ char\ |\ string \\
special & \rightarrow & \texttt{(}\ |\ \texttt{)}\ |\ \texttt{,}\ |\ \texttt{;}\ |\ \texttt{[}\ |\ \texttt{]}\ |\ \texttt{`}\ |\ \texttt{\{}\ |\ \texttt{\}} \\
\\
whitespace & \rightarrow & whitestuff\ \{whitestuff\} \\
whitestuff & \rightarrow & whitechar\ |\ comment\ |\ ncomment \\
whitechar & \rightarrow & newline\ |\ vertab\ |\ space\ |\ tab\ |\ uniWhite \\
newline & \rightarrow & return\ linefeed\ |\ return\ |\ linefeed\ |\ formfeed \\
return & \rightarrow & \text{a carriage return} \\
linefeed & \rightarrow & \text{a line feed} \\
vertab & \rightarrow & \text{a vertical tab} \\
formfeed & \rightarrow & \text{a form feed} \\
space & \rightarrow & \text{a space} \\
tab & \rightarrow & \text{a horizontal tab} \\
uniWhite & \rightarrow & \text{any Unicode character defined as whitespace} \\
\\
comment & \rightarrow & dashes\ [\ any_{\langle symbol\rangle}\ \{any\}\ ]\ newline \\
dashes & \rightarrow & \texttt{--}\ \{\texttt{-}\} \\
opencom & \rightarrow & \texttt{\{-} \\
closecom & \rightarrow & \texttt{-\}} \\
ncomment & \rightarrow & opencom\ ANYseq\ \{ncomment\ ANYseq\}\ closecom \\
ANYseq & \rightarrow & \{ANY\}_{\langle\{ANY\}\ (\ opencom\ |\ closecom\ )\ \{ANY\}\rangle} \\
ANY & \rightarrow & graphic\ |\ whitechar \\
any & \rightarrow & graphic\ |\ space\ |\ tab \\
graphic & \rightarrow & small\ |\ large\ |\ symbol\ |\ digit\ |\ special\ |\ \texttt{:}\ |\ \texttt{"}\ |\ \texttt{'} \\
\\
small & \rightarrow & ascSmall\ |\ uniSmall\ |\ \_ \\
ascSmall & \rightarrow & \texttt{a}\ |\ \texttt{b}\ |\ \ldots\ |\ \texttt{z}
\end{array}
$$

uniSmall	$\rightarrow$	any Unicode lowercase letter

large	$\rightarrow$	*ascLarge* | *uniLarge*
ascLarge	$\rightarrow$	A | B | ... | Z
uniLarge	$\rightarrow$	any uppercase or titlecase Unicode letter
symbol	$\rightarrow$	*ascSymbol* | *uniSymbol*⟨*special* | _ | : | " | '⟩

ascSymbol	$\rightarrow$	! | # | $ | % | & | * | + | . | / | < | = | > | ? | @
	|	\ | ^ | | | - | ~
uniSymbol	$\rightarrow$	any Unicode symbol or punctuation
digit	$\rightarrow$	*ascDigit* | *uniDigit*
ascDigit	$\rightarrow$	0 | 1 | ... | 9
uniDigit	$\rightarrow$	any Unicode decimal digit
octit	$\rightarrow$	0 | 1 | ... | 7
hexit	$\rightarrow$	*digit* | A | ... | F | a | ... | f

Lexical analysis should use the "maximal munch" rule: at each point, the longest possible lexeme satisfying the *lexeme* production is read. So, although case is a reserved word, cases is not. Similarly, although = is reserved, == and ~= are not.

Any kind of *whitespace* is also a proper delimiter for lexemes.

Characters not in the category *ANY* are not valid in Haskell programs and should result in a lexing error.

2.3 Comments

Comments are valid whitespace.

An ordinary comment begins with a sequence of two or more consecutive dashes (e.g. --) and extends to the following newline. *The sequence of dashes must not form part of a legal lexeme.* For example, "-->" or "|--" do *not* begin a comment, because both of these are legal lexemes; however "--foo" does start a comment.

A nested comment begins with "{-" and ends with "-}". No legal lexeme starts with "{-"; hence, for example, "{---" starts a nested comment despite the trailing dashes.

The comment itself is not lexically analysed. Instead, the first unmatched occurrence of the string "-}" terminates the nested comment. Nested comments may be nested to any depth: any occurrence of the string "{-" within the nested comment starts a new nested comment, terminated by "-}". Within a nested comment, each "{-" is matched by a corresponding occurrence of "-}".

In an ordinary comment, the character sequences "{-" and "-}" have no special significance, and, in a nested comment, a sequence of dashes has no special significance.

Nested comments are also used for compiler pragmas, as explained in Chapter 11.

If some code is commented out using a nested comment, then any occurrence of {- or -} within a string or within an end-of-line comment in that code will interfere with the nested comments.

2.4   Identifiers and Operators

$$
\begin{array}{lcl}
varid & \to & (small \ \{small \mid large \mid digit \mid \text{'} \ \})_{\langle reservedid \rangle} \\
conid & \to & large \ \{small \mid large \mid digit \mid \text{'} \ \} \\
reservedid & \to & \texttt{case} \mid \texttt{class} \mid \texttt{data} \mid \texttt{default} \mid \texttt{deriving} \mid \texttt{do} \mid \texttt{else} \\
& \mid & \texttt{if} \mid \texttt{import} \mid \texttt{in} \mid \texttt{infix} \mid \texttt{infixl} \mid \texttt{infixr} \mid \texttt{instance} \\
& \mid & \texttt{let} \mid \texttt{module} \mid \texttt{newtype} \mid \texttt{of} \mid \texttt{then} \mid \texttt{type} \mid \texttt{where} \mid \_
\end{array}
$$

An identifier consists of a letter followed by zero or more letters, digits, underscores, and single quotes. Identifiers are lexically distinguished into two namespaces (Section 1.4): those that begin with a lower-case letter (variable identifiers) and those that begin with an upper-case letter (constructor identifiers). Identifiers are case sensitive: `name`, `naMe`, and `Name` are three distinct identifiers (the first two are variable identifiers, the last is a constructor identifier).

Underscore, "_", is treated as a lower-case letter, and can occur wherever a lower-case letter can. However, "_" all by itself is a reserved identifier, used as wild card in patterns. Compilers that offer warnings for unused identifiers are encouraged to suppress such warnings for identifiers beginning with underscore. This allows programmers to use "_foo" for a parameter that they expect to be unused.

$$
\begin{array}{lcl}
varsym & \to & (\ symbol \ \{symbol \mid : \} \ )_{\langle reservedop \mid dashes \rangle} \\
consym & \to & (: \ \{symbol \mid : \})_{\langle reservedop \rangle} \\
reservedop & \to & \texttt{..} \mid : \mid :: \mid = \mid \backslash \mid \mid \mid \texttt{<-} \mid \texttt{->} \mid @ \mid \text{\textasciitilde} \mid \texttt{=>}
\end{array}
$$

Operator symbols are formed from one or more symbol characters, as defined above, and are lexically distinguished into two namespaces (Section 1.4):

- An operator symbol starting with a colon is a constructor.

- An operator symbol starting with any other character is an ordinary identifier.

Notice that a colon by itself, "`:`", is reserved solely for use as the Haskell list constructor; this makes its treatment uniform with other parts of list syntax, such as "`[ ]`" and "`[a,b]`".

Other than the special syntax for prefix negation, all operators are infix, although each infix operator can be used in a *section* to yield partially applied operators (see Section 3.5). All of the standard infix operators are just predefined symbols and may be rebound.

In the remainder of the report six different kinds of names will be used:

varid			(variables)
conid			(constructors)
tyvar	$\rightarrow$	*varid*	(type variables)
tycon	$\rightarrow$	*conid*	(type constructors)
tycls	$\rightarrow$	*conid*	(type classes)
modid	$\rightarrow$	*conid*	(modules)

Variables and type variables are represented by identifiers beginning with small letters, and the other four by identifiers beginning with capitals; also, variables and constructors have infix forms, the other four do not. Namespaces are also discussed in Section 1.4.

A name may optionally be *qualified* in certain circumstances by prepending them with a module identifier. This applies to variable, constructor, type constructor and type class names, but not type variables or module names. Qualified names are discussed in detail in Chapter 5.

qvarid	$\rightarrow$	[*modid* .] *varid*
qconid	$\rightarrow$	[*modid* .] *conid*
qtycon	$\rightarrow$	[*modid* .] *tycon*
qtycls	$\rightarrow$	[*modid* .] *tycls*
qvarsym	$\rightarrow$	[*modid* .] *varsym*
qconsym	$\rightarrow$	[*modid* .] *consym*

Since a qualified name is a lexeme, no spaces are allowed between the qualifier and the name. Sample lexical analyses are shown below.

This	Lexes as this	
`f.g`	`f . g`	(three tokens)
`F.g`	`F.g`	(qualified 'g')
`f..`	`f ..`	(two tokens)
`F..`	`F..`	(qualified '.')
`F.`	`F .`	(two tokens)

The qualifier does not change the syntactic treatment of a name; for example, `Prelude.+` is an infix operator with the same fixity as the definition of + in the Prelude (Section 4.4.2).

2.5 Numeric Literals

decimal	$\rightarrow$	*digit*{*digit*}
octal	$\rightarrow$	*octit*{*octit*}
hexadecimal	$\rightarrow$	*hexit*{*hexit*}

$$
\begin{array}{lll}
integer & \rightarrow & decimal \\
        & | & \texttt{0o}\ octal\ |\ \texttt{0O}\ octal \\
        & | & \texttt{0x}\ hexadecimal\ |\ \texttt{0X}\ hexadecimal
\end{array}
$$

$$
\begin{array}{lll}
float & \rightarrow & decimal\ \texttt{.}\ decimal\ [exponent] \\
      & | & decimal\ exponent
\end{array}
$$

$$
\begin{array}{lll}
exponent & \rightarrow & (\texttt{e}\ |\ \texttt{E})\ [\texttt{+}\ |\ \texttt{-}]\ decimal
\end{array}
$$

There are two distinct kinds of numeric literals: integer and floating. Integer literals may be given in decimal (the default), octal (prefixed by 0o or 0O) or hexadecimal notation (prefixed by 0x or 0X). Floating literals are always decimal. A floating literal must contain digits both before and after the decimal point; this ensures that a decimal point cannot be mistaken for another use of the dot character. Negative numeric literals are discussed in Section 3.4. The typing of numeric literals is discussed in Section 6.4.1.

2.6   Character and String Literals

$$
\begin{array}{lll}
char & \rightarrow & \texttt{'}\ (graphic_{\langle\,\texttt{'}\,|\,\backslash\rangle}\ |\ space\ |\ escape_{\langle\backslash\&\rangle})\ \texttt{'} \\
string & \rightarrow & \texttt{"}\ \{graphic_{\langle\texttt{"}\,|\,\backslash\rangle}\ |\ space\ |\ escape\ |\ gap\}\ \texttt{"} \\
escape & \rightarrow & \backslash\ (\ charesc\ |\ ascii\ |\ decimal\ |\ \texttt{o}\ octal\ |\ \texttt{x}\ hexadecimal\ ) \\
charesc & \rightarrow & \texttt{a}\ |\ \texttt{b}\ |\ \texttt{f}\ |\ \texttt{n}\ |\ \texttt{r}\ |\ \texttt{t}\ |\ \texttt{v}\ |\ \backslash\ |\ \texttt{"}\ |\ \texttt{'}\ |\ \texttt{\&} \\
ascii & \rightarrow & \texttt{\^{}}cntrl\ |\ \texttt{NUL}\ |\ \texttt{SOH}\ |\ \texttt{STX}\ |\ \texttt{ETX}\ |\ \texttt{EOT}\ |\ \texttt{ENQ}\ |\ \texttt{ACK} \\
      & | & \texttt{BEL}\ |\ \texttt{BS}\ |\ \texttt{HT}\ |\ \texttt{LF}\ |\ \texttt{VT}\ |\ \texttt{FF}\ |\ \texttt{CR}\ |\ \texttt{SO}\ |\ \texttt{SI}\ |\ \texttt{DLE} \\
      & | & \texttt{DC1}\ |\ \texttt{DC2}\ |\ \texttt{DC3}\ |\ \texttt{DC4}\ |\ \texttt{NAK}\ |\ \texttt{SYN}\ |\ \texttt{ETB}\ |\ \texttt{CAN} \\
      & | & \texttt{EM}\ |\ \texttt{SUB}\ |\ \texttt{ESC}\ |\ \texttt{FS}\ |\ \texttt{GS}\ |\ \texttt{RS}\ |\ \texttt{US}\ |\ \texttt{SP}\ |\ \texttt{DEL} \\
cntrl & \rightarrow & ascLarge\ |\ \texttt{@}\ |\ \texttt{[}\ |\ \backslash\ |\ \texttt{]}\ |\ \texttt{\^{}}\ |\ \texttt{\_} \\
gap & \rightarrow & \backslash\ whitechar\ \{whitechar\}\ \backslash
\end{array}
$$

Character literals are written between single quotes, as in 'a', and strings between double quotes, as in "Hello".

Escape codes may be used in characters and strings to represent special characters. Note that a single quote ' may be used in a string, but must be escaped in a character; similarly, a double quote " may be used in a character, but must be escaped in a string. \ must always be escaped. The category charesc also includes portable representations for the characters "alert" (\a), "backspace" (\b), "form feed" (\f), "new line" (\n), "carriage return" (\r), "horizontal tab" (\t), and "vertical tab" (\v).

Escape characters for the Unicode character set, including control characters such as \^X, are also provided. Numeric escapes such as \137 are used to designate the character with decimal representation 137; octal (e.g. \o137) and hexadecimal (e.g. \x37) representations are also allowed.

Consistent with the "maximal munch" rule, numeric escape characters in strings consist of all consecutive digits and may be of arbitrary length. Similarly, the one ambiguous ASCII escape code, `"\SOH"`, is parsed as a string of length 1. The escape character `\&` is provided as a "null character" to allow strings such as `"\137\&9"` and `"\SO\&H"` to be constructed (both of length two). Thus `"\&"` is equivalent to `""` and the character `'\&'` is disallowed. Further equivalences of characters are defined in Section 6.1.2.

A string may include a "gap" – two backslants enclosing white characters – which is ignored. This allows one to write long strings on more than one line by writing a backslant at the end of one line and at the start of the next. For example,

```
"Here is a backslant \\ as well as \137, \
      \a numeric escape character, and \^X, a control character."
```

String literals are actually abbreviations for lists of characters (see Section 3.7).

2.7 Layout

Haskell permits the omission of the braces and semicolons used in several grammar productions, by using *layout* to convey the same information. This allows both layout-sensitive and layout-insensitive styles of coding, which can be freely mixed within one program. Because layout is not required, Haskell programs can be straightforwardly produced by other programs.

The effect of layout on the meaning of a Haskell program can be completely specified by adding braces and semicolons in places determined by the layout. The meaning of this augmented program is now layout insensitive.

Informally stated, the braces and semicolons are inserted as follows. The layout (or "off-side") rule takes effect whenever the open brace is omitted after the keyword `where`, `let`, `do`, or `of`. When this happens, the indentation of the next lexeme (whether or not on a new line) is remembered and the omitted open brace is inserted (the whitespace preceding the lexeme may include comments). For each subsequent line, if it contains only whitespace or is indented more, then the previous item is continued (nothing is inserted); if it is indented the same amount, then a new item begins (a semicolon is inserted); and if it is indented less, then the layout list ends (a close brace is inserted). If the indentation of the non-brace lexeme immediately following a `where`, `let`, `do` or `of` is less than or equal to the current indentation level, then instead of starting a layout, an empty list "`{}`" is inserted, and layout processing occurs for the current level (i.e. insert a semicolon or close brace). A close brace is also inserted whenever the syntactic category containing the layout list ends; that is, if an illegal lexeme is encountered at a point where a close brace would be legal, a close brace is inserted. The layout rule matches only those open braces that it has inserted; an explicit open brace must be matched by an explicit close brace. Within these explicit open braces, *no* layout processing is performed for constructs outside the braces, even if a line is indented to the left of an earlier implicit open brace.

Section 9.3 gives a more precise definition of the layout rules.

Given these rules, a single newline may actually terminate several layout lists. Also, these rules permit:

```
f x = let a = 1; b = 2
          g y = exp2
      in exp1
```

making a, b and g all part of the same layout list.

As an example, Figure 2.1 shows a (somewhat contrived) module and Figure 2.2 shows the result of applying the layout rule to it. Note in particular: (a) the line beginning `}};pop`, where the termination of the previous line invokes three applications of the layout rule, corresponding to the depth (3) of the nested `where` clauses, (b) the close braces in the `where` clause nested within the tuple and `case` expression, inserted because the end of the tuple was detected, and (c) the close brace at the very end, inserted because of the column 0 indentation of the end-of-file token.

```
module AStack( Stack, push, pop, top, size ) where
data Stack a = Empty
             | MkStack a (Stack a)

push :: a -> Stack a -> Stack a
push x s = MkStack x s

size :: Stack a -> Int
size s = length (stkToLst s)   where
           stkToLst  Empty        = []
           stkToLst (MkStack x s)  = x:xs where xs = stkToLst s
pop :: Stack a -> (a, Stack a)
pop (MkStack x s)
  = (x, case s of r -> i r where i x = x)
                               -- (pop Empty) is an error
top :: Stack a -> a
top (MkStack x s) = x           -- (top Empty) is an error
```

Figure 2.1: A sample program

```
module AStack( Stack, push, pop, top, size ) where
{data Stack a = Empty
              | MkStack a (Stack a)

;push :: a -> Stack a -> Stack a
;push x s = MkStack x s

;size :: Stack a -> Int
;size s = length (stkToLst s)   where
           {stkToLst  Empty        = []
           ;stkToLst (MkStack x s)  = x:xs where {xs = stkToLst s
}};pop :: Stack a -> (a, Stack a)
;pop (MkStack x s)
  = (x, case s of {r -> i r where {i x = x}})
                               -- (pop Empty) is an error
;top :: Stack a -> a
;top (MkStack x s) = x           -- (top Empty) is an error
}
```

Figure 2.2: Sample program with layout expanded

JFP **13** (1): 17–38, January 2003. © 2003 Cambridge University Press
DOI: 10.1017/S0956796803000510   Printed in the United Kingdom

Chapter 3

Expressions

In this chapter, we describe the syntax and informal semantics of Haskell *expressions*, including their translations into the Haskell kernel, where appropriate. Except in the case of `let` expressions, these translations preserve both the static and dynamic semantics. Free variables and constructors used in these translations always refer to entities defined by the `Prelude`. For example, "`concatMap`" used in the translation of list comprehensions (Section 3.11) means the `concatMap` defined by the `Prelude`, regardless of whether or not the identifier "`concatMap`" is in scope where the list comprehension is used, and (if it is in scope) what it is bound to.

In the syntax that follows, there are some families of nonterminals indexed by precedence levels (written as a superscript). Similarly, the nonterminals *op*, *varop*, and *conop* may have a double index: a letter l, r, or n for left-, right- or non-associativity and a precedence level. A precedence-level variable i ranges from 0 to 9; an associativity variable a varies over $\{l,\ r,\ n\}$. For example

$$aexp \quad \rightarrow \quad (\ exp^{i+1}\ qop^{(a,i)}\ )$$

actually stands for 30 productions, with 10 substitutions for i and 3 for a.

exp	$\rightarrow$	exp^{0} `::` $[context$ `=>`$]\ type$	(expression type signature)
	|	exp^{0}	
exp^{i}	$\rightarrow$	$exp^{i+1}\ [qop^{(n,i)}\ exp^{i+1}]$	
	|	$lexp^{i}$	
	|	$rexp^{i}$	
$lexp^{i}$	$\rightarrow$	$(lexp^{i}\ $|$\ exp^{i+1})\ qop^{(l,i)}\ exp^{i+1}$	
$lexp^{6}$	$\rightarrow$	$-\ exp^{7}$	

$rexp^i$	$\rightarrow$	$exp^{i+1}\ qop^{(\mathrm{r},i)}\ (\,rexp^i\ \vert\ exp^{i+1}\,)$	
exp^{10}	$\rightarrow$	$\backslash\ apat_1\ \ldots\ apat_n\ \texttt{->}\ exp$	(lambda abstraction, $n \geq 1$)
	$\vert$	$\texttt{let}\ decls\ \texttt{in}\ exp$	(let expression)
	$\vert$	$\texttt{if}\ exp\ \texttt{then}\ exp\ \texttt{else}\ exp$	(conditional)
	$\vert$	$\texttt{case}\ exp\ \texttt{of}\ \texttt{\{}\ alts\ \texttt{\}}$	(case expression)
	$\vert$	$\texttt{do}\ \texttt{\{}\ stmts\ \texttt{\}}$	(do expression)
	$\vert$	$fexp$	
$fexp$	$\rightarrow$	$[fexp]\ aexp$	(function application)
$aexp$	$\rightarrow$	$qvar$	(variable)
	$\vert$	$gcon$	(general constructor)
	$\vert$	$literal$	
	$\vert$	$(\ exp\ )$	(parenthesized expression)
	$\vert$	$(\ exp_1\ \texttt{,}\ \ldots\ \texttt{,}\ exp_k\ )$	(tuple, $k \geq 2$)
	$\vert$	$[\ exp_1\ \texttt{,}\ \ldots\ \texttt{,}\ exp_k\ ]$	(list, $k \geq 1$)
	$\vert$	$[\ exp_1\ [\texttt{,}\ exp_2]\ \texttt{..}\ [exp_3]\ ]$	(arithmetic sequence)
	$\vert$	$[\ exp\ \vert\ qual_1\ \texttt{,}\ \ldots\ \texttt{,}\ qual_n\ ]$	(list comprehension, $n \geq 1$)
	$\vert$	$(\ exp^{i+1}\ qop^{(a,i)}\ )$	(left section)
	$\vert$	$(\ lexp^i\ qop^{(l,i)}\ )$	(left section)
	$\vert$	$(\ qop^{(a,i)}_{\langle-\rangle}\ exp^{i+1}\ )$	(right section)
	$\vert$	$(\ qop^{(r,i)}_{\langle-\rangle}\ rexp^i\ )$	(right section)
	$\vert$	$qcon\ \texttt{\{}\ fbind_1\ \texttt{,}\ \ldots\ \texttt{,}\ fbind_n\ \texttt{\}}$	(labeled construction, $n \geq 0$)
	$\vert$	$aexp_{\langle qcon\rangle}\ \texttt{\{}\ fbind_1\ \texttt{,}\ \ldots\ \texttt{,}\ fbind_n\ \texttt{\}}$	(labeled update, $n \geq 1$)

Expressions involving infix operators are disambiguated by the operator's fixity (see Section 4.4.2). Consecutive unparenthesized operators with the same precedence must both be either left or right associative to avoid a syntax error. Given an unparenthesized expression "$x\ qop^{(a,i)}\ y\ qop^{(b,j)}\ z$", parentheses must be added around either "$x\ qop^{(a,i)}\ y$" or "$y\ qop^{(b,j)}z$" when $i = j$ unless $a = b = $ l or $a = b = $ r.

Negation is the only prefix operator in Haskell; it has the same precedence as the infix $-$ operator defined in the Prelude (see Section 4.4.2, Figure 4.1).

The grammar is ambiguous regarding the extent of lambda abstractions, let expressions, and conditionals. The ambiguity is resolved by the meta-rule that each of these constructs extends as far to the right as possible.

Sample parses are shown below.

This	Parses as
`f x + g y`	`(f x) + (g y)`
`- f x + y`	`(- (f x)) + y`
`let { ... } in x + y`	`let { ... } in (x + y)`
`z + let { ... } in x + y`	`z + (let { ... } in (x + y))`
`f x y :: Int`	`(f x y) :: Int`
`\ x -> a+b :: Int`	`\ x -> ((a+b) :: Int)`

A note about parsing. Expressions that involve the interaction of fixities with the let/lambda meta-rule may be hard to parse. For example, the expression

```
let x = True in x == x == True
```

cannot possibly mean

```
let x = True in (x == x == True)
```

because (`==`) is a non-associative operator; so the expression must parse thus:

```
(let x = True in (x == x)) == True
```

However, implementations may well use a post-parsing pass to deal with fixities, so they may well incorrectly deliver the former parse. Programmers are advised to avoid constructs whose parsing involves an interaction of (lack of) associativity with the let/lambda meta-rule.

For the sake of clarity, the rest of this section shows the syntax of expressions without their precedences.

3.1 Errors

Errors during expression evaluation, denoted by $\bot$, are indistinguishable by a Haskell program from non-termination. Since Haskell is a non-strict language, all Haskell types include $\bot$. That is, a value of any type may be bound to a computation that, when demanded, results in an error. When evaluated, errors cause immediate program termination and cannot be caught by the user. The Prelude provides two functions to directly cause such errors:

```
error     :: String -> a
undefined :: a
```

A call to `error` terminates execution of the program and returns an appropriate error indication to the operating system. It should also display the string in some system-dependent manner. When `undefined` is used, the error message is created by the compiler.

Translations of Haskell expressions use `error` and `undefined` to explicitly indicate where execution time errors may occur. The actual program behavior when an error occurs is up to the implementation. The messages passed to the `error` function in these translations are only suggestions; implementations may choose to display more or less information when an error occurs.

3.2   Variables, Constructors, Operators, and Literals

aexp	$\rightarrow$	*qvar*	(variable)
	|	*gcon*	(general constructor)
	|	*literal*	

gcon	$\rightarrow$	( )	
	|	[ ]	
	|	(, { , })	
	|	*qcon*	

var	$\rightarrow$	*varid* | (*varsym*)	(variable)
qvar	$\rightarrow$	*qvarid* | (*qvarsym*)	(qualified variable)
con	$\rightarrow$	*conid* | (*consym*)	(constructor)
qcon	$\rightarrow$	*qconid* | (*gconsym*)	(qualified constructor)
varop	$\rightarrow$	*varsym* | ` *varid* `	(variable operator)
qvarop	$\rightarrow$	*qvarsym* | ` *qvarid* `	(qualified variable operator)
conop	$\rightarrow$	*consym* | ` *conid* `	(constructor operator)
qconop	$\rightarrow$	*gconsym* | ` *qconid* `	(qualified constructor operator)
op	$\rightarrow$	*varop* | *conop*	(operator)
qop	$\rightarrow$	*qvarop* | *qconop*	(qualified operator)
gconsym	$\rightarrow$	: | *qconsym*	

Haskell provides special syntax to support infix notation. An *operator* is a function that can be applied using infix syntax (Section 3.4), or partially applied using a *section* (Section 3.5).

An *operator* is either an *operator symbol*, such as `+` or `$$`, or is an ordinary identifier enclosed in grave accents (backquotes), such as `` `op` ``. For example, instead of writing the prefix application `op x y`, one can write the infix application `x `op` y`. If no fixity declaration is given for `` `op` `` then it defaults to highest precedence and left associativity (see Section 4.4.2).

Dually, an operator symbol can be converted to an ordinary identifier by enclosing it in parentheses. For example, `(+) x y` is equivalent to `x + y`, and `foldr (*) 1 xs` is equivalent to `foldr (\x y -> x*y) 1 xs`.

Special syntax is used to name some constructors for some of the built-in types, as found in the production for *gcon* and *literal*. These are described in Section 6.1.

An integer literal represents the application of the function `fromInteger` to the appropriate value of type `Integer`. Similarly, a floating point literal stands for an application of `fromRational` to a value of type `Rational` (that is, `Ratio Integer`).

Translation: The integer literal i is equivalent to `fromInteger` i, where `fromInteger` is a method in class `Num` (see Section 6.4.1).

The floating point literal f is equivalent to `fromRational` (n `Ratio.%` d), where `fromRational` is a method in class `Fractional` and `Ratio.%` constructs a rational from two integers, as defined in the `Ratio` library. The integers n and d are chosen so that $n/d = f$.

3.3 Curried Applications and Lambda Abstractions

fexp	$\rightarrow$	$[fexp]\ aexp$	(function application)
exp	$\rightarrow$	$\backslash\ apat_1\ \ldots\ apat_n\ \texttt{->}\ exp$	(lambda abstraction, $n \geq 1$)

Function application is written $e_1\ e_2$. Application associates to the left, so the parentheses may be omitted in (`f x`) `y`. Because e_1 could be a data constructor, partial applications of data constructors are allowed.

Lambda abstractions are written $\backslash\ p_1\ \ldots\ p_n\ \texttt{->}\ e$, where the p_i are *patterns*. An expression such as `\x:xs->x` is syntactically incorrect; it may legally be written as `\(x:xs)->x`.

The set of patterns must be *linear* – no variable may appear more than once in the set.

Translation: The following identity holds:

$$\backslash\ p_1\ \ldots\ p_n\ \texttt{->}\ e\ =\ \backslash\ x_1\ \ldots\ x_n\ \texttt{->}\ \texttt{case}\ (x_1,\ \ldots,\ x_n)\ \texttt{of}\ (p_1,\ \ldots,\ p_n)\ \texttt{->}\ e$$

where the x_i are new identifiers.

Given this translation combined with the semantics of case expressions and pattern matching described in Section 3.17.3, if the pattern fails to match, then the result is $\bot$.

3.4 Operator Applications

exp	$\rightarrow$	$exp_1\ qop\ exp_2$	
	$\mid$	$-\ exp$	(prefix negation)
qop	$\rightarrow$	$qvarop \mid qconop$	(qualified operator)

The form e_1 *qop* e_2 is the infix application of binary operator *qop* to expressions e_1 and e_2.

The special form $-e$ denotes prefix negation, the only prefix operator in Haskell, and is syntax for `negate` (e). The binary $-$ operator does not necessarily refer to the definition of $-$ in the Prelude; it may be rebound by the module system. However, unary $-$ will always refer to the `negate` function defined in the Prelude. There is no link between the local meaning of the $-$ operator and unary negation.

Prefix negation has the same precedence as the infix operator $-$ defined in the Prelude (see Table 4.1, p. 57). Because `e1-e2` parses as an infix application of the binary operator $-$, one must write `e1(-e2)` for the alternative parsing. Similarly, `(-)` is syntax for `(\ x y -> x-y)`, as with any infix operator, and does not denote `(\ x -> -x)` – one must use `negate` for that.

Translation: The following identities hold:

$$e_1 \; op \; e_2 \quad = \quad (\, op \,) \; e_1 \; e_2$$
$$-e \qquad = \quad \texttt{negate} \; (e)$$

3.5   Sections

aexp	$\rightarrow$	$(\; exp^{i+1} \; qop^{(a,i)} \;)$	(left section)
	$\mid$	$(\; lexp^{i} \; qop^{(l,i)} \;)$	(left section)
	$\mid$	$(\; qop^{(a,i)}_{(-)} \; exp^{i+1} \;)$	(right section)
	$\mid$	$(\; qop^{(r,i)}_{(-)} \; rexp^{i} \;)$	(right section)

Sections are written as (*op e*) or (*e op*), where *op* is a binary operator and *e* is an expression. Sections are a convenient syntax for partial application of binary operators.

Syntactic precedence rules apply to sections as follows. (*op e*) is legal if and only if (x *op e*) parses in the same way as (x *op* (*e*)); and similarly for (*e op*). For example, `(*a+b)` is syntactically invalid, but `(+a*b)` and `(*(a+b))` are valid. Because `(+)` is left associative, `(a+b+)` is syntactically correct, but `(+a+b)` is not; the latter may legally be written as `(+(a+b))`. As another example, the expression

```
(let n = 10 in n +)
```

is invalid because, by the let/lambda meta-rule (Section 3), the expression

```
(let n = 10 in n + x)
```

parses as

```
(let n = 10 in (n + x))
```

rather than

```
((let n = 10 in n) + x)
```

Because – is treated specially in the grammar, (– *exp*) is not a section, but an application of prefix negation, as described in the preceding section. However, there is a `subtract` function defined in the Prelude such that (`subtract` *exp*) is equivalent to the disallowed section. The expression (+ (– *exp*)) can serve the same purpose.

Translation: The following identities hold:

$$(op\ e)\quad =\quad \backslash\ x\ ->\ x\ op\ e$$
$$(e\ op)\quad =\quad \backslash\ x\ ->\ e\ op\ x$$

where *op* is a binary operator, *e* is an expression, and *x* is a variable that does not occur free in *e*.

3.6 Conditionals

$exp \qquad \rightarrow \qquad$ if exp_1 then exp_2 else exp_3

A *conditional expression* has the form if e_1 then e_2 else e_3 and returns the value of e_2 if the value of e_1 is `True`, e_3 if e_1 is `False`, and $\perp$ otherwise.

Translation: The following identity holds:

if e_1 then e_2 else e_3 =   case e_1 of { True -> e_2 ; False -> e_3 }

where `True` and `False` are the two nullary constructors from the type `Bool`, as defined in the Prelude. The type of e_1 must be `Bool`; e_2 and e_3 must have the same type, which is also the type of the entire conditional expression.

3.7 Lists

$$exp \qquad \rightarrow \qquad exp_1\ qop\ exp_2$$
$$aexp \qquad \rightarrow \qquad [\ exp_1\ ,\ \ldots\ ,\ exp_k\ ] \qquad\qquad (k \geq 1)$$
$$\qquad\qquad\quad |\qquad gcon$$
$$gcon \qquad \rightarrow \qquad [\ ]$$
$$\qquad\qquad\quad |\qquad qcon$$

qcon	$\rightarrow$	(*gconsym*)
qop	$\rightarrow$	*qconop*
qconop	$\rightarrow$	*gconsym*
gconsym	$\rightarrow$	:

Lists are written [e_1 , ..., e_k], where $k \geq 1$. The list constructor is :, and the empty list is denoted [ ]. Standard operations on lists are given in the Prelude (see Section 6.1.3, and Chapter 8 notably Section 8.2).

Translation: The following identity holds:

$$[e_1 , \ldots , e_k] \;=\; e_1 : (e_2 : (\ldots (e_k : [ ])))$$

where : and [ ] are constructors for lists, as defined in the Prelude (see Section 6.1.3). The types of e_1 through e_k must all be the same (call it t), and the type of the overall expression is [t] (see Section 4.1.2).

The constructor ":" is reserved solely for list construction; like [ ], it is considered part of the language syntax, and cannot be hidden or redefined. It is a right-associative operator, with precedence level 5 (Section 4.4.2).

3.8   Tuples

aexp	$\rightarrow$	(exp_1 , ... , exp_k)	$(k \geq 2)$
	|	*qcon*	
qcon	$\rightarrow$	(, { , })	

Tuples are written (e_1 , ..., e_k), and may be of arbitrary length $k \geq 2$. The constructor for an n-tuple is denoted by (, ... ,), where there are $n - 1$ commas. Thus (a,b,c) and (, ,) a b c denote the same value. Standard operations on tuples are given in the Prelude (see Section 6.1.4 and Chapter 8).

Translation: (e_1 , ..., e_k) for $k \geq 2$ is an instance of a k-tuple as defined in the Prelude, and requires no translation. If t_1 through t_k are the types of e_1 through e_k, respectively, then the type of the resulting tuple is (t_1 , ..., t_k) (see Section 4.1.2).

3.9 Unit Expressions and Parenthesized Expressions

$$
\begin{array}{rcl}
aexp & \to & gcon \\
& | & (\ exp\ ) \\
gcon & \to & (\,)
\end{array}
$$

The form $(\,e\,)$ is simply a *parenthesized expression*, and is equivalent to e. The *unit expression* $(\,)$ has type $(\,)$ (see Section 4.1.2). It is the only member of that type apart from $\bot$, and can be thought of as the "nullary tuple" (see Section 6.1.5).

Translation: $(\ e\ )$ is equivalent to e.

3.10 Arithmetic Sequences

$$
aexp \quad \to \quad [\ exp_1\ [,\ exp_2]\ ..\ [exp_3]\ ]
$$

The *arithmetic sequence* $[\ e_1\ ,\ e_2\ ..\ e_3\ ]$ denotes a list of values of type t, where each of the e_i has type t, and t is an instance of class `Enum`.

Translation: Arithmetic sequences satisfy these identities:

$$
\begin{array}{rcl}
[\ e_1\ ..\ ] & = & \text{enumFrom } e_1 \\
[\ e_1\ ,\ e_2\ ..\ ] & = & \text{enumFromThen } e_1\ e_2 \\
[\ e_1\ ..\ e_3\ ] & = & \text{enumFromTo } e_1\ e_3 \\
[\ e_1\ ,\ e_2\ ..\ e_3\ ] & = & \text{enumFromThenTo } e_1\ e_2\ e_3
\end{array}
$$

where `enumFrom`, `enumFromThen`, `enumFromTo`, and `enumFromThenTo` are class methods in the class `Enum` as defined in the Prelude (see Figure 6.1, p. 85).

The semantics of arithmetic sequences therefore depends entirely on the instance declaration for the type t. See Section 6.3.4 for more details of which `Prelude` types are in `Enum` and their semantics.

3.11 List Comprehensions

$$
\begin{array}{rcll}
aexp & \to & [\ exp\ |\ qual_1\ ,\ ...\ ,\ qual_n\ ] & \text{(list comprehension, } n \geq 1) \\
qual & \to & pat\ \text{<-}\ exp & \text{(generator)} \\
& | & \text{let } decls & \text{(local declaration)} \\
& | & exp & \text{(guard)}
\end{array}
$$

A *list comprehension* has the form [e | q_1 , ..., q_n], $n \geq 1$, where the q_i qualifiers are either

- *generators* of the form p <- e, where p is a pattern (see Section 3.17) of type t and e is an expression of type [t]

- *guards*, which are arbitrary expressions of type `Bool`

- *local bindings* that provide new definitions for use in the generated expression e or subsequent guards and generators.

Such a list comprehension returns the list of elements produced by evaluating e in the successive environments created by the nested, depth-first evaluation of the generators in the qualifier list. Binding of variables occurs according to the normal pattern matching rules (see Section 3.17), and if a match fails then that element of the list is simply skipped over. Thus:

```
[ x |   xs    <- [ [(1,2),(3,4)], [(5,4),(3,2)] ],
        (3,x) <- xs ]
```

yields the list [4,2]. If a qualifier is a guard, it must evaluate to `True` for the previous pattern match to succeed. As usual, bindings in list comprehensions can shadow those in outer scopes; for example:

```
[ x | x <- x, x <- x ]  =  [ z | y <- x, z <- y]
```

Translation: List comprehensions satisfy these identities, which may be used as a translation into the kernel:

$$
\begin{array}{lcl}
[\ e\ |\ \text{True}\ ] & = & [\,e\,] \\
[\ e\ |\ q\ ] & = & [\ e\ |\ q\text{, True}\ ] \\
[\ e\ |\ b,\ Q\ ] & = & \text{if}\ b\ \text{then}\ [\ e\ |\ Q\ ]\ \text{else}\ [\,] \\
[\ e\ |\ p <\!\!-\,l,\ Q\ ] & = & \text{let}\ \text{ok}\ p = [\ e\ |\ Q\ ] \\
 & & \phantom{\text{let }}\text{ok}\ \_ \ = [\,] \\
 & & \text{in concatMap ok}\ l \\
[\ e\ |\ \text{let}\ decls,\ Q\ ] & = & \text{let}\ decls\ \text{in}\ [\ e\ |\ Q\ ]
\end{array}
$$

where e ranges over expressions, p over patterns, l over list-valued expressions, b over boolean expressions, *decls* over declaration lists, q over qualifiers, and Q over sequences of qualifiers. ok is a fresh variable. The function `concatMap`, and boolean value `True`, are defined in the Prelude.

As indicated by the translation of list comprehensions, variables bound by `let` have fully polymorphic types while those defined by `<-` are lambda bound and are thus monomorphic (see Section 4.5.4).

3.12 Let Expressions

$exp \quad \rightarrow \quad$ let *decls* in *exp*

Let expressions have the general form let $\{\ d_1\ ;\ \ldots\ ;\ d_n\ \}$ in e, and introduce a nested, lexically-scoped, mutually-recursive list of declarations (let is often called letrec in other languages). The scope of the declarations is the expression e and the right hand side of the declarations. Declarations are described in Chapter 4. Pattern bindings are matched lazily; an implicit ˜ makes these patterns irrefutable. For example,

```
let (x,y) = undefined in e
```

does not cause an execution-time error until x or y is evaluated.

Translation: The dynamic semantics of the expression let $\{\ d_1\ ;\ \ldots\ ;\ d_n\ \}$ in e_0 are captured by this translation: After removing all type signatures, each declaration d_i is translated into an equation of the form $p_i = e_i$, where p_i and e_i are patterns and expressions respectively, using the translation in Section 4.4.3. Once done, these identities hold, which may be used as a translation into the kernel:

$$
\begin{aligned}
\text{let } \{p_1{=}e_1;\ \ldots\ ;\ p_n{=}e_n\} \text{ in } e_0 \ &=\ \text{let } (\tilde{\ }p_1,\ \ldots\ ,\tilde{\ }p_n)\ =\ (e_1,\ \ldots\ ,e_n)\ \text{ in } e_0 \\
\text{let } p\ =\ e_1\ \text{ in } e_0 \ &=\ \text{case } e_1 \text{ of } \tilde{\ }p \text{ -> } e_0 \\
&\qquad \text{where no variable in } p \text{ appears free in } e_1 \\
\text{let } p\ =\ e_1\ \text{ in } e_0 \ &=\ \text{let } p\ =\ \text{fix } (\ \backslash\ \tilde{\ }p \text{ -> } e_1)\ \text{ in } e_0
\end{aligned}
$$

where fix is the least fixpoint operator. Note the use of the irrefutable patterns ˜p. This translation does not preserve the static semantics because the use of case precludes a fully polymorphic typing of the bound variables. The static semantics of the bindings in a let expression are described in Section 4.4.3.

3.13 Case Expressions

$$
\begin{array}{lll}
exp & \rightarrow & \text{case } exp \text{ of } \{\ alts\ \} \\
alts & \rightarrow & alt_1\ ;\ \ldots\ ;\ alt_n \qquad\qquad\qquad (n \geq 1) \\
alt & \rightarrow & pat \text{ -> } exp\ [\text{where } decls] \\
& | & pat\ gdpat\ [\text{where } decls] \\
& | & \qquad\qquad\qquad\qquad\qquad\qquad (empty\ alternative) \\
\\
gdpat & \rightarrow & gd \text{ -> } exp\ [\ gdpat\ ] \\
gd & \rightarrow & |\ exp^0
\end{array}
$$

A *case expression* has the general form

$$\text{case } e \text{ of } \{\ p_1\ match_1\ ;\ \ldots\ ;\ p_n\ match_n\ \}$$

where each $match_i$ is of the general form

$$| \; g_{i1} \qquad \texttt{->} \; e_{i1}$$
$$\dots$$
$$| \; g_{im_i} \quad \texttt{->} \; e_{im_i}$$
$$\texttt{where} \; decls_i$$

(Notice that in the syntax rule for gd, the "$|$" is a terminal symbol, not the syntactic metasymbol for alternation.) Each alternative p_i $match_i$ consists of a pattern p_i and its matches, $match_i$. Each match in turn consists of a sequence of pairs of guards g_{ij} and bodies e_{ij} (expressions), followed by optional bindings ($decls_i$) that scope over all of the guards and expressions of the alternative. An alternative of the form

$$pat \; \texttt{->} \; exp \; \texttt{where} \; decls$$

is treated as shorthand for:

$$pat \; | \; \texttt{True} \quad \texttt{->} \; exp$$
$$\texttt{where} \; decls$$

A case expression must have at least one alternative and each alternative must have at least one body. Each body must have the same type, and the type of the whole expression is that type.

A case expression is evaluated by pattern matching the expression e against the individual alternatives. The alternatives are tried sequentially, from top to bottom. If e matches the pattern in the alternative, the guards for that alternative are tried sequentially from top to bottom, in the environment of the case expression extended first by the bindings created during the matching of the pattern, and then by the $decls_i$ in the **where** clause associated with that alternative. If one of the guards evaluates to **True**, the corresponding right-hand side is evaluated in the same environment as the guard. If all the guards evaluate to **False**, matching continues with the next alternative. If no match succeeds, the result is $\bot$. Pattern matching is described in Section 3.17, with the formal semantics of case expressions in Section 3.17.3.

A note about parsing. The expression

```
case x of { (a,_) | let b = not a in b :: Bool -> a }
```

is tricky to parse correctly. It has a single unambiguous parse, namely

```
case x of { (a,_) | (let b = not a in b :: Bool) -> a }
```

However, the phrase `Bool -> a` is syntactically valid as a type, and parsers with limited lookahead may incorrectly commit to this choice, and hence reject the program. Programmers are advised, therefore, to avoid guards that end with a type signature – indeed that is why a gd contains an exp^0 not an exp.

3.14 Do Expressions

exp	$\rightarrow$	`do {` *stmts* `}`	(do expression)
stmts	$\rightarrow$	*stmt$_1$* `...` *stmt$_n$* *exp* [`;`]	($n \geq 0$)
stmt	$\rightarrow$	*exp* `;`	
	|	*pat* `<-` *exp* `;`	
	|	`let` *decls* `;`	
	|	`;`	(*empty statement*)

A *do expression* provides a more conventional syntax for monadic programming. It allows an expression such as

```
putStr "x: "    >>
getLine         >>= \l ->
return (words l)
```

to be written in a more traditional way as:

```
do putStr "x: "
   l <- getLine
   return (words l)
```

Translation: Do expressions satisfy these identities, which may be used as a translation into the kernel, after eliminating empty *stmts*:

```
do {e}              =  e
do {e; stmts}       =  e >> do {stmts}
do {p <- e; stmts}  =  let ok p = do {stmts}
                           ok _ = fail "..."
                       in e >>= ok
do {let decls; stmts} =  let decls in do {stmts}
```

The ellipsis `"..."` stands for a compiler-generated error message, passed to `fail`, preferably giving some indication of the location of the pattern-match failure; the functions `>>`, `>>=`, and `fail` are operations in the class `Monad`, as defined in the Prelude; and `ok` is a fresh identifier.

As indicated by the translation of `do`, variables bound by `let` have fully polymorphic types while those defined by `<-` are lambda bound and are thus monomorphic.

3.15 Datatypes with Field Labels

A datatype declaration may optionally define field labels (see Section 4.2.1). These field labels can be used to construct, select from, and update fields in a manner that is independent of the overall structure of the datatype.

Different datatypes cannot share common field labels in the same scope. A field label can be used at most once in a constructor. Within a datatype, however, a field label can be used in more than one constructor provided the field has the same typing in all constructors. To illustrate the last point, consider:

```
data S = S1 { x :: Int } | S2 { x :: Int }    -- OK
data T = T1 { y :: Int } | T2 { y :: Bool }    -- BAD
```

Here S is legal but T is not, because y is given inconsistent typings in the latter.

3.15.1 Field Selection

$aexp \quad \rightarrow \quad qvar$

Field labels are used as selector functions. When used as a variable, a field label serves as a function that extracts the field from an object. Selectors are top level bindings and so they may be shadowed by local variables but cannot conflict with other top level bindings of the same name. This shadowing only affects selector functions; in record construction (Section 3.15.2) and update (Section 3.15.3), field labels cannot be confused with ordinary variables.

Translation: A field label f introduces a selector function defined as:

f x   =   case x of { $C_1\ p_{11}\ \ldots\ p_{1k}$ -> e_1 ; $\ldots$; $C_n\ p_{n1}\ \ldots\ p_{nk}$ -> e_n }

where $C_1\ \ldots\ C_n$ are all the constructors of the datatype containing a field labeled with f, p_{ij} is y when f labels the jth component of C_i or _ otherwise, and e_i is y when some field in C_i has a label of f or undefined otherwise.

3.15.2 Construction Using Field Labels

$aexp \quad \rightarrow \quad qcon\ \{\ fbind_1\ ,\ \ldots\ ,\ fbind_n\ \}$ (labeled construction, $n \geq 0$)
$fbind \quad \rightarrow \quad qvar = exp$

A constructor with labeled fields may be used to construct a value in which the components are specified by name rather than by position. Unlike the braces used in declaration lists, these are not subject to layout; the { and } characters must be explicit. (This is also true of field updates and field patterns.) Construction using field labels is subject to the following constraints:

- Only field labels declared with the specified constructor may be mentioned.

- A field label may not be mentioned more than once.

- Fields not mentioned are initialized to $\bot$.

- A compile-time error occurs when any strict fields (fields whose declared types are prefixed by !) are omitted during construction. Strict fields are discussed in Section 4.2.1.

The expression F {}, where F is a data constructor, is legal *whether or not F was declared with record syntax* (provided F has no strict fields – see the third bullet above); it denotes F $\perp_1$ ... $\perp_n$, where n is the arity of F.

Translation: In the binding $f = v$, the field f labels v.

$$C \{ bs \} = C (pick_1^C \; bs \; \texttt{undefined}) \; ... \; (pick_k^C \; bs \; \texttt{undefined})$$

where k is the arity of C.
The auxiliary function $pick_i^C \; bs \; d$ is defined as follows:

> If the ith component of a constructor C has the field label f, and if $f = v$ appears in the binding list bs, then $pick_i^C \; bs \; d$ is v. Otherwise, $pick_i^C \; bs \; d$ is the default value d.

3.15.3 Updates Using Field Labels

$$aexp \quad \rightarrow \quad aexp_{\langle qcon \rangle} \{ fbind_1 , \; ... \; , fbind_n \} \qquad \text{(labeled update, } n \geq 1)$$

Values belonging to a datatype with field labels may be non-destructively updated. This creates a new value in which the specified field values replace those in the existing value. Updates are restricted in the following ways:

- All labels must be taken from the same datatype.

- At least one constructor must define all of the labels mentioned in the update.

- No label may be mentioned more than once.

- An execution error occurs when the value being updated does not contain all of the specified labels.

Translation: Using the prior definition of $pick$,

$$e \{ bs \} = \texttt{case } e \texttt{ of}$$
$$C_1 \; v_1 \; ... \; v_{k_1} \; \texttt{->} \; C_1 \; (pick_1^{C_1} \; bs \; v_1) \; ... \; (pick_{k_1}^{C_1} \; bs \; v_{k_1})$$
$$...$$
$$C_j \; v_1 \; ... \; v_{k_j} \; \texttt{->} \; C_j \; (pick_1^{C_j} \; bs \; v_1) \; ... \; (pick_{k_j}^{C_j} \; bs \; v_{k_j})$$
$$\_ \; \texttt{-> error "Update error"}$$

where $\{ C_1, ..., C_j \}$ is the set of constructors containing all labels in bs, and k_i is the arity of C_i.

Here are some examples using labeled fields:

```
data T    = C1 {f1,f2 :: Int}
          | C2 {f1 :: Int,
                f3,f4 :: Char}
```

Expression	Translation
C1 {f1 = 3}	C1 3 undefined
C2 {f1 = 1, f4 = 'A', f3 = 'B'}	C2 1 'B' 'A'
x {f1 = 1}	case x of C1 _ f2 -> C1 1 f2
	C2 _ f3 f4 -> C2 1 f3 f4

The field f1 is common to both constructors in T. This example translates expressions using constructors in field-label notation into equivalent expressions using the same constructors without field labels. A compile-time error will result if no single constructor defines the set of field labels used in an update, such as x {f2 = 1, f3 = 'x'}.

3.16   Expression Type-Signatures

$$exp \quad \rightarrow \quad exp :: [context =>] type$$

Expression type-signatures have the form $e :: t$, where e is an expression and t is a type (Section 4.1.2); they are used to type an expression explicitly and may be used to resolve ambiguous typings due to overloading (see Section 4.3.4). The value of the expression is just that of exp. As with normal type signatures (see Section 4.4.1), the declared type may be more specific than the principal type derivable from exp, but it is an error to give a type that is more general than, or not comparable to, the principal type.

Translation:
$$e :: t \;=\; \texttt{let \{}\, v :: t; \quad v = e \,\texttt{\} in } v$$

3.17   Pattern Matching

Patterns appear in lambda abstractions, function definitions, pattern bindings, list comprehensions, do expressions, and case expressions. However, the first five of these ultimately translate into case expressions, so defining the semantics of pattern matching for case expressions is sufficient.

3.17.1   Patterns

Patterns have this syntax:

pat	$\rightarrow$	var + $integer$	(successor pattern)
	|	pat^0	
pat^i	$\rightarrow$	pat^{i+1} $[qconop^{(n,i)}$ $pat^{i+1}]$	
	|	$lpat^i$	
	|	$rpat^i$	
$lpat^i$	$\rightarrow$	$(lpat^i$ | $pat^{i+1})$ $qconop^{(l,i)}$ pat^{i+1}	
$lpat^6$	$\rightarrow$	$-$ ($integer$ | $float$)	(negative literal)
$rpat^i$	$\rightarrow$	pat^{i+1} $qconop^{(r,i)}$ ($rpat^i$ | pat^{i+1})	
pat^{10}	$\rightarrow$	$apat$	
	|	$gcon$ $apat_1$ ... $apat_k$	(arity $gcon$ = k, $k \geq 1$)
$apat$	$\rightarrow$	var $[$ @ $apat]$	(as pattern)
	|	$gcon$	(arity $gcon$ = 0)
	|	$qcon$ { $fpat_1$, ... , $fpat_k$ }	(labeled pattern, $k \geq 0$)
	|	$literal$	
	|	$\_$	(wildcard)
	|	(pat)	(parenthesized pattern)
	|	(pat_1 , ... , pat_k)	(tuple pattern, $k \geq 2$)
	|	[pat_1 , ... , pat_k]	(list pattern, $k \geq 1$)
	|	~ $apat$	(irrefutable pattern)
$fpat$	$\rightarrow$	$qvar$ = pat	

The arity of a constructor must match the number of sub-patterns associated with it; one cannot match against a partially-applied constructor.

All patterns must be *linear* – no variable may appear more than once. For example, this definition is illegal:

```
f (x,x) = x    -- ILLEGAL; x used twice in pattern
```

Patterns of the form *var*@*pat* are called *as-patterns*, and allow one to use *var* as a name for the value being matched by *pat*. For example,

```
case e of { xs@(x:rest) -> if x==0 then rest else xs }
```

is equivalent to:

```
let { xs = e } in
   case xs of { (x:rest) -> if x==0 then rest else xs }
```

Patterns of the form _ are *wildcards* and are useful when some part of a pattern is not referenced on the right-hand side. It is as if an identifier not used elsewhere were put in its place. For example,

```
case e of { [x,_,_]  ->  if x==0 then True else False }
```

is equivalent to:

```
case e of { [x,y,z]   ->   if x==0 then True else False }
```

3.17.2   Informal Semantics of Pattern Matching

Patterns are matched against values. Attempting to match a pattern can have one of three results:
it may *fail*; it may *succeed*, returning a binding for each variable in the pattern; or it may *diverge*
(i.e. return $\perp$). Pattern matching proceeds from left to right, and outside to inside, according to the
following rules:

1. Matching the pattern *var* against a value v always succeeds and binds *var* to v.

2. Matching the pattern ˜*apat* against a value v always succeeds. The free variables in *apat* are
    bound to the appropriate values if matching *apat* against v would otherwise succeed, and to
    $\perp$ if matching *apat* against v fails or diverges. (Binding does *not* imply evaluation.)

    Operationally, this means that no matching is done on a ˜*apat* pattern until one of the vari-
    ables in *apat* is used. At that point the entire pattern is matched against the value, and if the
    match fails or diverges, so does the overall computation.

3. Matching the wildcard pattern _ against any value always succeeds, and no binding is done.

4. Matching the pattern *con pat* against a value, where *con* is a constructor defined by `newtype`,
    depends on the value:

    -   If the value is of the form *con v*, then *pat* is matched against v.
    -   If the value is $\perp$, then *pat* is matched against $\perp$.

    That is, constructors associated with `newtype` serve only to change the type of a value.

5. Matching the pattern *con pat₁ ... patₙ* against a value, where *con* is a constructor defined
    by `data`, depends on the value:

    -   If the value is of the form *con v₁ ... vₙ*, sub-patterns are matched left-to-right against
        the components of the data value; if all matches succeed, the overall match succeeds;
        the first to fail or diverge causes the overall match to fail or diverge, respectively.
    -   If the value is of the form *con' v₁ ... vₘ*, where *con* is a different constructor to *con'*,
        the match fails.
    -   If the value is $\perp$, the match diverges.

6. Matching against a constructor using labeled fields is the same as matching ordinary con-
    structor patterns except that the fields are matched in the order they are named in the field
    list. All fields listed must be declared by the constructor; fields may not be named more than
    once. Fields not named by the pattern are ignored (matched against _).

7. Matching a numeric, character, or string literal pattern k against a value v succeeds if v `==` k, where `==` is overloaded based on the type of the pattern. The match diverges if this test diverges.

   The interpretation of numeric literals is exactly as described in Section 3.2; that is, the overloaded function `fromInteger` or `fromRational` is applied to an `Integer` or `Rational` literal (resp) to convert it to the appropriate type.

8. Matching an $n+k$ pattern (where n is a variable and k is a positive integer literal) against a value v succeeds if x `>=` k, resulting in the binding of n to $x - k$, and fails otherwise. Again, the functions `>=` and `-` are overloaded, depending on the type of the pattern. The match diverges if the comparison diverges.

   The interpretation of the literal k is the same as in numeric literal patterns, except that only integer literals are allowed.

9. Matching an as-pattern $var\,@\,apat$ against a value v is the result of matching $apat$ against v, augmented with the binding of var to v. If the match of $apat$ against v fails or diverges, then so does the overall match.

Aside from the obvious static type constraints (for example, it is a static error to match a character against a boolean), the following static class constraints hold:

- An integer literal pattern can only be matched against a value in the class `Num`.

- A floating literal pattern can only be matched against a value in the class `Fractional`.

- An $n+k$ pattern can only be matched against a value in the class `Integral`.

Many people feel that $n+k$ patterns should not be used. These patterns may be removed or changed in future versions of Haskell.

It is sometimes helpful to distinguish two kinds of patterns. Matching an *irrefutable pattern* is non-strict: the pattern matches even if the value to be matched is $\bot$. Matching a *refutable* pattern is strict: if the value to be matched is $\bot$ the match diverges. The irrefutable patterns are as follows: a variable, a wildcard, $N\ apat$ where N is a constructor defined by `newtype` and $apat$ is irrefutable (see Section 4.2.3), $var\,@\,apat$ where $apat$ is irrefutable, or of the form $\tilde{}\,apat$ (whether or not $apat$ is irrefutable). All other patterns are *refutable*.

Here are some examples:

1. If the pattern `[ 'a' , 'b' ]` is matched against `[ 'x' , ⊥ ]`, then `'a'` *fails* to match against `'x'`, and the result is a failed match. But if `[ 'a' , 'b' ]` is matched against `[ ⊥ , 'x' ]`, then attempting to match `'a'` against $\bot$ causes the match to *diverge*.

2. These examples demonstrate refutable vs. irrefutable matching:

   ```
   (\ ~(x,y) -> 0) ⊥      ⇒      0
   (\  (x,y) -> 0) ⊥      ⇒      ⊥
   ```

```
(\ ~[x] -> 0) []        ⇒       0
(\ ~[x] -> x) []        ⇒       ⊥

(\ ~[x,~(a,b)] -> x) [(0,1),⊥]     ⇒       (0,1)
(\ ~[x, (a,b)] -> x) [(0,1),⊥]     ⇒       ⊥

(\  (x:xs) -> x:x:xs) ⊥    ⇒    ⊥
(\ ~(x:xs) -> x:x:xs) ⊥    ⇒    ⊥:⊥:⊥
```

3. Consider the following declarations:

```
newtype N = N Bool
data     D = D !Bool
```

These examples illustrate the difference in pattern matching between types defined by `data` and `newtype`:

```
(\  (N True) -> True) ⊥      ⇒       ⊥
(\  (D True) -> True) ⊥      ⇒       ⊥
(\ ~(D True) -> True) ⊥      ⇒       True
```

Additional examples may be found in Section 4.2.3.

Top level patterns in case expressions and the set of top level patterns in function or pattern bindings may have zero or more associated *guards*. A guard is a boolean expression that is evaluated only after all of the arguments have been successfully matched, and it must be true for the overall pattern match to succeed. The environment of the guard is the same as the right-hand-side of the case-expression alternative, function definition, or pattern binding to which it is attached.

The guard semantics have an obvious influence on the strictness characteristics of a function or case expression. In particular, an otherwise irrefutable pattern may be evaluated because of a guard. For example, in

```
f :: (Int,Int,Int) -> [Int] -> Int
f ~(x,y,z) [a] | (a == y) = 1
```

both a and y will be evaluated by == in the guard.

3.17.3   Formal Semantics of Pattern Matching

The semantics of all pattern matching constructs other than `case` expressions are defined by giving identities that relate those constructs to `case` expressions. The semantics of `case` expressions themselves are in turn given as a series of identities, in Figures 3.1 and 3.2. Any implementation should behave so that these identities hold; it is not expected that it will use them directly, since that would generate rather inefficient code.

```
(a)    case e of { alts } = (\v -> case v of { alts }) e
       where v is a new variable
(b)    case v of { p₁ match₁;  ...  ; pₙ matchₙ }
       =  case v of { p₁ match₁ ;
                         _  -> ... case v of {
                                     pₙ matchₙ ;
                                     _ -> error "No match" }...}
       where each matchᵢ has the form:
          | gᵢ,₁ -> eᵢ,₁ ;  ... ;  | gᵢ,mᵢ -> eᵢ,mᵢ where { declsᵢ }
(c)    case v of { p | g₁ -> e₁ ; ...
                     | gₙ -> eₙ where { decls }
                     _      -> e' }
       = case e' of
         {y -> (where y is a new variable)
          case v of {
                 p -> let { decls } in
                         if g₁ then e₁ ... else if gₙ then eₙ else y ;
                 _ -> y }}
(d)    case v of { ~p -> e; _ -> e' }
       = (\x₁...xₙ ->e ) (case v of { p-> x₁ }) ...(case v of { p -> xₙ})
       where x₁,...,xₙ are all the variables in p
(e)    case v of { x@p -> e; _ -> e' }
       = case v of { p -> ( \ x -> e ) v ; _ -> e' }
(f)    case v of { _ -> e; _ -> e' } = e
```

Figure 3.1: Semantics of Case Expressions, Part 1

In Figures 3.1 and 3.2: e, e' and e_i are expressions; g and g_i are boolean-valued expressions; p and p_i are patterns; v, x, and x_i are variables; K and K' are algebraic datatype (`data`) constructors (including tuple constructors); and N is a `newtype` constructor.

Rule (b) matches a general source-language `case` expression, regardless of whether it actually includes guards – if no guards are written, then `True` is substituted for the guards $g_{i,j}$ in the $match_i$ forms. Subsequent identities manipulate the resulting `case` expression into simpler and simpler forms.

Rule (h) in Figure 3.2 involves the overloaded operator ==; it is this rule that defines the meaning of pattern matching against overloaded constants.

These identities all preserve the static semantics. Rules (d), (e), (j), (q), and (s) use a lambda rather than a `let`; this indicates that variables bound by `case` are monomorphically typed (Section 4.1.4).

(g)　　`case` v `of {` $K\, p_1 \ldots p_n$ `-> ` e `; _ -> ` e' `}`
　　　　`= case` v `of {`
　　　　　　　　$K\, x_1 \ldots x_n$ `-> case ` x_1 ` of {`
　　　　　　　　　　　　　　　　p_1 `-> ... case ` x_n ` of {` p_n `-> ` e ` ; _ -> ` e' `}` `...`
　　　　　　　　　　　　　　　　`_ -> ` e' `}`
　　　　　　　　`_ -> ` e' `}`
　　　　at least one of $p_1, \ldots, p_n$ is not a variable; $x_1, \ldots, x_n$ are new variables

(h)　　`case` v `of {` k `-> ` e `; _ -> ` e' `} = if (` $v==k$ `) then ` e ` else ` e'
　　　　where k is a numeric, character, or string literal.

(i)　　`case` v `of {` x `-> ` e `; _ -> ` e' `} = case` v `of {` x `-> ` e `}`

(j)　　`case` v `of {` x `-> ` e `} = ( \` x `-> ` e ` ) ` v

(k)　　`case` $N\, v$ `of {` $N\, p$ `-> ` e `; _ -> ` e' `}`
　　　　`= case` v `of {` p `-> ` e `; _ -> ` e' `}`
　　　　where N is a `newtype` constructor

(l)　　`case` $\bot$ `of {` $N\, p$ `-> ` e `; _ -> ` e' `} = case` $\bot$ `of {` p `-> ` e `}`
　　　　where N is a `newtype` constructor

(m)　　`case` v `of {` K `{` f_1 `=` p_1 `,` f_2 `=` p_2 `, ...} -> ` e `; _ -> ` e' `}`
　　　　`= case` e' `of {`
　　　　　　y `->`
　　　　　　`case` v `of {`
　　　　　　　　K `{` f_1 `=` p_1 `} ->`
　　　　　　　　　　`case` v `of {` K `{` f_2 `=` p_2 `, ... } -> ` e `; _ -> ` y `};`
　　　　　　　　　　`_ -> ` y `}}`
　　　　where $f_1, f_2, \ldots$ are fields of constructor K; y is a new variable

(n)　　`case` v `of {` K `{` f `=` p `} -> ` e `; _ -> ` e' `}`
　　　　`= case` v `of {`
　　　　　　$K\, p_1 \ldots p_n$ `-> ` e `; _ -> ` e' `}`
　　　　where p_i is p if f labels the ith component of K, _ otherwise

(o)　　`case` v `of {` K `{} -> ` e `; _ -> ` e' `}`
　　　　`= case` v `of {`
　　　　　　K `_ ... _ -> ` e `; _ -> ` e' `}`

(p)　　`case (` $K'\, e_1 \ldots e_m$ `) of {` $K\, x_1 \ldots x_n$ `-> ` e `; _ -> ` e' `} = ` e'
　　　　where K and K' are distinct `data` constructors of arity n and m, respectively

(q)　　`case (` $K\, e_1 \ldots e_n$ `) of {` $K\, x_1 \ldots x_n$ `-> ` e `; _ -> ` e' `}`
　　　　`= (\` $x_1 \ldots x_n$ `-> ` e `)` $e_1 \ldots e_n$
　　　　where K is a `data` constructor of arity n

(r)　　`case` $\bot$ `of {` $K\, x_1 \ldots x_n$ `-> ` e `; _ -> ` e' `} = ` $\bot$
　　　　where K is a `data` constructor of arity n

(s)　　`case` v `of {` $x{+}k$ `-> ` e `; _ -> ` e' `}`
　　　　`= if` $v \geq k$ `then (\` x `-> ` e `)(` $v{-}k$ `) else ` e'
　　　　where k is a numeric literal

Figure 3.2: Semantics of Case Expressions, Part 2

JFP **13** (1): 39–66, January 2003. © 2003 Cambridge University Press
DOI: 10.1017/S0956796803000613   Printed in the United Kingdom

Chapter 4

Declarations and Bindings

In this chapter, we describe the syntax and informal semantics of Haskell *declarations*.

module	$\rightarrow$	**module** *modid* [*exports*] **where** *body*
	|	*body*
body	$\rightarrow$	{ *impdecls* ; *topdecls* }
	|	{ *impdecls* }
	|	{ *topdecls* }

topdecls	$\rightarrow$	*topdecl$_1$* ; ... ; *topdecl$_n$*	$(n \geq 1)$
topdecl	$\rightarrow$	**type** *simpletype* = *type*	
	|	**data** [*context* =>] *simpletype* = *constrs* [*deriving*]	
	|	**newtype** [*context* =>] *simpletype* = *newconstr* [*deriving*]	
	|	**class** [*scontext* =>] *tycls tyvar* [**where** *cdecls*]	
	|	**instance** [*scontext* =>] *qtycls inst* [**where** *idecls*]	
	|	**default** (*type$_1$* , ... , *type$_n$*)	$(n \geq 0)$
	|	*decl*	

decls	$\rightarrow$	{ *decl$_1$* ; ... ; *decl$_n$* }	$(n \geq 0)$
decl	$\rightarrow$	*gendecl*	
	|	(*funlhs* | *pat^0*) *rhs*	

cdecls	$\rightarrow$	{ *cdecl$_1$* ; ... ; *cdecl$_n$* }	$(n \geq 0)$
cdecl	$\rightarrow$	*gendecl*	
	|	(*funlhs* | *var*) *rhs*	

$$
\begin{array}{llll}
idecls & \to & \{\ idecl_1\ ;\ \dots\ ;\ idecl_n\ \} & (n \geq 0) \\
idecl & \to & (funlhs \mid var)\ rhs & \\
& \mid & & (\text{empty}) \\
\\
gendecl & \to & vars\ ::\ [context =>]\ type & (\text{type signature}) \\
& \mid & fixity\ [integer]\ ops & (\text{fixity declaration}) \\
& \mid & & (\text{empty declaration}) \\
\\
ops & \to & op_1\ ,\ \dots\ ,\ op_n & (n \geq 1) \\
vars & \to & var_1\ ,\ \dots\ ,\ var_n & (n \geq 1) \\
fixity & \to & \texttt{infixl} \mid \texttt{infixr} \mid \texttt{infix} &
\end{array}
$$

The declarations in the syntactic category *topdecls* are only allowed at the top level of a Haskell module (see Chapter 5), whereas *decls* may be used either at the top level or in nested scopes (i.e. those within a `let` or `where` construct).

For exposition, we divide the declarations into three groups: user-defined datatypes, consisting of `type`, `newtype`, and `data` declarations (Section 4.2); type classes and overloading, consisting of `class`, `instance`, and `default` declarations (Section 4.3); and nested declarations, consisting of value bindings, type signatures, and fixity declarations (Section 4.4).

Haskell has several primitive datatypes that are "hard-wired" (such as integers and floating-point numbers), but most "built-in" datatypes are defined with normal Haskell code, using normal `type` and `data` declarations. These "built-in" datatypes are described in detail in Section 6.1.

4.1   Overview of Types and Classes

Haskell uses a traditional Hindley–Milner polymorphic type system to provide a static type semantics [5, 8], but the type system has been extended with *type classes* (or just *classes*) that provide a structured way to introduce *overloaded* functions.

A `class` declaration (Section 4.3.1) introduces a new *type class* and the overloaded operations that must be supported by any type that is an instance of that class. An `instance` declaration (Section 4.3.2) declares that a type is an *instance* of a class and includes the definitions of the overloaded operations – called *class methods* – instantiated on the named type.

For example, suppose we wish to overload the operations `(+)` and `negate` on types `Int` and `Float`. We introduce a new type class called `Num`:

```
class Num a  where          --  simplified class declaration for Num
    (+)      :: a -> a -> a  --  (Num is defined in the Prelude)
    negate :: a -> a
```

This declaration may be read "a type `a` is an instance of the class `Num` if there are class methods `(+)` and `negate`, of the given types, defined on it."

We may then declare `Int` and `Float` to be instances of this class:

```
instance Num Int  where      -- simplified instance of Num Int
   x + y      =  addInt x y
   negate x   =  negateInt x
instance Num Float  where    -- simplified instance of Num Float
   x + y      =  addFloat x y
   negate x   =  negateFloat x
```

where `addInt`, `negateInt`, `addFloat`, and `negateFloat` are assumed in this case to be primitive functions, but in general could be any user-defined function. The first declaration above may be read "`Int` is an instance of the class `Num` as witnessed by these definitions (i.e. class methods) for `(+)` and `negate`."

More examples of type classes can be found in the papers by Jones [10] or Wadler and Blott [16]. The term "type class" was used to describe the original Haskell 1.0 type system; "constructor class" was used to describe an extension to the original type classes. There is no longer any reason to use two different terms: in this report, "type class" includes both the original Haskell type classes and the constructor classes introduced by Jones.

4.1.1 Kinds

To ensure that they are valid, type expressions are classified into different *kinds*, which take one of two possible forms:

- The symbol $*$ represents the kind of all nullary type constructors.

- If κ_1 and κ_2 are kinds, then $\kappa_1 \to \kappa_2$ is the kind of types that take a type of kind κ_1 and return a type of kind κ_2.

Kind inference checks the validity of type expressions in a similar way that type inference checks the validity of value expressions. However, unlike types, kinds are entirely implicit and are not a visible part of the language. Kind inference is discussed in Section 4.6.

4.1.2 Syntax of Types

type	$\to$	*btype* [`->` *type*]	(function type)
btype	$\to$	[*btype*] *atype*	(type application)
atype	$\to$	*gtycon*	
	$\mid$	*tyvar*	
	$\mid$	(*type₁* , ... , *typeₖ*)	(tuple type, $k \geq 2$)
	$\mid$	[*type*]	(list type)

| (*type*)   (parenthesised constructor)

gtycon   →   *qtycon*
| ( )   (unit type)
| [ ]   (list constructor)
| (->)   (function constructor)
| (,{,})   (tupling constructors)

The syntax for Haskell type expressions is given above. Just as data values are built using data constructors, type values are built from *type constructors*. As with data constructors, the names of type constructors start with uppercase letters. Unlike data constructors, infix type constructors are not allowed (other than (->)).

The main forms of type expression are as follows:

1. Type variables, written as identifiers beginning with a lowercase letter. The kind of a variable is determined implicitly by the context in which it appears.

2. Type constructors. Most type constructors are written as an identifier beginning with an uppercase letter. For example:

   - Char, Int, Integer, Float, Double and Bool are type constants with kind $*$.

   - Maybe and IO are unary type constructors, and treated as types with kind $* \rightarrow *$.

   - The declarations data T ... or newtype T ... add the type constructor T to the type vocabulary. The kind of T is determined by kind inference.

   Special syntax is provided for certain built-in type constructors:

   - The *trivial type* is written as ( ) and has kind $*$. It denotes the "nullary tuple" type, and has exactly one value, also written ( ) (see Sections 3.9 and 6.1.5).

   - The *function type* is written as (->) and has kind $* \rightarrow * \rightarrow *$.

   - The *list type* is written as [ ] and has kind $* \rightarrow *$.

   - The *tuple types* are written as (,), (,,), and so on. Their kinds are $* \rightarrow * \rightarrow *$, $* \rightarrow * \rightarrow * \rightarrow *$, and so on.

   Use of the (->) and [ ] constants is described in more detail below.

3. Type application. If t_1 is a type of kind $\kappa_1 \rightarrow \kappa_2$ and t_2 is a type of kind κ_1, then $t_1\ t_2$ is a type expression of kind κ_2.

4. A *parenthesized type*, having form (t), is identical to the type t.

For example, the type expression IO a can be understood as the application of a constant, IO, to the variable a. Since the IO type constructor has kind $* \rightarrow *$, it follows that both the variable a and the whole expression, IO a, must have kind $*$. In general, a process of *kind inference* (see

Section 4.6) is needed to determine appropriate kinds for user-defined datatypes, type synonyms, and classes.

Special syntax is provided to allow certain type expressions to be written in a more traditional style:

1. A *function type* has the form t_1 -> t_2, which is equivalent to the type (->) t_1 t_2. Function arrows associate to the right. For example, `Int -> Int -> Float` means `Int -> (Int -> Float)`.

2. A *tuple type* has the form (t_1, ... , t_k) where $k \geq 2$, which is equivalent to the type (,...,) t_1 ... t_k where there are $k - 1$ commas between the parenthesis. It denotes the type of k-tuples with the first component of type t_1, the second component of type t_2, and so on (see Sections 3.8 and 6.1.4).

3. A *list type* has the form [t], which is equivalent to the type [ ] t. It denotes the type of lists with elements of type t (see Sections 3.7 and 6.1.3).

These special syntactic forms always denote the built-in type constructors for functions, tuples, and lists, regardless of what is in scope. In a similar way, the prefix type constructors (->), [ ], ( ), (,), and so on, always denote the built-in type constructors; they cannot be qualified, nor mentioned in import or export lists (Chapter 5). (Hence the special production, "gtycon", above.)

Although the list and tuple types have special syntax, their semantics is the same as the equivalent user-defined algebraic data types.

Notice that expressions and types have a consistent syntax. If t_i is the type of expression or pattern e_i, then the expressions (\ e_1 -> e_2), [e_1], and (e_1, e_2) have the types (t_1 -> t_2), [t_1], and (t_1, t_2), respectively.

With one exception (that of the distinguished type variable in a class declaration (Section 4.3.1)), the type variables in a Haskell type expression are all assumed to be universally quantified; there is no explicit syntax for universal quantification [5]. For example, the type expression a -> a denotes the type $\forall\, a.\, a \rightarrow a$. For clarity, however, we often write quantification explicitly when discussing the types of Haskell programs. When we write an explicitly quantified type, the scope of the $\forall$ extends as far to the right as possible; for example, $\forall\, a.\, a \rightarrow a$ means $\forall\, a.\, (a \rightarrow a)$.

4.1.3   Syntax of Class Assertions and Contexts

context	$\rightarrow$	*class*	
	|	(*class$_1$* , ... , *class$_n$*)	($n \geq 0$)
class	$\rightarrow$	*qtycls tyvar*	
	|	*qtycls* (*tyvar atype$_1$* ... *atype$_n$*)	($n \geq 1$)
qtycls	$\rightarrow$	[*modid* .] *tycls*	
tycls	$\rightarrow$	*conid*	
tyvar	$\rightarrow$	*varid*	

A *class assertion* has form *qtycls tyvar*, and indicates the membership of the type *tyvar* in the class *qtycls*. A class identifier begins with an uppercase letter. A *context* consists of zero or more class assertions, and has the general form

$$(\; C_1 \; u_1, \; \ldots, \; C_n \; u_n \;)$$

where C_1, ..., C_n are class identifiers, and each of the u_1, ..., u_n is either a type variable, or the application of type variable to one or more types. The outer parentheses may be omitted when $n = 1$. In general, we use cx to denote a context and we write $cx \Rightarrow t$ to indicate the type t restricted by the context cx. The context cx must only contain type variables referenced in t. For convenience, we write $cx \Rightarrow t$ even if the context cx is empty, although in this case the concrete syntax contains no =>.

4.1.4   Semantics of Types and Classes

In this subsection, we provide informal details of the type system. (Wadler and Blott [16] and Jones [10] discuss type and constructor classes, respectively, in more detail.)

The Haskell type system attributes a *type* to each expression in the program. In general, a type is of the form $\forall \, \overline{u}. \; cx \; \Rightarrow \; t$, where $\overline{u}$ is a set of type variables u_1, ..., u_n. In any such type, any of the universally-quantified type variables u_i that are free in cx must also be free in t. Furthermore, the context cx must be of the form given above in Section 4.1.3. For example, here are some valid types:

```
Eq a => a -> a
(Eq a, Show a, Eq b) => [a] -> [b] -> String
(Eq (f a), Functor f) => (a -> b) -> f a -> f b -> Bool
```

In the third type, the constraint Eq (f a) cannot be made simpler because f is universally quantified.

The type of an expression e depends on a *type environment* that gives types for the free variables in e, and a *class environment* that declares which types are instances of which classes (a type becomes an instance of a class only via the presence of an instance declaration or a deriving clause).

Types are related by a generalization preorder (specified below); the most general type, up to the equivalence induced by the generalization preorder, that can be assigned to a particular expression (in a given environment) is called its *principal type*. Haskell's extended Hindley–Milner type system can infer the principal type of all expressions, including the proper use of overloaded class methods (although certain ambiguous overloadings could arise, as described in Section 4.3.4). Therefore, explicit typings (called *type signatures*) are usually optional (see Sections 3.16 and 4.4.1).

The type $\forall \, \overline{u}. \; cx_1 \; \Rightarrow \; t_1$ is *more general than* the type $\forall \, \overline{w}. \; cx_2 \; \Rightarrow \; t_2$ if and only if there is a substitution S whose domain is $\overline{u}$ such that:

- t_2 is identical to $S(t_1)$.

- Whenever cx_2 holds in the class environment, $S(cx_1)$ also holds.

A value of type $\forall\,\overline{u}.\ cx\ \Rightarrow\ t$, may be instantiated at types $\overline{s}$ if and only if the context $cx[\overline{s}/\overline{u}]$ holds. For example, consider the function `double`:

```
double x = x + x
```

The most general type of `double` is $\forall\,a.\ \text{Num}\ a\ \Rightarrow\ a\ \rightarrow\ a$. `double` may be applied to values of type `Int` (instantiating a to `Int`), since `Num Int` holds, because `Int` is an instance of the class `Num`. However, `double` may not normally be applied to values of type `Char`, because `Char` is not normally an instance of class `Num`. The user may choose to declare such an instance, in which case `double` may indeed be applied to a `Char`.

4.2 User-Defined Datatypes

In this section, we describe algebraic datatypes (`data` declarations), renamed datatypes (`newtype` declarations), and type synonyms (`type` declarations). These declarations may only appear at the top level of a module.

4.2.1 Algebraic Datatype Declarations

topdecl	$\rightarrow$	`data` $[context \Rightarrow]$ *simpletype* = *constrs* $[deriving]$	
simpletype	$\rightarrow$	*tycon* $tyvar_1$ ... $tyvar_k$	$(k \geq 0)$
constrs	$\rightarrow$	$constr_1$ | ... | $constr_n$	$(n \geq 1)$
constr	$\rightarrow$	*con* $[!]$ $atype_1$ ... $[!]$ $atype_k$	(arity *con* $=\ k,\ k \geq 0$)
	|	$(btype\ \|\ !\ atype)$ *conop* $(btype\ \|\ !\ atype)$	(infix *conop*)
	|	*con* { $fielddecl_1$, ... , $fielddecl_n$ }	$(n \geq 0)$
fielddecl	$\rightarrow$	*vars* `::` $(type\ \|\ !\ atype)$	
deriving	$\rightarrow$	`deriving` $(dclass\ \|\ (dclass_1 ,\ ... ,\ dclass_n))$	$(n \geq 0)$
dclass	$\rightarrow$	*qtycls*	

The precedence for *constr* is the same as that for expressions – normal constructor application has higher precedence than infix constructor application (thus a `:` Foo a parses as a `:` (Foo a)).

An algebraic datatype declaration has the form:

$$\texttt{data}\ cx \Rightarrow T\ u_1\ ...\ u_k = K_1\ t_{11}\ ...\ t_{1k_1}\ |\ \cdots\ |\ K_n\ t_{n1}\ ...\ t_{nk_n}$$

where cx is a context. This declaration introduces a new *type constructor* T with one or more constituent *data constructors* K_1, ..., K_n. In this Report, the unqualified term "constructor" always means "data constructor".

The types of the data constructors are given by:

$$K_i \; :: \; \forall \, u_1 \; \ldots \; u_k. \; cx_i \; \Rightarrow \; t_{i1} \; \rightarrow \; \cdots \; \rightarrow \; t_{ik_i} \; \rightarrow \; (T \; u_1 \; \ldots \; u_k)$$

where cx_i is the largest subset of cx that constrains only those type variables free in the types $t_{i1}, \ldots, t_{ik_i}$. The type variables u_1 through u_k must be distinct and may appear in cx and the t_{ij}; it is a static error for any other type variable to appear in cx or on the right-hand-side. The new type constant T has a kind of the form $\kappa_1 \rightarrow \ldots \rightarrow \kappa_k \rightarrow *$ where the kinds κ_i of the argument variables u_i are determined by kind inference as described in Section 4.6. This means that T may be used in type expressions with anywhere between 0 and k arguments.

For example, the declaration

```
    data Eq a => Set a = NilSet | ConsSet a (Set a)
```

introduces a type constructor `Set` of kind $* \rightarrow *$, and constructors `NilSet` and `ConsSet` with types

$$\text{NilSet} \quad :: \; \forall \, a. \; \text{Set} \; a$$
$$\text{ConsSet} \quad :: \; \forall \, a. \; \text{Eq} \; a \Rightarrow a \rightarrow \text{Set} \; a \rightarrow \text{Set} \; a$$

In the example given, the overloaded type for `ConsSet` ensures that `ConsSet` can only be applied to values whose type is an instance of the class `Eq`. Pattern matching against `ConsSet` also gives rise to an `Eq a` constraint. For example:

```
    f (ConsSet a s) = a
```

the function `f` has inferred type `Eq a => Set a -> a`. The context in the `data` declaration has no other effect whatsoever.

The visibility of a datatype's constructors (i.e. the "abstractness" of the datatype) outside of the module in which the datatype is defined is controlled by the form of the datatype's name in the export list as described in Section 5.8.

The optional `deriving` part of a `data` declaration has to do with *derived instances*, and is described in Section 4.3.3.

Labelled Fields   A data constructor of arity k creates an object with k components. These components are normally accessed positionally as arguments to the constructor in expressions or patterns. For large datatypes it is useful to assign *field labels* to the components of a data object. This allows a specific field to be referenced independently of its location within the constructor.

A constructor definition in a `data` declaration may assign labels to the fields of the constructor, using the record syntax (C { ... }). Constructors using field labels may be freely mixed with constructors without them. A constructor with associated field labels may still be used as an ordinary constructor; features using labels are simply a shorthand for operations using an underlying positional constructor. The arguments to the positional constructor occur in the same order as the labeled fields. For example, the declaration

```
data C = F { f1,f2 :: Int, f3 :: Bool }
```

defines a type and constructor identical to the one produced by

```
data C = F Int Int Bool
```

Operations using field labels are described in Section 3.15. A `data` declaration may use the same field label in multiple constructors as long as the typing of the field is the same in all cases after type synonym expansion. A label cannot be shared by more than one type in scope. Field names share the top level namespace with ordinary variables and class methods and must not conflict with other top level names in scope.

The pattern `F {}` matches any value built with constructor `F`, *whether or not* `F` *was declared with record syntax.*

Strictness Flags   Whenever a data constructor is applied, each argument to the constructor is evaluated if and only if the corresponding type in the algebraic datatype declaration has a strictness flag, denoted by an exclamation point, "`!`". Lexically, "`!`" is an ordinary varsym not a *reservedop*; it has special significance only in the context of the argument types of a data declaration.

Translation: A declaration of the form

$$\text{data } cx => T \ u_1 \ \dots \ u_k = \dots \ | \ K \ s_1 \ \dots \ s_n \ | \ \dots$$

where each s_i is either of the form `!` t_i or t_i, replaces every occurrence of K in an expression by

$$(\backslash \ x_1 \ \dots \ x_n -> (\ ((K \ op_1 \ x_1) \ op_2 \ x_2) \ \dots) \ op_n \ x_n)$$

where op_i is the non-strict apply function `$` if s_i is of the form t_i, and op_i is the strict apply function `$!` (see Section 6.2) if s_i is of the form `!` t_i. Pattern matching on K is not affected by strictness flags.

4.2.2   Type Synonym Declarations

topdecl	$\rightarrow$	**type** *simpletype* = *type*
simpletype	$\rightarrow$	*tycon tyvar$_1$* ... *tyvar$_k$* $(k \geq 0)$

A type synonym declaration introduces a new type that is equivalent to an old type. It has the form

$$\text{type } T \ u_1 \ \dots \ u_k = t$$

which introduces a new type constructor, T. The type $(T \ t_1 \ \dots t_k)$ is equivalent to the type $t[t_1/u_1, \ \dots, \ t_k/u_k]$. The type variables u_1 through u_k must be distinct and are scoped only over t; it is a static error for any other type variable to appear in t. The kind of the new type constructor T

is of the form $\kappa_1 \rightarrow \ldots \rightarrow \kappa_k \rightarrow \kappa$ where the kinds κ_i of the arguments u_i and κ of the right hand side t are determined by kind inference as described in Section 4.6. For example, the following definition can be used to provide an alternative way of writing the list type constructor:

```
type List = []
```

Type constructor symbols T introduced by type synonym declarations cannot be partially applied; it is a static error to use T without the full number of arguments.

Although recursive and mutually recursive datatypes are allowed, this is not so for type synonyms, *unless an algebraic datatype intervenes*. For example,

```
type Rec a  =  [Circ a]
data Circ a  =  Tag [Rec a]
```

is allowed, whereas

```
type Rec a   =  [Circ a]        -- invalid
type Circ a  =  [Rec a]         -- invalid
```

is not. Similarly, `type Rec a = [Rec a]` is not allowed.

Type synonyms are a convenient, but strictly syntactic, mechanism to make type signatures more readable. A synonym and its definition are completely interchangeable, except in the instance type of an `instance` declaration (Section 4.3.2).

4.2.3   Datatype Renamings

topdecl	$\rightarrow$	`newtype` $[context \Rightarrow]$ *simpletype* = *newconstr* $[deriving]$
newconstr	$\rightarrow$	*con atype*
	$\mid$	*con* { *var* :: *type* }
simpletype	$\rightarrow$	*tycon* $tyvar_1 \ldots tyvar_k$ $(k \geq 0)$

A declaration of the form
$$\texttt{newtype } cx \Rightarrow T \; u_1 \; \ldots \; u_k = N \; t$$

introduces a new type whose representation is the same as an existing type. The type ($T \; u_1 \ldots u_k$) renames the datatype t. It differs from a type synonym in that it creates a distinct type that must be explicitly coerced to or from the original type. Also, unlike type synonyms, `newtype` may be used to define recursive types. The constructor N in an expression coerces a value from type t to type ($T \; u_1 \; \ldots \; u_k$). Using N in a pattern coerces a value from type ($T \; u_1 \; \ldots \; u_k$) to type t. These coercions may be implemented without execution time overhead; `newtype` does not change the underlying representation of an object.

New instances (see Section 4.3.2) can be defined for a type defined by `newtype` but may not be defined for a type synonym. A type created by `newtype` differs from an algebraic datatype in that the representation of an algebraic datatype has an extra level of indirection. This difference may make access to the representation less efficient. The difference is reflected in different rules for pattern matching (see Section 3.17). Unlike algebraic datatypes, the newtype constructor N is *unlifted*, so that $N \perp$ is the same as $\perp$.

The following examples clarify the differences between `data` (algebraic datatypes), `type` (type synonyms), and `newtype` (renaming types.) Given the declarations

```
data D1 = D1 Int
data D2 = D2 !Int
type S = Int
newtype N = N Int
d1 (D1 i) = 42
d2 (D2 i) = 42
s i = 42
n (N i) = 42
```

the expressions (`d1` $\perp$), (`d2` $\perp$) and (`d2` (`D2` $\perp$)) are all equivalent to $\perp$, whereas (`n` $\perp$), (`n` (`N` $\perp$)), (`d1` (`D1` $\perp$)) and (`s` $\perp$) are all equivalent to `42`. In particular, (`N` $\perp$) is equivalent to $\perp$ while (`D1` $\perp$) is not equivalent to $\perp$.

The optional deriving part of a `newtype` declaration is treated in the same way as the deriving component of a `data` declaration; see Section 4.3.3.

A `newtype` declaration may use field-naming syntax, though of course there may only be one field. Thus:

```
newtype Age = Age { unAge :: Int }
```

brings into scope both a constructor and a de-constructor:

```
Age    :: Int -> Age
unAge :: Age -> Int
```

4.3 Type Classes and Overloading

4.3.1 Class Declarations

topdecl	$\rightarrow$	**class** $[scontext =>]$ *tycls tyvar* [**where** *cdecls*]	
scontext	$\rightarrow$	*simpleclass*	
	|	(*simpleclass$_1$* , ... , *simpleclass$_n$*)	$(n \geq 0)$
simpleclass	$\rightarrow$	*qtycls tyvar*	
cdecls	$\rightarrow$	{ *cdecl$_1$* ; ... ; *cdecl$_n$* }	$(n \geq 0)$
cdecl	$\rightarrow$	*gendecl*	
	|	(*funlhs* | *var*) *rhs*	

A *class declaration* introduces a new class and the operations (*class methods*) on it. A class declaration has the general form:

$$\texttt{class } cx \texttt{ => } C \ u \texttt{ where } cdecls$$

This introduces a new class name C; the type variable u is scoped only over the class method signatures in the class body. The context cx specifies the superclasses of C, as described below; the only type variable that may be referred to in cx is u.

The superclass relation must not be cyclic, i.e. it must form a directed acyclic graph.

The *cdecls* part of a `class` declaration contains three kinds of declarations:

- The class declaration introduces new *class methods* v_i, whose scope extends outside the `class` declaration. The class methods of a class declaration are precisely the v_i for which there is an explicit type signature

  $$v_i \texttt{ :: } cx_i \texttt{ => } t_i$$

  in *cdecls*. Class methods share the top level namespace with variable bindings and field names; they must not conflict with other top level bindings in scope. That is, a class method can not have the same name as a top level definition, a field name, or another class method.

  The type of the top-level class method v_i is:

  $$v_i :: \forall u, \overline{w}. \ (Cu, cx_i) \Rightarrow t_i$$

  The t_i must mention u; it may mention type variables $\overline{w}$ other than u, in which case the type of v_i is polymorphic in both u and $\overline{w}$. The cx_i may constrain only $\overline{w}$; in particular, the cx_i may not constrain u. For example:

  ```
  class Foo a where
      op :: Num b => a -> b -> a
  ```

  Here the type of op is $\forall a, b. (\texttt{Foo } a, \texttt{Num } b) \Rightarrow a \rightarrow b \rightarrow a$.

- The *cdecls* may also contain a *fixity declaration* for any of the class methods (but for no other values). However, since class methods declare top-level values, the fixity declaration for a class method may alternatively appear at top level, outside the class declaration.

- Lastly, the *cdecls* may contain a *default class method* for any of the v_i. The default class method for v_i is used if no binding for it is given in a particular `instance` declaration (see Section 4.3.2). The default method declaration is a normal value definition, except that the left hand side may only be a variable or function definition. For example:

  ```
  class Foo a where
      op1, op2 :: a -> a
      (op1, op2) = ...
  ```

  is not permitted, because the left hand side of the default declaration is a pattern.

Other than these cases, no other declarations are permitted in *cdecls*.

A `class` declaration with no `where` part may be useful for combining a collection of classes into a larger one that inherits all of the class methods in the original ones. For example:

```
class   (Read a, Show a) => Textual  a
```

In such a case, if a type is an instance of all superclasses, it is not *automatically* an instance of the subclass, even though the subclass has no immediate class methods. The `instance` declaration must be given explicitly with no `where` part.

4.3.2   Instance Declarations

topdecl	$\rightarrow$	`instance` [*scontext* =>] *qtycls inst* [`where` *idecls*]	
inst	$\rightarrow$	*gtycon*	
	|	(*gtycon tyvar$_1$* ... *tyvar$_k$*)	($k \geq 0$, *tyvars* distinct)
	|	(*tyvar$_1$* , ... , *tyvar$_k$*)	($k \geq 2$, *tyvars* distinct)
	|	[*tyvar*]	
	|	(*tyvar$_1$* -> *tyvar$_2$*)	(*tyvar$_1$* and *tyvar$_2$* distinct)
idecls	$\rightarrow$	{ *idecl$_1$* ; ... ; *idecl$_n$* }	($n \geq 0$)
idecl	$\rightarrow$	(*funlhs* | *var*) *rhs*	
	|		(*empty*)

An *instance declaration* introduces an instance of a class. Let

$$\texttt{class } cx \texttt{ => } C \ u \texttt{ where } \{ \ cbody \ \}$$

be a `class` declaration. The general form of the corresponding instance declaration is:

$$\texttt{instance } cx' \texttt{ => } C \ (T \ u_1 \ ... \ u_k) \texttt{ where } \{ \ d \ \}$$

where $k \geq 0$. The type $(T \ u_1 \ ... \ u_k)$ must take the form of a type constructor T applied to simple type variables $u_1, \ ... \ u_k$; furthermore, T must not be a type synonym, and the u_i must all be distinct.

This prohibits instance declarations such as:

```
        instance  C  (a,a)  where ...
        instance  C  (Int,a)  where ...
        instance  C  [[a]]  where ...
```

The declarations d may contain bindings only for the class methods of C. It is illegal to give a binding for a class method that is not in scope, but the name under which it is in scope is immaterial; in particular, it may be a qualified name. (This rule is identical to that used for subordinate names in export lists – Section 5.2.) For example, this is legal, even though `range` is in scope only with the qualified name `Ix.range`.

```
module A where
  import qualified Ix

  instance Ix.Ix T where
    range = ...
```

The declarations may not contain any type signatures or fixity declarations, since these have already been given in the `class` declaration. As in the case of default class methods (Section 4.3.1), the method declarations must take the form of a variable or function definition.

If no binding is given for some class method then the corresponding default class method in the `class` declaration is used (if present); if such a default does not exist then the class method of this instance is bound to `undefined` and no compile-time error results.

An `instance` declaration that makes the type T to be an instance of class C is called a *C-T instance declaration* and is subject to these static restrictions:

- A type may not be declared as an instance of a particular class more than once in the program.

- The class and type must have the same kind; this can be determined using kind inference as described in Section 4.6.

- Assume that the type variables in the instance type $(T\ u_1\ \ldots\ u_k)$ satisfy the constraints in the instance context cx'. Under this assumption, the following two conditions must also be satisfied:

  1. The constraints expressed by the superclass context $cx[(T\ u1\ \ldots\ uk)/u]$ of C must be satisfied. In other words, T must be an instance of each of C's superclasses and the contexts of all superclass instances must be implied by cx'.

  2. Any constraints on the type variables in the instance type that are required for the class method declarations in d to be well-typed must also be satisfied.

  In fact, except in pathological cases it is possible to infer from the instance declaration the most general instance context cx' satisfying the above two constraints, but it is nevertheless mandatory to write an explicit instance context.

The following example illustrates the restrictions imposed by superclass instances:

```
class Foo a => Bar a where ...

instance (Eq a, Show a) => Foo [a] where ...

instance Num a => Bar [a] where ...
```

This example is valid Haskell. Since `Foo` is a superclass of `Bar`, the second instance declaration is only valid if `[a]` is an instance of `Foo` under the assumption `Num a`. The first instance declaration does indeed say that `[a]` is an instance of `Foo` under this assumption, because `Eq` and `Show` are superclasses of `Num`.

If the two instance declarations instead read like this:

```
instance Num a => Foo [a] where ...
instance (Eq a, Show a) => Bar [a] where ...
```

then the program would be invalid. The second instance declaration is valid only if [a] is an instance of Foo under the assumptions (Eq a, Show a). But this does not hold, since [a] is only an instance of Foo under the stronger assumption Num a.

Further examples of instance declarations may be found in Chapter 8.

4.3.3 Derived Instances

As mentioned in Section 4.2.1, data and newtype declarations contain an optional deriving form. If the form is included, then *derived instance declarations* are automatically generated for the datatype in each of the named classes. These instances are subject to the same restrictions as user-defined instances. When deriving a class C for a type T, instances for all superclasses of C must exist for T, either via an explicit instance declaration or by including the superclass in the deriving clause.

Derived instances provide convenient commonly-used operations for user-defined datatypes. For example, derived instances for datatypes in the class Eq define the operations == and /=, freeing the programmer from the need to define them.

The only classes in the Prelude for which derived instances are allowed are Eq, Ord, Enum, Bounded, Show, and Read, all mentioned in Figure 6.1, page 85. The precise details of how the derived instances are generated for each of these classes are provided in Chapter 10, including a specification of when such derived instances are possible. Classes defined by the standard libraries may also be derivable.

A static error results if it is not possible to derive an instance declaration over a class named in a deriving form. For example, not all datatypes can properly support class methods in Enum. It is also a static error to give an explicit instance declaration for a class that is also derived.

If the deriving form is omitted from a data or newtype declaration, then *no* instance declarations are derived for that datatype; that is, omitting a deriving form is equivalent to including an empty deriving form: deriving ().

4.3.4 Ambiguous Types, and Defaults for Overloaded Numeric Operations

topdecl   →   default (*type₁* , ... , *typeₙ*) $(n \geq 0)$

A problem inherent with Haskell-style overloading is the possibility of an *ambiguous type*. For example, using the read and show functions defined in Chapter 10, and supposing that just Int and Bool are members of Read and Show, then the expression

```
let x = read "..." in show x   -- invalid
```

is ambiguous, because the types for `show` and `read`,

$$\text{show} \; :: \; \forall \, a . \, \text{Show} \; a \; \Rightarrow \; a \; \rightarrow \; \text{String}$$
$$\text{read} \; :: \; \forall \, a . \, \text{Read} \; a \; \Rightarrow \; \text{String} \; \rightarrow \; a$$

could be satisfied by instantiating `a` as either `Int` in both cases, or `Bool`. Such expressions are considered ill-typed, a static error.

We say that an expression `e` has an *ambiguous type* if, in its type $\forall \, \overline{u} . \, cx \; \Rightarrow \; t$, there is a type variable u in $\overline{u}$ that occurs in cx but not in t. Such types are invalid.

For example, the earlier expression involving `show` and `read` has an ambiguous type since its type is $\forall \, a . \, \text{Show} \; a , \, \text{Read} \; a \; \Rightarrow \; \text{String}$.

Ambiguous types can only be circumvented by input from the user. One way is through the use of *expression type-signatures* as described in Section 3.16. For example, for the ambiguous expression given earlier, one could write:

```
let x = read "..." in show (x::Bool)
```

which disambiguates the type.

Occasionally, an otherwise ambiguous expression needs to be made the same type as some variable, rather than being given a fixed type with an expression type-signature. This is the purpose of the function `asTypeOf` (Chapter 8): x `'asTypeOf'` y has the value of x, but x and y are forced to have the same type. For example,

```
approxSqrt x = encodeFloat 1 (exponent x 'div' 2) 'asTypeOf' x
```

(See Section 6.4.6 for a description of `encodeFloat` and `exponent`.)

Ambiguities in the class `Num` are most common, so Haskell provides another way to resolve them – with a *default declaration*:

$$\text{default} \; (\, t_1 \, , \; \dots \, , \, t_n \,)$$

where $n \geq 0$, and each t_i must be a type for which `Num` t_i holds. In situations where an ambiguous type is discovered, an ambiguous type variable, v, is *defaultable* if:

- v appears only in constraints of the form $C \; v$, where C is a class, and

- at least one of these classes is a numeric class, (that is, `Num` or a subclass of `Num`), and

- all of these classes are defined in the Prelude or a standard library (Figures 6.2 and 6.3, pages 93–94 show the numeric classes, and Figure 6.1, page 85, shows the classes defined in the Prelude.)

Each defaultable variable is replaced by the first type in the default list that is an instance of all the ambiguous variable's classes. It is a static error if no such type is found.

Only one default declaration is permitted per module, and its effect is limited to that module. If no default declaration is given in a module then it assumed to be:

```
default (Integer, Double)
```

The empty default declaration, `default ()`, turns off all defaults in a module.

4.4 Nested Declarations

The following declarations may be used in any declaration list, including the top level of a module.

4.4.1 Type Signatures

gendecl	$\rightarrow$	*vars* **::** [*context* **=>**] *type*
vars	$\rightarrow$	*var_1* **,** ..., *var_n* $(n \geq 1)$

A type signature specifies types for variables, possibly with respect to a context. A type signature has the form:

$$v_1, \ldots, v_n \texttt{ :: } cx \texttt{ => } t$$

which is equivalent to asserting v_i **::** cx **=>** t for each i from 1 to n. Each v_i must have a value binding in the same declaration list that contains the type signature; i.e. it is invalid to give a type signature for a variable bound in an outer scope. Moreover, it is invalid to give more than one type signature for one variable, even if the signatures are identical.

As mentioned in Section 4.1.2, every type variable appearing in a signature is universally quantified over that signature, and hence the scope of a type variable is limited to the type signature that contains it. For example, in the following declarations

```
f :: a -> a
f x = x :: a                    -- invalid
```

the a's in the two type signatures are quite distinct. Indeed, these declarations contain a static error, since x does not have type $\forall a. a$. (The type of x is dependent on the type of f; there is currently no way in Haskell to specify a signature for a variable with a dependent type; this is explained in Section 4.5.4.)

If a given program includes a signature for a variable f, then each use of f is treated as having the declared type. It is a static error if the same type cannot also be inferred for the defining occurrence of f.

If a variable f is defined without providing a corresponding type signature declaration, then each use of f outside its own declaration group (see Section 4.5) is treated as having the corresponding inferred, or *principal* type. However, to ensure that type inference is still possible, the defining occurrence, and all uses of f within its declaration group must have the same monomorphic type (from which the principal type is obtained by generalization, as described in Section 4.5.2).

For example, if we define

```
sqr x  =  x*x
```

then the principal type is `sqr` :: $\forall\, a.$ `Num` $a \Rightarrow a \rightarrow a$, which allows applications such as `sqr 5` or `sqr 0.1`. It is also valid to declare a more specific type, such as

```
sqr :: Int -> Int
```

but now applications such as `sqr 0.1` are invalid. Type signatures such as

```
sqr :: (Num a, Num b) => a -> b        -- invalid
sqr :: a -> a                          -- invalid
```

are invalid, as they are more general than the principal type of `sqr`.

Type signatures can also be used to support *polymorphic recursion*. The following definition is pathological, but illustrates how a type signature can be used to specify a type more general than the one that would be inferred:

```
data T a  =   K (T Int) (T a)
f         :: T a -> a
f (K x y) =   if f x == 1 then f y else undefined
```

If we remove the signature declaration, the type of `f` will be inferred as `T Int -> Int` due to the first recursive call for which the argument to `f` is `T Int`. Polymorphic recursion allows the user to supply the more general type signature, `T a -> a`.

4.4.2 Fixity Declarations

gendecl	$\rightarrow$	*fixity* [*integer*] *ops*
fixity	$\rightarrow$	`infixl` | `infixr` | `infix`
ops	$\rightarrow$	op_1 , ... , op_n $(n \geq 1)$
op	$\rightarrow$	*varop* | *conop*

A fixity declaration gives the fixity and binding precedence of one or more operators. The *integer* in a fixity declaration must be in the range *0* to *9*. A fixity declaration may appear anywhere that a type signature appears and, like a type signature, declares a property of a particular operator. Also like a type signature, a fixity declaration can only occur in the same sequence of declarations as the declaration of the operator itself, and at most one fixity declaration may be given for any

Table 4.1: Precedences and fixities of prelude operators

Precedence	Left associative operators	Non-associative operators	Right associative operators
9	`!!`		`.`
8			`^, ^^, **`
7	`*, /, 'div',` `'mod', 'rem', 'quot'`		
6	`+, -`		
5			`:, ++`
4		`==, /=, <, <=, >, >=,` `'elem', 'notElem'`	
3			`&&`
2			`||`
1	`>>, >>=`		
0			`$, $!, 'seq'`

operator. (Class methods are a minor exception; their fixity declarations can occur either in the class declaration itself or at top level.)

There are three kinds of fixity, non-, left- and right-associativity (`infix`, `infixl`, and `infixr`, respectively), and ten precedence levels, 0 to 9 inclusive (level 0 binds least tightly, and level 9 binds most tightly). If the *digit* is omitted, level 9 is assumed. Any operator lacking a fixity declaration is assumed to be `infixl` 9 (See Section 3 for more on the use of fixities). Table 4.1 lists the fixities and precedences of the operators defined in the Prelude.

Fixity is a property of a particular entity (constructor or variable), just like its type; fixity is not a property of that entity's *name*. For example:

```
module Bar( op ) where
  infixr 7 'op'
  op = ...
module Foo where
  import qualified Bar
  infix 3 'op'

  a 'op' b = (a 'Bar.op' b) + 1

  f x = let
          p 'op' q = (p 'Foo.op' q) * 2
        in ...
```

Here, `'Bar.op'` is `infixr` 7, `'Foo.op'` is `infix` 3, and the nested definition of op in f's right-hand side has the default fixity of `infixl` 9. (It would also be possible to give a fixity to the nested definition of `'op'` with a nested fixity declaration.)

4.4.3   Function and Pattern Bindings

$decl$ $\rightarrow$ $(funlhs \mid pat^0)\ rhs$

$funlhs$ $\rightarrow$ $var\ apat\ \{\ apat\ \}$
     $\mid$ $pat^{i+1}\ varop^{(a,i)}\ pat^{i+1}$
     $\mid$ $lpat^i\ varop^{(l,i)}\ pat^{i+1}$
     $\mid$ $pat^{i+1}\ varop^{(r,i)}\ rpat^i$
     $\mid$ $(\ funlhs\ )\ apat\ \{\ apat\ \}$

rhs $\rightarrow$ $=\ exp\ [\textbf{where}\ decls]$
     $\mid$ $gdrhs\ [\textbf{where}\ decls]$

$gdrhs$ $\rightarrow$ $gd\ =\ exp\ [gdrhs]$

gd $\rightarrow$ $\mid\ exp^0$

We distinguish two cases within this syntax: a *pattern binding* occurs when the left hand side is a pat^0; otherwise, the binding is called a *function binding*. Either binding may appear at the top-level of a module or within a `where` or `let` construct.

4.4.3.1   Function bindings.

A function binding binds a variable to a function value. The general form of a function binding for variable x is:

$$x \quad p_{11}\ \ldots\ p_{1k} \quad match_1$$
$$\ldots$$
$$x \quad p_{n1}\ \ldots\ p_{nk} \quad match_n$$

where each p_{ij} is a pattern, and where each $match_i$ is of the general form:

$$=\ e_i\ \textbf{where}\ \{\ decls_i\ \}$$

or

$$\mid\ g_{i1} \quad =\ e_{i1}$$
$$\ldots$$
$$\mid\ g_{im_i} \quad =\ e_{im_i}$$
$$\textbf{where}\ \{\ decls_i\ \}$$

and where $n \geq 1$, $1 \leq i \leq n$, $m_i \geq 1$. The former is treated as shorthand for a particular case of the latter, namely:

$$\mid\ \textbf{True}\ =\ e_i\ \textbf{where}\ \{\ decls_i\ \}$$

Note that all clauses defining a function must be contiguous, and the number of patterns in each clause must be the same. The set of patterns corresponding to each match must be *linear* – no variable is allowed to appear more than once in the entire set.

Alternative syntax is provided for binding functional values to infix operators. For example, these three function definitions are all equivalent:

```
plus x y z = x+y+z
x `plus` y = \ z -> x+y+z
(x `plus` y) z = x+y+z
```

Translation: The general binding form for functions is semantically equivalent to the equation (i.e. simple pattern binding):

$$x = \ x_1 \ \ldots \ x_k \ \text{->} \ \texttt{case} \ (x_1, \ \ldots, \ x_k) \ \texttt{of} \ (p_{11}, \ \ldots, \ p_{1k}) \ match_1$$
$$\ldots$$
$$(p_{n1}, \ \ldots, \ p_{nk}) \ match_n$$

where the x_i are new identifiers.

4.4.3.2 Pattern bindings.

A pattern binding binds variables to values. A *simple* pattern binding has form $p = e$. The pattern p is matched "lazily" as an irrefutable pattern, as if there were an implicit ~ in front of it. See the translation in Section 3.12.

The *general* form of a pattern binding is p *match*, where a *match* is the same structure as for function bindings above; in other words, a pattern binding is:

$$p \quad | \ g_1 \quad = e_1$$
$$| \ g_2 \quad = e_2$$
$$\ldots$$
$$| \ g_m \quad = e_m$$
$$\texttt{where} \ \{ \ decls \ \}$$

Translation: The pattern binding above is semantically equivalent to this simple pattern binding:

$$p \ = \ \texttt{let} \ decls \ \texttt{in}$$
$$\texttt{if} \ g_1 \ \texttt{then} \ e_1 \ \texttt{else}$$
$$\texttt{if} \ g_2 \ \texttt{then} \ e_2 \ \texttt{else}$$
$$\ldots$$
$$\texttt{if} \ g_m \ \texttt{then} \ e_m \ \texttt{else error} \ \texttt{"Unmatched pattern"}$$

A note about syntax. It is usually straightforward to tell whether a binding is a pattern binding or a function binding, but the existence of n+k patterns sometimes confuses the issue. Here are four examples:

```
x + 1 = ...              -- Function binding, defines (+)
                         -- Equivalent to   (+) x 1 = ...

(x + 1) = ...            -- Pattern binding, defines x

(x + 1) * y = ...        -- Function binding, defines (*)
                         -- Equivalent to   (*) (x+1) y = ...

(x + 1) y = ...          -- Function binding, defines (+)
                         -- Equivalent to   (+) x 1 y = ...
```

The first two can be distinguished because a pattern binding has a pat^0 on the left hand side, not a pat – the former cannot be an unparenthesised n+k pattern.

4.5   Static Semantics of Function and Pattern Bindings

The static semantics of the function and pattern bindings of a `let` expression or `where` clause are discussed in this section.

4.5.1   Dependency Analysis

In general the static semantics are given by the normal Hindley–Milner inference rules. A *dependency analysis transformation* is first performed to increase polymorphism. Two variables bound by value declarations are in the same *declaration group* if either

1. they are bound by the same pattern binding, or

2. their bindings are mutually recursive (perhaps via some other declarations that are also part of the group).

Application of the following rules causes each `let` or `where` construct (including the `where` defining the top level bindings in a module) to bind only the variables of a single declaration group, thus capturing the required dependency analysis:[1]

1. The order of declarations in `where`/`let` constructs is irrelevant.

2. `let` $\{d_1 ;\ d_2\}$ `in` $e =$ `let` $\{d_1\}$ `in` (`let` $\{d_2\}$ `in` e)
   (when no identifier bound in d_2 appears free in d_1)

---

[1]A similar transformation is described in Peyton Jones' book [14].

4.5.2 Generalization

The Hindley–Milner type system assigns types to a `let`-expression in two stages. First, the right-hand side of the declaration is typed, giving a type with no universal quantification. Second, all type variables that occur in this type are universally quantified unless they are associated with bound variables in the type environment; this is called *generalization*. Finally, the body of the `let`-expression is typed.

For example, consider the declaration

```
f x = let g y = (y,y)
        in ...
```

The type of `g`'s definition is $a \rightarrow (a, a)$. The generalization step attributes to `g` the polymorphic type $\forall u.\ u \rightarrow (a, a)$, after which the typing of the "`...`" part can proceed.

When typing overloaded definitions, all the overloading constraints from a single declaration group are collected together, to form the context for the type of each variable declared in the group. For example, in the definition:

```
f x = let g1 x y = if x>y then show x else g2 y x
          g2 p q = g1 q p
        in ...
```

The types of the definitions of `g1` and `g2` are both $a \rightarrow a \rightarrow$ `String`, and the accumulated constraints are `Ord` a (arising from the use of `>`), and `Show` a (arising from the use of `show`). The type variables appearing in this collection of constraints are called the *constrained type variables*.

The generalization step attributes to both `g1` and `g2` the type

$$\forall a.\ (\text{Ord } a,\ \text{Show } a) \Rightarrow a \rightarrow a \rightarrow \text{String}$$

Notice that `g2` is overloaded in the same way as `g1` even though the occurrences of `>` and `show` are in the definition of `g1`.

If the programmer supplies explicit type signatures for more than one variable in a declaration group, the contexts of these signatures must be identical up to renaming of the type variables.

4.5.3 Context Reduction Errors

As mentioned in Section 4.1.4, the context of a type may constrain only a type variable, or the application of a type variable to one or more types. Hence, types produced by generalization must be expressed in a form in which all context constraints have be reduced to this "head normal form". Consider, for example, the definition:

```
f xs y  =  xs == [y]
```

Its type is given by

```
f :: Eq a => [a] -> a -> Bool
```

and not

```
f :: Eq [a] => [a] -> a -> Bool
```

Even though the equality is taken at the list type, the context must be simplified, using the instance declaration for `Eq` on lists, before generalization. If no such instance is in scope, a static error occurs.

Here is an example that shows the need for a constraint of the form $C\ (m\ t)$ where m is one of the type variables being generalized; that is, where the class C applies to a type expression that is not a type variable or a type constructor. Consider:

```
f :: (Monad m, Eq (m a)) => a -> m a -> Bool
f x y = return x == y
```

The type of `return` is `Monad m => a -> m a`; the type of `(==)` is `Eq a => a -> a -> Bool`. The type of f should be therefore `(Monad m, Eq (m a)) => a -> m a -> Bool`, and the context cannot be simplified further.

The instance declaration derived from a data type `deriving` clause (see Section 4.3.3) must, like any instance declaration, have a *simple* context; that is, all the constraints must be of the form $C\ a$, where a is a type variable. For example, in the type

```
data Apply a b = App (a b)   deriving Show
```

the derived Show instance will produce a context `Show (a b)`, which cannot be reduced and is not simple; thus a static error results.

4.5.4   Monomorphism

Sometimes it is not possible to generalize over all the type variables used in the type of the definition. For example, consider the declaration

```
f x = let g y z = ([x,y], z)
          in ...
```

In an environment where x has type a, the type of g's definition is $a \rightarrow b \rightarrow ([a], b)$. The generalization step attributes to g the type $\forall\ b.\ a \rightarrow b \rightarrow ([a], b)$; only b can be universally quantified because a occurs in the type environment. We say that the type of g is *monomorphic in the type variable* a.

The effect of such monomorphism is that the first argument of all applications of g must be of a single type. For example, it would be valid for the "..." to be

```
(g True, g False)
```

(which would, incidentally, force x to have type Bool) but invalid for it to be

```
(g True, g 'c')
```

In general, a type $\forall \overline{u}. cx \Rightarrow t$ is said to be *monomorphic* in the type variable a if a is free in $\forall \overline{u}. cx \Rightarrow t$.

It is worth noting that the explicit type signatures provided by Haskell are not powerful enough to express types that include monomorphic type variables. For example, we cannot write

```
f x = let
         g :: a -> b -> ([a],b)
         g y z = ([x,y], z)
      in ...
```

because that would claim that g was polymorphic in both a and b (Section 4.4.1). In this program, g can only be given a type signature if its first argument is restricted to a type not involving type variables; for example

```
g :: Int -> b -> ([Int],b)
```

This signature would also cause x to have type Int.

4.5.5 The Monomorphism Restriction

Haskell places certain extra restrictions on the generalization step, beyond the standard Hindley–Milner restriction described above, which further reduces polymorphism in particular cases.

The monomorphism restriction depends on the binding syntax of a variable. Recall that a variable is bound by either a *function binding* or a *pattern binding*, and that a *simple* pattern binding is a pattern binding in which the pattern consists of only a single variable (Section 4.4.3).

The following two rules define the monomorphism restriction:

The monomorphism restriction

Rule 1. We say that a given declaration group is *unrestricted* if and only if:

> **(a):** every variable in the group is bound by a function binding or a simple pattern binding (Section 4.4.3.2), *and*

> **(b):** an explicit type signature is given for every variable in the group that is bound by simple pattern binding.

> The usual Hindley–Milner restriction on polymorphism is that only type variables that do not occur free in the environment may be generalized. In addition, *the constrained type variables of a restricted declaration group may not be generalized* in the generalization step for that group. (Recall that a type variable is constrained if it must belong to some type class; see Section 4.5.2.)

Rule 2. Any monomorphic type variables that remain when type inference for an entire module is complete, are considered *ambiguous*, and are resolved to particular types using the defaulting rules (Section 4.3.4).

Motivation   Rule 1 is required for two reasons, both of which are fairly subtle.

- *Rule 1 prevents computations from being unexpectedly repeated:* e.g. `genericLength` is a standard function (in library `List`) whose type is given by

    ```
    genericLength :: Num a => [b] -> a
    ```

    Now consider the following expression:

    ```
    let { len = genericLength xs } in (len, len)
    ```

    It looks as if `len` should be computed only once, but without Rule 1 it might be computed twice, once at each of two different overloadings. If the programmer does actually wish the computation to be repeated, an explicit type signature may be added:

    ```
    let { len :: Num a => a; len = genericLength xs } in (len, len)
    ```

- *Rule 1 prevents ambiguity:* e.g. consider the declaration group

    ```
    [(n,s)] = reads t
    ```

    Recall that `reads` is a standard function whose type is given by the signature

    ```
    reads :: (Read a) => String -> [(a,String)]
    ```

    Without Rule 1, n would be assigned the type $\forall$ a. Read a $\Rightarrow$ a and s the type $\forall$ a. Read a $\Rightarrow$ String. The latter is an invalid type, because it is inherently ambiguous. It is not possible to determine at what overloading to use s, nor can this be solved by adding a type signature for s. Hence, when *non-simple* pattern bindings are used (Section 4.4.3.2), the types inferred are always monomorphic in their constrained type variables, irrespective of whether a type signature is provided. In this case, both n and s are monomorphic in a.

The same constraint applies to pattern-bound functions. For example, in

```
(f,g) = ((+),(-))
```

both f and g are monomorphic regardless of any type signatures supplied for f or g.

Rule 2 is required because there is no way to enforce monomorphic use of an *exported* binding, except by performing type inference on modules outside the current module. Rule 2 states that the exact types of all the variables bound in a module must be determined by that module alone, and not by any modules that import it.

```
module M1(len1) where
  default( Int, Double )
  len1 = genericLength "Hello"

module M2 where
  import M1(len1)
  len2 = (2*len1) :: Rational
```

When type inference on module M1 is complete, len1 has the monomorphic type Num a => a (by Rule 1). Rule 2 now states that the monomorphic type variable a is ambiguous, and must be resolved using the defaulting rules of Section 4.3.4. Hence, len1 gets type Int, and its use in len2 is type-incorrect. (If the above code is actually what is wanted, a type signature on len1 would solve the problem.)

This issue does not arise for nested bindings, because their entire scope is visible to the compiler.

Consequences   The monomorphism rule has a number of consequences for the programmer. Anything defined with function syntax usually generalizes as a function is expected to. Thus in

```
f x y = x+y
```

the function f may be used at any overloading in class Num. There is no danger of recomputation here. However, the same function defined with pattern syntax:

```
f = \x -> \y -> x+y
```

requires a type signature if f is to be fully overloaded. Many functions are most naturally defined using simple pattern bindings; the user must be careful to affix these with type signatures to retain full overloading. The standard prelude contains many examples of this:

```
sum  :: (Num a) => [a] -> a
sum  =  foldl (+) 0
```

Rule 1 applies to both top-level and nested definitions. Consider

```
module M where
  len1 = genericLength "Hello"
  len2 = (2*len1) :: Rational
```

Here, type inference finds that len1 has the monomorphic type (Num a => a); and the type variable a is resolved to Rational when performing type inference on len2.

4.6   Kind Inference

This section describes the rules that are used to perform *kind inference*, i.e. to calculate a suitable kind for each type constructor and class appearing in a given program.

The first step in the kind inference process is to arrange the set of datatype, synonym, and class definitions into dependency groups. This can be achieved in much the same way as the dependency analysis for value declarations that was described in Section 4.5. For example, the following program fragment includes the definition of a datatype constructor D, a synonym S and a class C, all of which would be included in the same dependency group:

```
data C a => D a = Foo (S a)
type S a = [D a]
class C a where
     bar :: a -> D a -> Bool
```

The kinds of variables, constructors, and classes within each group are determined using standard techniques of type inference and kind-preserving unification [10]. For example, in the definitions above, the parameter a appears as an argument of the function constructor (->) in the type of bar and hence must have kind $*$. It follows that both D and S must have kind $* \rightarrow *$ and that every instance of class C must have kind $*$.

It is possible that some parts of an inferred kind may not be fully determined by the corresponding definitions; in such cases, a default of $*$ is assumed. For example, we could assume an arbitrary kind κ for the a parameter in each of the following examples:

```
data App f a = A (f a)
data Tree a  = Leaf | Fork (Tree a) (Tree a)
```

This would give kinds $(\kappa \rightarrow *) \rightarrow \kappa \rightarrow *$ and $\kappa \rightarrow *$ for App and Tree, respectively, for any kind κ, and would require an extension to allow polymorphic kinds. Instead, using the default binding $\kappa = *$, the actual kinds for these two constructors are $(* \rightarrow *) \rightarrow * \rightarrow *$ and $* \rightarrow *$, respectively.

Defaults are applied to each dependency group without consideration of the ways in which particular type constructor constants or classes are used in later dependency groups or elsewhere in the program. For example, adding the following definition to those above does not influence the kind inferred for Tree (by changing it to $(* \rightarrow *) \rightarrow *$, for instance), and instead generates a static error because the kind of [ ], $* \rightarrow *$, does not match the kind $*$ that is expected for an argument of Tree:

```
type FunnyTree = Tree []      -- invalid
```

This is important because it ensures that each constructor and class are used consistently with the same kind whenever they are in scope.

JFP **13** (1): 67–80, January 2003. © 2003 Cambridge University Press

DOI: 10.1017/S0956796803000716 Printed in the United Kingdom

Chapter 5

Modules

A module defines a collection of values, datatypes, type synonyms, classes, etc. (see Chapter 4), in an environment created by a set of *imports* (resources brought into scope from other modules). It *exports* some of these resources, making them available to other modules. We use the term *entity* to refer to a value, type, or class defined in, imported into, or perhaps exported from a module.

A Haskell *program* is a collection of modules, one of which, by convention, must be called `Main` and must export the value `main`. The *value* of the program is the value of the identifier `main` in module `Main`, which must be a computation of type `IO` τ for some type τ (see Chapter 7). When the program is executed, the computation `main` is performed, and its result (of type τ) is discarded.

Modules may reference other modules via explicit `import` declarations, each giving the name of a module to be imported and specifying its entities to be imported. Modules may be mutually recursive.

Modules are used for name-space control, and are not first class values. A multi-module Haskell program can be converted into a single-module program by giving each entity a unique name, changing all occurrences to refer to the appropriate unique name, and then concatenating all the module bodies[1]. For example, here is a three-module program:

---

[1]There are two minor exceptions to this statement. First, `default` declarations scope over a single module (see Section 4.3.4). Second, Rule 2 of the monomorphism restriction (see Section 4.5.5) is affected by module boundaries.

```
module Main where
  import A
  import B
  main = A.f >> B.f

module A where
  f = ...

module B where
  f = ...
```

It is equivalent to the following single-module program:

```
module Main where
  main = af >> bf

  af = ...

  bf = ...
```

Because they are allowed to be mutually recursive, modules allow a program to be partitioned freely without regard to dependencies.

The name-space for modules themselves is flat, with each module being associated with a unique module name (which are Haskell identifiers beginning with a capital letter; i.e. *modid*). There is one distinguished module, `Prelude`, which is imported into all modules by default (see Section 5.6), plus a set of standard library modules that may be imported as required (see Part II).

5.1   Module Structure

A module defines a mutually recursive scope containing declarations for value bindings, data types, type synonyms, classes, etc. (see Chapter 4).

module	$\rightarrow$	**module** *modid* [*exports*] **where** *body*
	|	*body*
body	$\rightarrow$	{ *impdecls* ; *topdecls* }
	|	{ *impdecls* }
	|	{ *topdecls* }

modid	$\rightarrow$	*conid*	
impdecls	$\rightarrow$	*impdecl$_1$* ; ... ; *impdecl$_n$*	$(n \geq 1)$
topdecls	$\rightarrow$	*topdecl$_1$* ; ... ; *topdecl$_n$*	$(n \geq 1)$

A module begins with a header: the keyword **module**, the module name, and a list of entities (enclosed in round parentheses) to be exported. The header is followed by a possibly-empty list of **import** declarations (*impdecls*, Section 5.3) that specify modules to be imported, optionally restricting the imported bindings. This is followed by a possibly-empty list of top-level declarations (*topdecls*, Chapter 4).

An abbreviated form of module, consisting only of the module body, is permitted. If this is used, the header is assumed to be 'module Main(main) where'. If the first lexeme in the abbreviated module is not a {, then the layout rule applies for the top level of the module.

5.2 Export Lists

$$
\begin{array}{lll}
exports & \rightarrow & (\ export_1\ ,\ \ldots\ ,\ export_n\ [\ ,\ ]\ ) \qquad\qquad (n \geq 0) \\[1ex]
export & \rightarrow & qvar \\
 & | & qtycon\ [(\ ..\ )\ |\ (\ cname_1\ ,\ \ldots\ ,\ cname_n\ )] \quad (n > 0) \\
 & | & qtycls\ [(\ ..\ )\ |\ (\ var_1\ ,\ \ldots\ ,\ var_n\ )] \qquad (n \geq 0) \\
 & | & \texttt{module}\ modid \\[1ex]
cname & \rightarrow & var\ |\ con
\end{array}
$$

An *export list* identifies the entities to be exported by a module declaration. A module implementation may only export an entity that it declares, or that it imports from some other module. If the export list is omitted, all values, types and classes defined in the module are exported, *but not those that are imported*.

Entities in an export list may be named as follows:

1. A value, field name, or class method, whether declared in the module body or imported, may be named by giving the name of the value as a *qvarid*, which must be in scope. Operators should be enclosed in parentheses to turn them into *qvarid*s.

2. An algebraic datatype T declared by a data or newtype declaration may be named in one of three ways:

   - The form T names the type *but not the constructors or field names*. The ability to export a type without its constructors allows the construction of abstract datatypes (see Section 5.8).

   - The form $T\,(c_1,\ \ldots,c_n)$, names the type and some or all of its constructors and field names.

   - The abbreviated form $T\,(\,..\,)$ names the type and all its constructors and field names that are currently in scope (whether qualified or not).

   In all cases, the (possibly-qualified) type constructor T must be in scope. The constructor and field names c_i in the second form are unqualified; one of these subordinate names is legal if and only if (a) it names a constructor or field of T, and (b) the constructor or field is in scope in the module body *regardless of whether it is in scope under a qualified or unqualified name*. For example, the following is legal

```
module A( Mb.Maybe( Nothing, Just ) ) where
    import qualified Maybe as Mb
```

Data constructors cannot be named in export lists except as subordinate names, because they cannot otherwise be distinguished from type constructors.

3. A type synonym T declared by a `type` declaration may be named by the form T, where T is in scope.

4. A class C with operations $f_1, \ldots, f_n$ declared in a `class` declaration may be named in one of three ways:

   - The form C names the class *but not the class methods*.
   - The form $C(f_1, \ldots, f_n)$, names the class and some or all of its methods.
   - The abbreviated form $C(..)$ names the class and all its methods that are in scope (whether qualified or not).

   In all cases, C must be in scope. In the second form, one of the (unqualified) subordinate names f_i is legal if and only if (a) it names a class method of C, and (b) the class method is in scope in the module body regardless of whether it is in scope under a qualified or unqualified name.

5. The form "`module M`" names the set of all entities that are in scope with both an unqualified name e and a qualified name M.e. This set may be empty. For example:

   ```
   module Queue( module Stack, enqueue, dequeue ) where
           import Stack
               ...
   ```

   Here the module `Queue` uses the module name `Stack` in its export list to abbreviate all the entities imported from `Stack`.

   A module can name its own local definitions in its export list using its own name in the "`module M`" syntax, because a local declaration brings into scope both a qualified and unqualified name (Section 5.5.1). For example:

   ```
   module Mod1( module Mod1, module Mod2 ) where
   import Mod2
   import Mod3
   ```

   Here module `Mod1` exports all local definitions as well as those imported from `Mod2` but not those imported from `Mod3`.

   It is an error to use `module M` in an export list unless M is the module bearing the export list, or M is imported by at least one import declaration (qualified or unqualified).

Exports lists are cumulative: the set of entities exported by an export list is the union of the entities exported by the individual items of the list.

It makes no difference to an importing module how an entity was exported. For example, a field name f from data type T may be exported individually (f, item (1) above); or as an explicitly-named member of its data type (T(f), item (2)); or as an implicitly-named member (T(..), item(2)); or by exporting an entire module (module M, item (5)).

The *unqualified* names of the entities exported by a module must all be distinct (within their respective namespace). For example

```
module A ( C.f, C.g, g, module B ) where    -- an invalid module
import B(f)
import qualified C(f,g)
g = f True
```

There are no name clashes within module A itself, but there are name clashes in the export list between C.g and g (assuming C.g and g are different entities – remember, modules can import each other recursively), and between module B and C.f (assuming B.f and C.f are different entities).

5.3 Import Declarations

impdecl	$\rightarrow$	import [qualified] *modid* [as *modid*] [*impspec*]	
			(*empty declaration*)
impspec	$\rightarrow$	(*import₁* , ... , *importₙ* [,])	($n \geq 0$)
		hiding (*import₁* , ... , *importₙ* [,])	($n \geq 0$)
import	$\rightarrow$	*var*	
		tycon [(..)	(*cname₁* , ... , *cnameₙ*)]	($n \geq 0$)
		tycls [(..)	(*var₁* , ... , *varₙ*)]	($n \geq 0$)
cname	$\rightarrow$	*var*	*con*	

The entities exported by a module may be brought into scope in another module with an import declaration at the beginning of the module. The import declaration names the module to be imported and optionally specifies the entities to be imported. A single module may be imported by more than one import declaration. Imported names serve as top level declarations: they scope over the entire body of the module but may be shadowed by local non-top-level bindings.

The effect of multiple import declarations is strictly cumulative: an entity is in scope if it is imported by any of the import declarations in a module. The ordering of import declarations is irrelevant.

Lexically, the terminal symbols "as", "qualified" and "hiding" are each a *varid* rather than a *reservedid*. They have special significance only in the context of an import declaration; they may also be used as variables.

5.3.1   What is Imported

Exactly which entities are to be imported can be specified in one of the following three ways:

1. The imported entities can be specified explicitly by listing them in parentheses. Items in the list have the same form as those in export lists, except qualifiers are not permitted and the 'module *modid*' entity is not permitted. When the (..) form of import is used for a type or class, the (..) refers to all of the constructors, methods, or field names exported from the module.

   The list must name only entities exported by the imported module. The list may be empty, in which case nothing except the instances is imported.

2. Entities can be excluded by using the form `hiding(` *import₁* `,` ... `,` *importₙ* `)`, which specifies that all entities exported by the named module should be imported except for those named in the list. Data constructors may be named directly in hiding lists without being prefixed by the associated type. Thus, in

   ```
   import M hiding (C)
   ```

   any constructor, class, or type named C is excluded. In contrast, using C in an import list names only a class or type.

   It is an error to hide an entity that is not, in fact, exported by the imported module.

3. Finally, if *impspec* is omitted then all the entities exported by the specified module are imported.

5.3.2   Qualified Import

For each entity imported under the rules of Section 5.3.1, the top-level environment is extended. If the import declaration used the `qualified` keyword, only the *qualified name* of the entity is brought into scope. If the `qualified` keyword is omitted, then *both* the qualified *and* unqualified name of the entity is brought into scope. Section 5.5.1 describes qualified names in more detail.

The qualifier on the imported name is either the name of the imported module, or the local alias given in the `as` clause (Section 5.3.3) on the `import` statement. Hence, *the qualifier is not necessarily the name of the module in which the entity was originally declared.*

The ability to exclude the unqualified names allows full programmer control of the unqualified namespace: a locally defined entity can share the same name as a qualified import:

```
module Ring where
import qualified Prelude    -- All Prelude names must be qualified
import List( nub )

l1 + l2 = l1 Prelude.++ l2 -- + differs from that in the Prelude
l1 * l2 = nub (l1 + l2)     -- * differs from that in the Prelude

succ = (Prelude.+ 1)
```

5.3.3 Local Aliases

Imported modules may be assigned a local alias in the importing module using the `as` clause. For example, in

```
import qualified VeryLongModuleName as C
```

entities must be referenced using 'C.' as a qualifier instead of 'VeryLongModuleName.'. This also allows a different module to be substituted for VeryLongModuleName without changing the qualifiers used for the imported module. It is legal for more than one module in scope to use the same qualifier, provided that all names can still be resolved unambiguously. For example:

```
module M where
    import qualified Foo as A
    import qualified Baz as A
    x = A.f
```

This module is legal provided only that Foo and Baz do not both export f.

An `as` clause may also be used on an un-`qualified` `import` statement:

```
import Foo as A(f)
```

This declaration brings into scope f and A.f.

5.3.4 Examples

To clarify the above import rules, suppose the module A exports x and y. Then this table shows what names are brought into scope by the specified import statement:

Import declaration	Names brought into scope
`import A`	x, y, A.x, A.y
`import A()`	(nothing)
`import A(x)`	x, A.x
`import qualified A`	A.x, A.y
`import qualified A()`	(nothing)
`import qualified A(x)`	A.x
`import A hiding ()`	x, y, A.x, A.y
`import A hiding (x)`	y, A.y
`import qualified A hiding ()`	A.x, A.y
`import qualified A hiding (x)`	A.y
`import A as B`	x, y, B.x, B.y
`import A as B(x)`	x, B.x
`import qualified A as B`	B.x, B.y

In all cases, all instance declarations in scope in module A are imported (Section 5.4).

5.4   Importing and Exporting Instance Declarations

Instance declarations cannot be explicitly named on import or export lists. All instances in scope within a module are *always* exported and any import brings *all* instances in from the imported module. Thus, an instance declaration is in scope if and only if a chain of `import` declarations leads to the module containing the instance declaration.

For example, `import M()` does not bring any new names in scope from module M, but does bring in any instances visible in M. A module whose only purpose is to provide instance declarations can have an empty export list. For example

```
module MyInstances() where
   instance Show (a -> b) where
      show fn = "<<function>>"
   instance Show (IO a) where
      show io = "<<IO action>>"
```

5.5   Name Clashes and Closure

5.5.1   Qualified Names

A *qualified name* is written as *modid* **.** *name* (Section 2.4). A qualified name is brought into scope:

- *By a top level declaration.* A top-level declaration brings into scope both the unqualified *and* the qualified name of the entity being defined. Thus:

  ```
  module M where
     f x = ...
     g x = M.f x x
  ```

  is legal. The *defining* occurrence must mention the *unqualified* name; therefore, it is illegal to write

  ```
  module M where
     M.f x = ...                    -- ILLEGAL
     g x = let M.y = x+1 in ...    -- ILLEGAL
  ```

- *By an* `import` *declaration.* An `import` declaration, whether `qualified` or not, always brings into scope the qualified name of the imported entity (Section 5.3). This allows a qualified import to be replaced with an unqualified one without forcing changes in the references to the imported names.

5.5.2 Name Clashes

If a module contains a bound occurrence of a name, such as `f` or `A.f`, it must be possible unambiguously to resolve which entity is thereby referred to; that is, there must be only one binding for `f` or `A.f` respectively.

It is *not* an error for there to exist names that cannot be so resolved, provided that the program does not mention those names. For example:

```
module A where
   import B
   import C
   tup = (b, c, d, x)
module B( d, b, x, y ) where
   import D
   x = ...
   y = ...
   b = ...
module C( d, c, x, y ) where
   import D
   x = ...
   y = ...
   c = ...
module D( d ) where
   d = ...
```

Consider the definition of `tup`.

- The references to `b` and `c` can be unambiguously resolved to `b` declared in `B`, and `c` declared in `C` respectively.

- The reference to `d` is unambiguously resolved to `d` declared in `D`. In this case the same entity is brought into scope by two routes (the import of `B` and the import of `C`), and can be referred to in `A` by the names `d`, `B.d`, and `C.d`.

- The reference to `x` is ambiguous: it could mean `x` declared in `B`, or `x` declared in `C`. The ambiguity could be fixed by replacing the reference to `x` by `B.x` or `C.x`.

- There is no reference to `y`, so it is not erroneous that distinct entities called `y` are exported by both `B` and `C`. An error is only reported if `y` is actually mentioned.

The name occurring in a type signature or fixity declarations is always unqualified, and unambiguously refers to another declaration in the same declaration list (except that the fixity declaration for a class method can occur at top level – Section 4.4.2). For example, the following module is legal:

```
module F where
    sin :: Float -> Float
    sin x = (x::Float)

    f x = Prelude.sin (F.sin x)
```

The local declaration for `sin` is legal, even though the Prelude function `sin` is implicitly in scope. The references to `Prelude.sin` and `F.sin` must both be qualified to make it unambiguous which `sin` is meant. However, the unqualified name `sin` in the type signature in the first line of `F` unambiguously refers to the local declaration for `sin`.

5.5.3   Closure

Every module in a Haskell program must be *closed*. That is, every name explicitly mentioned by the source code must be either defined locally or imported from another module. However, entities that the compiler requires for type checking or other compile time analysis need not be imported if they are not mentioned by name. The Haskell compilation system is responsible for finding any information needed for compilation without the help of the programmer. That is, the import of a variable x does not require that the datatypes and classes in the signature of x be brought into the module along with x unless these entities are referenced by name in the user program. The Haskell system silently imports any information that must accompany an entity for type checking or any other purposes. Such entities need not even be explicitly exported: the following program is valid even though T does not escape M1:

```
module M1(x) where
    data T = T
    x = T
module M2 where
    import M1(x)
    y = x
```

In this example, there is no way to supply an explicit type signature for y since T is not in scope. Whether or not T is explicitly exported, module M2 knows enough about T to correctly type check the program.

The type of an exported entity is unaffected by non-exported type synonyms. For example, in

```
module M(x) where
    type T = Int
    x :: T
    x = 1
```

the type of x is both T and Int; these are interchangeable even when T is not in scope. That is, the definition of T is available to any module that encounters it whether or not the name T is in scope. The only reason to export T is to allow other modules to refer it by name; the type checker finds the definition of T if needed whether or not it is exported.

5.6 Standard Prelude

Many of the features of Haskell are defined in Haskell itself as a library of standard datatypes, classes, and functions, called the "Standard Prelude." In Haskell, the Prelude is contained in the module `Prelude`. There are also many predefined library modules, which provide less frequently used functions and types. For example, complex numbers, arrays and most of the input/output are all part of the standard libraries. These are defined in Part II. Separating libraries from the Prelude has the advantage of reducing the size and complexity of the Prelude, allowing it to be more easily assimilated, and increasing the space of useful names available to the programmer.

Prelude and library modules differ from other modules in that their semantics (but not their implementation) are a fixed part of the Haskell language definition. This means, for example, that a compiler may optimize calls to functions in the Prelude without consulting the source code of the Prelude.

5.6.1 The `Prelude` Module

The `Prelude` module is imported automatically into all modules as if by the statement 'import Prelude', if and only if it is not imported with an explicit `import` declaration. This provision for explicit import allows entities defined in the Prelude to be selectively imported, just like those from any other module.

The semantics of the entities in `Prelude` is specified by a reference implementation of `Prelude` written in Haskell, given in Chapter 8. Some datatypes (such as `Int`) and functions (such as `Int` addition) cannot be specified directly in Haskell. Since the treatment of such entities depends on the implementation, they are not formally defined in the appendix. The implementation of `Prelude` is also incomplete in its treatment of tuples: there should be an infinite family of tuples and their instance declarations, but the implementation only gives a scheme.

Chapter 8 defines the module `Prelude` using several other modules: `PreludeList`, `PreludeIO`, and so on. These modules are *not* part of Haskell 98, and they cannot be imported separately. They are simply there to help explain the structure of the `Prelude` module; they should be considered part of its implementation, not part of the language definition.

5.6.2 Shadowing Prelude Names

The rules about the Prelude have been cast so that it is possible to use Prelude names for nonstandard purposes; however, every module that does so must have an `import` declaration that makes this nonstandard usage explicit. For example:

```
module A( null, nonNull ) where
  import Prelude hiding( null )
  null, nonNull :: Int -> Bool
  null    x = x == 0
  nonNull x = not (null x)
```

Module A redefines `null`, and contains an unqualified reference to `null` on the right hand side of `nonNull`. The latter would be ambiguous without the `hiding(null)` on the `import Prelude` statement. Every module that imports A unqualified, and then makes an unqualified reference to `null` must also resolve the ambiguous use of `null` just as A does. Thus there is little danger of accidentally shadowing Prelude names.

It is possible to construct and use a different module to serve in place of the Prelude. Other than the fact that it is implicitly imported, the Prelude is an ordinary Haskell module; it is special only in that some objects in the Prelude are referenced by special syntactic constructs. Redefining names used by the Prelude does not affect the meaning of these special constructs. For example, in

```
module B where
   import Prelude()
   import MyPrelude
   f x = (x,x)
   g x = (,) x x
   h x = [x] ++ []
```

the explicit `import Prelude()` declaration prevents the automatic import of `Prelude`, while the declaration `import MyPrelude` brings the non-standard prelude into scope. The special syntax for tuples (such as `(x,x)` and `(,)`) and lists (such as `[x]` and `[]`) continues to refer to the tuples and lists defined by the standard `Prelude`; there is no way to redefine the meaning of `[x]`, for example, in terms of a different implementation of lists. On the other hand, the use of `++` is not special syntax, so it refers to `++` imported from `MyPrelude`.

It is not possible, however, to hide `instance` declarations in the `Prelude`. For example, one cannot define a new instance for `Show Char`.

5.7   Separate Compilation

Depending on the Haskell implementation used, separate compilation of mutually recursive modules may require that imported modules contain additional information so that they may be referenced before they are compiled. Explicit type signatures for all exported values may be necessary to deal with mutual recursion. The precise details of separate compilation are not defined by this report.

5.8   Abstract Datatypes

The ability to export a datatype without its constructors allows the construction of abstract datatypes (ADTs). For example, an ADT for stacks could be defined as:

```
module Stack( StkType, push, pop, empty ) where
   data StkType a = EmptyStk | Stk a (StkType a)
   push x s = Stk x s
   pop (Stk _ s) = s
   empty = EmptyStk
```

Modules importing `Stack` cannot construct values of type `StkType` because they do not have access to the constructors of the type. Instead, they must use `push`, `pop`, and `empty` to construct such values.

It is also possible to build an ADT on top of an existing type by using a `newtype` declaration. For example, stacks can be defined with lists:

```
module Stack( StkType, push, pop, empty ) where
   newtype StkType a = Stk [a]
   push x (Stk s) = Stk (x:s)
   pop (Stk (_:s)) = Stk s
   empty = Stk []
```

JFP **13** (1): 81–96, January 2003. © 2003 Cambridge University Press
DOI: 10.1017/S0956796803000819 Printed in the United Kingdom

Chapter 6

Predefined Types and Classes

The Haskell Prelude contains predefined classes, types, and functions that are implicitly imported into every Haskell program. In this chapter, we describe the types and classes found in the Prelude. Most functions are not described in detail here as they can easily be understood from their definitions as given in Chapter 8. Other predefined types such as arrays, complex numbers, and rationals are defined in Part II.

6.1 Standard Haskell Types

These types are defined by the Haskell Prelude. Numeric types are described in Section 6.4. When appropriate, the Haskell definition of the type is given. Some definitions may not be completely valid on syntactic grounds but they faithfully convey the meaning of the underlying type.

6.1.1 Booleans

```
data  Bool  =  False | True deriving
                        (Read, Show, Eq, Ord, Enum, Bounded)
```

The boolean type `Bool` is an enumeration. The basic boolean functions are `&&` (and), `||` (or), and `not`. The name `otherwise` is defined as `True` to make guarded expressions more readable.

6.1.2   Characters and Strings

The character type Char is an enumeration whose values represent Unicode characters [15]. The lexical syntax for characters is defined in Section 2.6; character literals are nullary constructors in the datatype Char. Type Char is an instance of the classes Read, Show, Eq, Ord, Enum, and Bounded. The toEnum and fromEnum functions, standard functions from class Enum, map characters to and from the Int type.

Note that ASCII control characters each have several representations in character literals: numeric escapes, ASCII mnemonic escapes, and the \^X notation. In addition, there are the following equivalences: \a and \BEL, \b and \BS, \f and \FF, \r and \CR, \t and \HT, \v and \VT, and \n and \LF.

A *string* is a list of characters:

```
type   String   =   [Char]
```

Strings may be abbreviated using the lexical syntax described in Section 2.6. For example, "A string" abbreviates

```
[ 'A',' ','s','t','r', 'i','n','g']
```

6.1.3   Lists

```
data  [a]  =  []  |  a : [a]   deriving (Eq, Ord)
```

Lists are an algebraic datatype of two constructors, although with special syntax, as described in Section 3.7. The first constructor is the null list, written '[ ]' ("nil"), and the second is ':' ("cons"). The module PreludeList (see Chapter 8.2) defines many standard list functions. Arithmetic sequences and list comprehensions, two convenient syntaxes for special kinds of lists, are described in Sections 3.10 and 3.11, respectively. Lists are an instance of classes Read, Show, Eq, Ord, Monad, Functor, and MonadPlus.

6.1.4   Tuples

Tuples are algebraic datatypes with special syntax, as defined in Section 3.8. Each tuple type has a single constructor. All tuples are instances of Eq, Ord, Bounded, Read, and Show (provided, of course, that all their component types are).

There is no upper bound on the size of a tuple, but some Haskell implementations may restrict the size of tuples, and limit the instances associated with larger tuples. However, every Haskell implementation must support tuples up to size 15, together with the instances for Eq, Ord, Bounded, Read, and Show. The Prelude and libraries define tuple functions such as zip for tuples up to a size of 7.

The constructor for a tuple is written by omitting the expressions surrounding the commas; thus `(x,y)` and `(,) x y` produce the same value. The same holds for tuple type constructors; thus, `(Int,Bool,Int)` and `(,,) Int Bool Int` denote the same type.

The following functions are defined for pairs (2-tuples): `fst`, `snd`, `curry`, and `uncurry`. Similar functions are not predefined for larger tuples.

6.1.5 The Unit Datatype

```
data  ()  =  ()  deriving  (Eq,  Ord,  Bounded,  Enum,  Read,  Show)
```

The unit datatype `()` has one non-$\perp$ member, the nullary constructor `()`. See also Section 3.9.

6.1.6 Function Types

Functions are an abstract type: no constructors directly create functional values. The following simple functions are found in the Prelude: `id`, `const`, `(.)`, `flip`, `($)`, and `until`.

6.1.7 The IO and IOError Types

The `IO` type serves as a tag for operations (actions) that interact with the outside world. The `IO` type is abstract: no constructors are visible to the user. `IO` is an instance of the `Monad` and `Functor` classes. Chapter 7 describes I/O operations.

`IOError` is an abstract type representing errors raised by I/O operations. It is an instance of `Show` and `Eq`. Values of this type are constructed by the various I/O functions and are not presented in any further detail in this report. The Prelude contains a few I/O functions (defined in Section 8.4), and the IO Library (Chapter 21) contains many more.

6.1.8 Other Types

```
data  Maybe a      =  Nothing | Just a   deriving (Eq, Ord, Read, Show)
data  Either a b   =  Left a  | Right b  deriving (Eq, Ord, Read, Show)
data  Ordering     =  LT | EQ | GT deriving
                                    (Eq, Ord, Bounded, Enum, Read, Show)
```

The `Maybe` type is an instance of classes `Functor`, `Monad`, and `MonadPlus`. The `Ordering` type is used by `compare` in the class `Ord`. The functions `maybe` and `either` are found in the Prelude.

6.2   Strict Evaluation

Function application in Haskell is non-strict; that is, a function argument is evaluated only when required. Sometimes it is desirable to force the evaluation of a value, using the `seq` function:

```
seq :: a -> b -> b
```

The function `seq` is defined by the equations:

$$\text{seq} \perp b = \perp$$
$$\text{seq } a\ b = b,\ if\ a \neq \perp$$

`seq` is usually introduced to improve performance by avoiding unneeded laziness. Strict datatypes (see Section 4.2.1) are defined in terms of the `$!` operator. However, the provision of `seq` has important semantic consequences, because it is available *at every type*. As a consequence, $\perp$ is not the same as `\x ->` $\perp$, since `seq` can be used to distinguish them. For the same reason, the existence of `seq` weakens Haskell's parametricity properties.

The operator `$!` is strict (call-by-value) application, and is defined in terms of `seq`. The Prelude also defines the `$` operator to perform non-strict application.

```
infixr 0 $, $!
($), ($!) :: (a -> b) -> a -> b
f $   x   =           f x
f $! x    =   x 'seq' f x
```

The non-strict application operator `$` may appear redundant, since ordinary application (`f x`) means the same as (`f $ x`). However, `$` has low, right-associative binding precedence, so it sometimes allows parentheses to be omitted; for example:

```
f $ g $ h x   =   f (g (h x))
```

It is also useful in higher-order situations, such as `map ($ 0) xs`, or `zipWith ($) fs xs`.

6.3   Standard Haskell Classes

Figure 6.1 shows the hierarchy of Haskell classes defined in the Prelude and the Prelude types that are instances of these classes.

Default class method declarations (Section 4.3) are provided for many of the methods in standard classes. A comment with each `class` declaration in Chapter 8 specifies the smallest collection of method definitions that, together with the default declarations, provide a reasonable definition for all the class methods. If there is no such comment, then all class methods must be given to fully specify an instance.

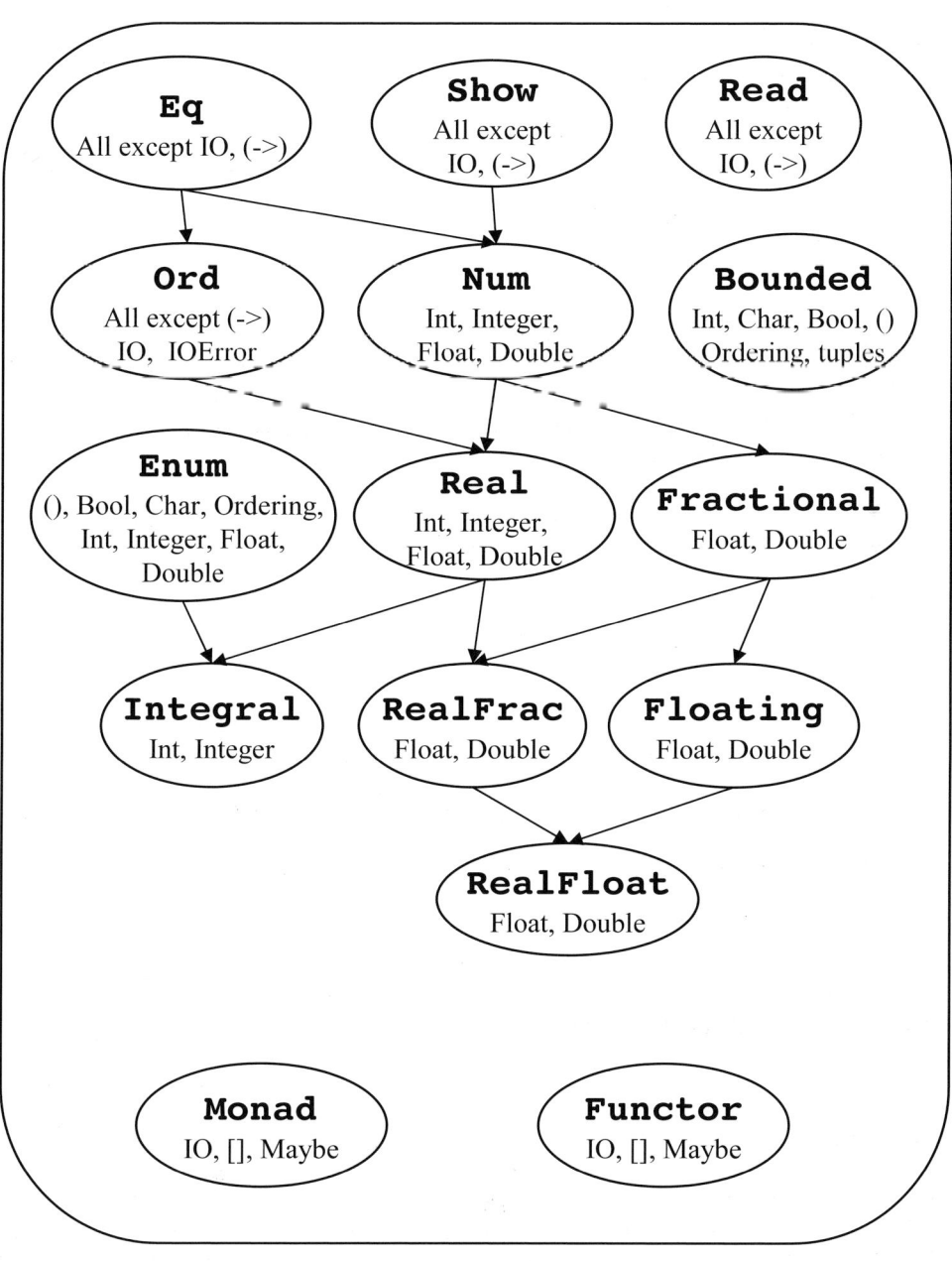

Figure 6.1: Standard Haskell Classes

6.3.1   The Eq Class

```
class  Eq a  where
      (==), (/=)  ::  a -> a -> Bool

      x /= y  = not (x == y)
      x == y  = not (x /= y)
```

The Eq class provides equality (==) and inequality (/=) methods. All basic datatypes except for functions and IO are instances of this class. Instances of Eq can be derived for any user-defined datatype whose constituents are also instances of Eq.

This declaration gives default method declarations for both /= and ==, each being defined in terms of the other. If an instance declaration for Eq defines neither == nor /=, then both will loop. If one is defined, the default method for the other will make use of the one that is defined. If both are defined, neither default method is used.

6.3.2   The Ord Class

```
class  (Eq a) => Ord a  where
   compare                 :: a -> a -> Ordering
   (<), (<=), (>=), (>) :: a -> a -> Bool
   max, min                :: a -> a -> a

   compare x y | x == y    = EQ
               | x <= y    = LT
               | otherwise = GT

   x <= y  = compare x y /= GT
   x <  y  = compare x y == LT
   x >= y  = compare x y /= LT
   x >  y  = compare x y == GT

   -- Note that (min x y, max x y) = (x,y) or (y,x)
   max x y | x <= y    =  y
           | otherwise =  x
   min x y | x <= y    =  x
           | otherwise =  y
```

The Ord class is used for totally ordered datatypes. All basic datatypes except for functions, IO, and IOError, are instances of this class. Instances of Ord can be derived for any user-defined datatype whose constituent types are in Ord. The declared order of the constructors in the data declaration determines the ordering in derived Ord instances. The Ordering datatype allows a single comparison to determine the precise ordering of two objects.

The default declarations allow a user to create an Ord instance either with a type-specific compare function or with type-specific == and <= functions.

6.3.3   The Read and Show Classes

```
type  ReadS a = String -> [(a,String)]
type  ShowS   = String -> String

class  Read a  where
    readsPrec :: Int -> ReadS a
    readList  :: ReadS [a]
    -- ... default decl for readList given in Prelude

class  Show a  where
    showsPrec :: Int -> a -> ShowS
    show      :: a -> String
    showList  :: [a] -> ShowS

    showsPrec _ x s   = show x ++ s
    show x            = showsPrec 0 x ""
    -- ... default decl for showList given in Prelude
```

The Read and Show classes are used to convert values to or from strings. The Int argument to showsPrec and readsPrec gives the operator precedence of the enclosing context (see Section 10.4).

showsPrec and showList return a String-to-String function, to allow constant-time concatenation of its results using function composition. A specialised variant, show, is also provided, which uses precedence context zero, and returns an ordinary String. The method showList is provided to allow the programmer to give a specialised way of showing lists of values. This is particularly useful for the Char type, where values of type String should be shown in double quotes, rather than between square brackets.

Derived instances of Read and Show replicate the style in which a constructor is declared: infix constructors and field names are used on input and output. Strings produced by showsPrec are usually readable by readsPrec.

All Prelude types, except function types and IO types, are instances of Show and Read. (If desired, a programmer can easily make functions and IO types into (vacuous) instances of Show, by providing an instance declaration.)

For convenience, the Prelude provides the following auxiliary functions:

```
reads   :: (Read a) => ReadS a
reads   =  readsPrec 0

shows   :: (Show a) => a -> ShowS
shows   =  showsPrec 0

read    :: (Read a) => String -> a
read s  =  case [x | (x,t) <- reads s, ("","") <- lex t] of
                [x] -> x
                []  -> error "PreludeText.read: no parse"
                _   -> error "PreludeText.read: ambiguous parse"
```

The shows and reads functions use a default precedence of 0. The read function reads input from a string, which must be completely consumed by the input process.

The function lex :: ReadS String, used by read, is also part of the Prelude. It reads a single lexeme from the input, discarding initial white space, and returning the characters that constitute the lexeme. If the input string contains only white space, lex returns a single successful "lexeme" consisting of the empty string. (Thus lex "" = [("","")].) If there is no legal lexeme at the beginning of the input string, lex fails (i.e. returns [ ]).

6.3.4 The Enum Class

```
class   Enum a   where
    succ, pred      :: a -> a
    toEnum          :: Int -> a
    fromEnum        :: a -> Int
    enumFrom        :: a -> [a]              -- [n..]
    enumFromThen    :: a -> a -> [a]         -- [n,n'..]
    enumFromTo      :: a -> a -> [a]         -- [n..m]
    enumFromThenTo  :: a -> a -> a -> [a]    -- [n,n'..m]

    -- Default declarations given in Prelude
```

Class Enum defines operations on sequentially ordered types. The functions succ and pred return the successor and predecessor, respectively, of a value. The functions fromEnum and toEnum map values from a type in Enum to and from Int. The enumFrom... methods are used when translating arithmetic sequences (Section 3.10).

Instances of Enum may be derived for any enumeration type (types whose constructors have no fields); see Chapter 10.

For any type that is an instance of class Bounded as well as Enum, the following should hold:

- The calls succ maxBound and pred minBound should result in a runtime error.

- fromEnum and toEnum should give a runtime error if the result value is not representable in the result type. For example, toEnum 7 :: Bool is an error.

- enumFrom and enumFromThen should be defined with an implicit bound, thus:

```
enumFrom     x   = enumFromTo     x maxBound
enumFromThen x y = enumFromThenTo x y bound
   where
      bound | fromEnum y >= fromEnum x = maxBound
            | otherwise                = minBound
```

The following `Prelude` types are instances of `Enum`:

- Enumeration types: `()`, `Bool`, and `Ordering`. The semantics of these instances is given by Chapter 10. For example, `[LT..]` is the list `[LT,EQ,GT]`.

- `Char`: the instance is given in Chapter 8, based on the primitive functions that convert between a `Char` and an `Int`. For example, `enumFromTo 'a' 'z'` denotes the list of lowercase letters in alphabetical order.

- Numeric types: `Int`, `Integer`, `Float`, `Double`. The semantics of these instances is given next.

For all four numeric types, `succ` adds 1, and `pred` subtracts 1. The conversions `fromEnum` and `toEnum` convert between the type and `Int`. In the case of `Float` and `Double`, the digits after the decimal point may be lost. It is implementation-dependent what `fromEnum` returns when applied to a value that is too large to fit in an `Int`.

For the types `Int` and `Integer`, the enumeration functions have the following meaning:

- The sequence `enumFrom` e_1 is the list $[e_1, e_1 + 1, e_1 + 2, \dots]$.

- The sequence `enumFromThen` e_1 e_2 is the list $[e_1, e_1 + i, e_1 + 2i, \dots]$, where the increment, i, is $e_2 - e_1$. The increment may be zero or negative. If the increment is zero, all the list elements are the same.

- The sequence `enumFromTo` e_1 e_3 is the list $[e_1, e_1 + 1, e_1 + 2, \dots e_3]$. The list is empty if $e_1 > e_3$.

- The sequence `enumFromThenTo` e_1 e_2 e_3 is the list $[e_1, e_1 + i, e_1 + 2i, \dots e_3]$, where the increment, i, is $e_2 - e_1$. If the increment is positive or zero, the list terminates when the next element would be greater than e_3; the list is empty if $e_1 > e_3$. If the increment is negative, the list terminates when the next element would be less than e_3; the list is empty if $e1 < e_3$.

For `Float` and `Double`, the semantics of the `enumFrom` family is given by the rules for `Int` above, except that the list terminates when the elements become greater than $e_3 + i/2$ for positive increment i, or when they become less than $e_3 + i/2$ for negative i.

For all four of these Prelude numeric types, all of the `enumFrom` family of functions are strict in all their arguments.

6.3.5 The Functor Class

```
class  Functor f  where
    fmap    :: (a -> b) -> f a -> f b
```

The `Functor` class is used for types that can be mapped over. Lists, `IO`, and `Maybe` are in this class.

Instances of `Functor` should satisfy the following laws:

$$
\begin{array}{lcl}
\texttt{fmap id} & = & \texttt{id} \\
\texttt{fmap (f . g)} & = & \texttt{fmap f . fmap g}
\end{array}
$$

All instances of `Functor` defined in the Prelude satisfy these laws.

6.3.6   The Monad Class

```
class  Monad m  where
    (>>=)    :: m a -> (a -> m b) -> m b
    (>>)     :: m a -> m b -> m b
    return   :: a -> m a
    fail     :: String -> m a

    m >> k  =  m >>= \_ -> k
    fail s  = error s
```

The `Monad` class defines the basic operations over a *monad*. See Chapter 7 for more information about monads.

"do" expressions provide a convenient syntax for writing monadic expressions (see Section 3.14). The `fail` method is invoked on pattern-match failure in a `do` expression.

In the Prelude, lists, `Maybe`, and `IO` are all instances of `Monad`. The `fail` method for lists returns the empty list [ ], for `Maybe` returns `Nothing`, and for `IO` raises a user exception in the IO monad (see Section 7.3).

Instances of `Monad` should satisfy the following laws:

$$
\begin{array}{lcl}
\texttt{return a >>= k} & = & \texttt{k a} \\
\texttt{m >>= return} & = & \texttt{m} \\
\texttt{m >>= (\textbackslash x -> k x >>= h)} & = & \texttt{(m >>= k) >>= h}
\end{array}
$$

Instances of both `Monad` and `Functor` should additionally satisfy the law:

$$
\texttt{fmap f xs} = \texttt{xs >>= return . f}
$$

All instances of `Monad` defined in the Prelude satisfy these laws.

The Prelude provides the following auxiliary functions:

```
sequence   :: Monad m => [m a] -> m [a]
sequence_  :: Monad m => [m a] -> m ()
mapM       :: Monad m => (a -> m b) -> [a] -> m [b]
mapM_      :: Monad m => (a -> m b) -> [a] -> m ()
(=<<)      :: Monad m => (a -> m b) -> m a -> m b
```

6.3.7 The Bounded Class

```
class  Bounded a  where
   minBound, maxBound :: a
```

The `Bounded` class is used to name the upper and lower limits of a type. `Ord` is not a superclass of `Bounded` since types that are not totally ordered may also have upper and lower bounds. The types `Int`, `Char`, `Bool`, `()`, `Ordering`, and all tuples are instances of `Bounded`. The `Bounded` class may be derived for any enumeration type; `minBound` is the first constructor listed in the `data` declaration and `maxBound` is the last. `Bounded` may also be derived for single-constructor datatypes whose constituent types are in `Bounded`.

6.4 Numbers

Haskell provides several kinds of numbers; the numeric types and the operations upon them have been heavily influenced by Common Lisp and Scheme. Numeric function names and operators are usually overloaded, using several type classes with an inclusion relation shown in Figure 6.1, page 85. The class `Num` of numeric types is a subclass of `Eq`, since all numbers may be compared for equality; its subclass `Real` is also a subclass of `Ord`, since the other comparison operations apply to all but complex numbers (defined in the `Complex` library). The class `Integral` contains integers of both limited and unlimited range; the class `Fractional` contains all non-integral types; and the class `Floating` contains all floating-point types, both real and complex.

The Prelude defines only the most basic numeric types: fixed sized integers (`Int`), arbitrary precision integers (`Integer`), single precision floating (`Float`), and double precision floating (`Double`). Other numeric types such as rationals and complex numbers are defined in libraries. In particular, the type `Rational` is a ratio of two `Integer` values, as defined in the `Ratio` library.

The default floating point operations defined by the Haskell Prelude do not conform to current language independent arithmetic (LIA) standards. These standards require considerably more complexity in the numeric structure and have thus been relegated to a library. Some, but not all, aspects of the IEEE floating point standard have been accounted for in Prelude class `RealFloat`.

The standard numeric types are listed in Table 6.1. The finite-precision integer type `Int` covers at least the range $[-2^{29}, 2^{29} - 1]$. As `Int` is an instance of the `Bounded` class, `maxBound` and `minBound` can be used to determine the exact `Int` range defined by an implementation. `Float` is implementation-defined; it is desirable that this type be at least equal in range and precision to the IEEE single-precision type. Similarly, `Double` should cover IEEE double-precision. The results of exceptional conditions (such as overflow or underflow) on the fixed-precision numeric types are undefined; an implementation may choose error ($\perp$, semantically), a truncated value, or a special value such as infinity, indefinite, etc.

The standard numeric classes and other numeric functions defined in the Prelude are shown in Figures 6.2 and 6.3. Figure 6.1 shows the class dependencies and built-in types that are instances of the numeric classes.

Table 6.1: Standard Numeric Types

Type	Class	Description
Integer	Integral	Arbitrary-precision integers
Int	Integral	Fixed-precision integers
(Integral a) => Ratio a	RealFrac	Rational numbers
Float	RealFloat	Real floating-point, single precision
Double	RealFloat	Real floating-point, double precision
(RealFloat a) => Complex a	Floating	Complex floating-point

6.4.1   Numeric Literals

The syntax of numeric literals is given in Section 2.5. An integer literal represents the application of the function `fromInteger` to the appropriate value of type `Integer`. Similarly, a floating literal stands for an application of `fromRational` to a value of type `Rational` (that is, `Ratio Integer`). Given the typings:

```
fromInteger  :: (Num a) => Integer -> a
fromRational :: (Fractional a) => Rational -> a
```

integer and floating literals have the typings `(Num a) => a` and `(Fractional a) => a`, respectively. Numeric literals are defined in this indirect way so that they may be interpreted as values of any appropriate numeric type. See Section 4.3.4 for a discussion of overloading ambiguity.

6.4.2   Arithmetic and Number-Theoretic Operations

The infix class methods (+), (*), (-), and the unary function `negate` (which can also be written as a prefix minus sign; see Section 3.4) apply to all numbers. The class methods `quot`, `rem`, `div`, and `mod` apply only to integral numbers, while the class method (/) applies only to fractional ones. The `quot`, `rem`, `div`, and `mod` class methods satisfy these laws if `y` is non-zero:

```
(x `quot` y)*y + (x `rem` y) == x
(x `div`  y)*y + (x `mod` y) == x
```

`quot` is integer division truncated toward zero, while the result of `div` is truncated toward negative infinity. The `quotRem` class method takes a dividend and a divisor as arguments and returns a (quotient, remainder) pair; `divMod` is defined similarly:

```
quotRem x y  =  (x `quot` y, x `rem` y)
divMod  x y  =  (x `div` y, x `mod` y)
```

Also available on integral numbers are the even and odd predicates:

```
even x =  x `rem` 2 == 0
odd    =  not . even
```

```
class  (Eq a, Show a) => Num a  where
    (+), (-), (*)   :: a -> a -> a
    negate          :: a -> a
    abs, signum     :: a -> a
    fromInteger     :: Integer -> a
class  (Num a, Ord a) => Real a  where
    toRational ::  a -> Rational
class  (Real a, Enum a) => Integral a  where
    quot, rem, div, mod :: a -> a -> a
    quotRem, divMod     :: a -> a -> (a,a)
    toInteger           :: a -> Integer
class  (Num a) => Fractional a  where
    (/)             :: a -> a -> a
    recip           :: a -> a
    fromRational :: Rational -> a
class  (Fractional a) => Floating a  where
    pi                  :: a
    exp, log, sqrt      :: a -> a
    (**), logBase       :: a -> a -> a
    sin, cos, tan       :: a -> a
    asin, acos, atan    :: a -> a
    sinh, cosh, tanh    :: a -> a
    asinh, acosh, atanh :: a -> a
```

Figure 6.2: Standard Numeric Classes and Related Operations, Part 1

Finally, there are the greatest common divisor and least common multiple functions. gcd x y is the greatest (positive) integer that divides both x and y; for example gcd (-3) 6 = 3, gcd (-3) (-6) = 3, gcd 0 4 = 4. gcd 0 0 raises a runtime error.

lcm x y is the smallest positive integer that both x and y divide.

6.4.3 Exponentiation and Logarithms

The one-argument exponential function exp and the logarithm function log act on floating-point numbers and use base e. logBase a x returns the logarithm of x in base a. sqrt returns the principal square root of a floating-point number. There are three two-argument exponentiation operations: (^) raises any number to a nonnegative integer power, (^^) raises a fractional number to any integer power, and (**) takes two floating-point arguments. The value of x^0 or x^^0 is

```
class  (Real a, Fractional a) => RealFrac a  where
    properFraction   :: (Integral b) => a -> (b,a)
    truncate, round  :: (Integral b) => a -> b
    ceiling, floor   :: (Integral b) => a -> b

class  (RealFrac a, Floating a) => RealFloat a  where
    floatRadix             :: a -> Integer
    floatDigits            :: a -> Int
    floatRange             :: a -> (Int,Int)
    decodeFloat            :: a -> (Integer,Int)
    encodeFloat            :: Integer -> Int -> a
    exponent               :: a -> Int
    significand            :: a -> a
    scaleFloat             :: Int -> a -> a
    isNaN, isInfinite, isDenormalized, isNegativeZero, isIEEE
                           :: a -> Bool
    atan2                  :: a -> a -> a

gcd, lcm :: (Integral a) => a -> a-> a
(^)        :: (Num a, Integral b) => a -> b -> a
(^^)       :: (Fractional a, Integral b) => a -> b -> a

fromIntegral :: (Integral a, Num b) => a -> b
realToFrac   :: (Real a, Fractional b) => a -> b
```

Figure 6.3: Standard Numeric Classes and Related Operations, Part 2

1 for any x, including zero; $0**y$ is undefined.

6.4.4 Magnitude and Sign

A number has a *magnitude* and a *sign*. The functions abs and signum apply to any number and satisfy the law:

```
abs x * signum x == x
```

For real numbers, these functions are defined by:

```
abs x      | x >= 0   = x
           | x <  0   = -x

signum x   | x >  0   = 1
           | x == 0   = 0
           | x <  0   = -1
```

6.4.5 Trigonometric Functions

Class `Floating` provides the circular and hyperbolic sine, cosine, and tangent functions and their inverses. Default implementations of `tan`, `tanh`, `logBase`, `**`, and `sqrt` are provided, but implementors are free to provide more accurate implementations.

Class `RealFloat` provides a version of arctangent taking two real floating-point arguments. For real floating x and y, `atan2` y x computes the angle (from the positive x-axis) of the vector from the origin to the point (x, y). `atan2` y x returns a value in the range `[-pi, pi]`. It follows the Common Lisp semantics for the origin when signed zeroes are supported. `atan2` y 1, with y in a type that is `RealFloat`, should return the same value as `atan` y. A default definition of `atan2` is provided, but implementors can provide a more accurate implementation.

The precise definition of the above functions is as in Common Lisp, which in turn follows Penfield's proposal for APL [13]. See these references for discussions of branch cuts, discontinuities, and implementation.

6.4.6 Coercions and Component Extraction

The `ceiling`, `floor`, `truncate`, and `round` functions each take a real fractional argument and return an integral result. `ceiling` x returns the least integer not less than x, and `floor` x, the greatest integer not greater than x. `truncate` x yields the integer nearest x between 0 and x, inclusive. `round` x returns the nearest integer to x, the even integer if x is equidistant between two integers.

The function `properFraction` takes a real fractional number x and returns a pair (n, f) such that $x = n + f$, and: n is an integral number with the same sign as x; and f is a fraction f with the same type and sign as x, and with absolute value less than 1. The `ceiling`, `floor`, `truncate`, and `round` functions can be defined in terms of `properFraction`.

Two functions convert numbers to type `Rational`: `toRational` returns the rational equivalent of its real argument with full precision; `approxRational` takes two real fractional arguments x and ϵ and returns the simplest rational number within ϵ of x, where a rational p/q in reduced form is *simpler* than another p'/q' if $|p| \leq |p'|$ and $q \leq q'$. Every real interval contains a unique simplest rational; in particular, note that $0/1$ is the simplest rational of all.

The class methods of class `RealFloat` allow efficient, machine-independent access to the components of a floating-point number. The functions `floatRadix`, `floatDigits`, and `floatRange` give the parameters of a floating-point type: the radix of the representation, the number of digits of this radix in the significand, and the lowest and highest values the exponent may assume, respectively. The function `decodeFloat` applied to a real floating-point number returns the significand expressed as an `Integer` and an appropriately scaled exponent (an `Int`). If `decodeFloat x` yields `(m, n)`, then x is equal in value to mb^n, where b is the floating-point radix, and furthermore, either m and n are both zero or else $b^{d-1} \leq m < b^d$, where d is the value of `floatDigits x`. `encodeFloat` performs the inverse of this transformation. The functions `significand` and exponent together provide the same information as decodeFloat, but rather than an Integer, significand x yields a value of the same type as x, scaled to lie in the open interval $(-1, 1)$. exponent 0 is zero. scaleFloat multiplies a floating-point number by an integer power of the radix.

The functions isNaN, isInfinite, isDenormalized, isNegativeZero, and isIEEE all support numbers represented using the IEEE standard. For non-IEEE floating point numbers, these may all return false.

Also available are the following coercion functions:

```
fromIntegral :: (Integral a, Num b)     => a -> b
realToFrac   :: (Real a, Fractional b) => a -> b
```

JFP **13** (1): 97–102, January 2003. © 2003 Cambridge University Press
DOI: 10.1017/S0956796803000911 Printed in the United Kingdom

Chapter 7

Basic Input/Output

The I/O system in Haskell is purely functional, yet has all of the expressive power found in conventional programming languages. To achieve this, Haskell uses a *monad* to integrate I/O operations into a purely functional context.

The I/O monad used by Haskell mediates between the *values* natural to a functional language and the *actions* that characterize I/O operations and imperative programming in general. The order of evaluation of expressions in Haskell is constrained only by data dependencies; an implementation has a great deal of freedom in choosing this order. Actions, however, must be ordered in a well-defined manner for program execution – and I/O in particular – to be meaningful. Haskell's I/O monad provides the user with a way to specify the sequential chaining of actions, and an implementation is obliged to preserve this order.

The term *monad* comes from a branch of mathematics known as *category theory*. From the perspective of a Haskell programmer, however, it is best to think of a monad as an *abstract datatype*. In the case of the I/O monad, the abstract values are the *actions* mentioned above. Some operations are primitive actions, corresponding to conventional I/O operations. Special operations (methods in the class `Monad`, see Section 6.3.6) sequentially compose actions, corresponding to sequencing operators (such as the semicolon) in imperative languages.

7.1 Standard I/O Functions

Although Haskell provides fairly sophisticated I/O facilities, as defined in the `IO` library, it is possible to write many Haskell programs using only the few simple functions that are exported from the Prelude, and which are described in this section.

All I/O functions defined here are character oriented. The treatment of the newline character will vary on different systems. For example, two characters of input, return and linefeed, may read as a single newline character. These functions cannot be used portably for binary I/O.

In the following, recall that `String` is a synonym for `[Char]` (Section 6.1.2).

Output Functions   These functions write to the standard output device (this is normally the user's terminal).

```
putChar  :: Char -> IO ()
putStr   :: String -> IO ()
putStrLn :: String -> IO ()   -- adds a newline
print    :: Show a => a -> IO ()
```

The `print` function outputs a value of any printable type to the standard output device. Printable types are those that are instances of class `Show`; `print` converts values to strings for output using the `show` operation and adds a newline.

For example, a program to print the first 20 integers and their powers of 2 could be written as:

```
main = print ([(n, 2^n) | n <- [0..19]])
```

Input Functions   These functions read input from the standard input device (normally the user's terminal).

```
getChar     :: IO Char
getLine     :: IO String
getContents :: IO String
interact    :: (String -> String) -> IO ()
readIO      :: Read a => String -> IO a
readLn      :: Read a => IO a
```

The `getChar` operation raises an exception (Section 7.3) on end-of-file; a predicate `isEOFError` that identifies this exception is defined in the `IO` library. The `getLine` operation raises an exception under the same circumstances as `hGetLine`, defined the `IO` library.

The `getContents` operation returns all user input as a single string, which is read lazily as it is needed. The `interact` function takes a function of type `String->String` as its argument. The entire input from the standard input device is passed to this function as its argument, and the resulting string is output on the standard output device.

Typically, the `read` operation from class `Read` is used to convert the string to a value. The `readIO` function is similar to `read` except that it signals parse failure to the I/O monad instead of terminating the program. The `readLn` function combines `getLine` and `readIO`.

The following program simply removes all non-ASCII characters from its standard input and echoes the result on its standard output. (The `isAscii` function is defined in a library.)

```
main = interact (filter isAscii)
```

Files   These functions operate on files of characters. Files are named by strings using some implementation-specific method to resolve strings as file names.

The `writeFile` and `appendFile` functions write or append the string, their second argument, to the file, their first argument. The `readFile` function reads a file and returns the contents of the file as a string. The file is read lazily, on demand, as with `getContents`.

```
type FilePath = String

writeFile  :: FilePath -> String -> IO ()
appendFile :: FilePath -> String -> IO ()
readFile   :: FilePath           -> IO String
```

Note that `writeFile` and `appendFile` write a literal string to a file. To write a value of any printable type, as with `print`, use the `show` function to convert the value to a string first.

```
main = appendFile "squares" (show [(x,x*x) | x <- [0,0.1..2]])
```

7.2   Sequencing I/O Operations

The type constructor `IO` is an instance of the `Monad` class. The two monadic binding functions, methods in the `Monad` class, are used to compose a series of I/O operations. The `>>` function is used where the result of the first operation is uninteresting, for example when it is `()`. The `>>=` operation passes the result of the first operation as an argument to the second operation.

```
(>>=) :: IO a -> (a -> IO b) -> IO b
(>>)  :: IO a -> IO b        -> IO b
```

For example,

```
main = readFile "input-file"                      >>= \ s ->
       writeFile "output-file" (filter isAscii s) >>
       putStr "Filtering successful\n"
```

is similar to the previous example using `interact`, but takes its input from `"input-file"` and writes its output to `"output-file"`. A message is printed on the standard output before the program completes.

The do notation allows programming in a more imperative syntactic style. A slightly more elaborate version of the previous example would be:

```
main = do
        putStr "Input file: "
        ifile <- getLine
        putStr "Output file: "
        ofile <- getLine
        s <- readFile ifile
        writeFile ofile (filter isAscii s)
        putStr "Filtering successful\n"
```

The return function is used to define the result of an I/O operation. For example, getLine is defined in terms of getChar, using return to define the result:

```
getLine :: IO String
getLine = do c <- getChar
             if c == '\n' then return ""
                          else do s <- getLine
                                  return (c:s)
```

7.3 Exception Handling in the I/O Monad

The I/O monad includes a simple exception handling system. Any I/O operation may raise an exception instead of returning a result.

Exceptions in the I/O monad are represented by values of type IOError. This is an abstract type: its constructors are hidden from the user. The IO library defines functions that construct and examine IOError values. The only Prelude function that creates an IOError value is userError. User error values include a string describing the error.

```
    userError :: String -> IOError
```

Exceptions are raised and caught using the following functions:

```
    ioError :: IOError -> IO a
    catch   :: IO a    -> (IOError -> IO a) -> IO a
```

The ioError function raises an exception; the catch function establishes a handler that receives any exception raised in the action protected by catch. An exception is caught by the most recent handler established by catch. These handlers are not selective: all exceptions are caught. Exception propagation must be explicitly provided in a handler by re-raising any unwanted exceptions. For example, in

```
f = catch g (\e -> if IO.isEOFError e
                   then return []
                   else ioError e)
```

the function f returns [ ] when an end-of-file exception occurs in g; otherwise, the exception is propagated to the next outer handler. The isEOFError function is part of IO library.

When an exception propagates outside the main program, the Haskell system prints the associated IOError value and exits the program.

The fail method of the IO instance of the Monad class (Section 6.3.6) raises a userError, thus:

```
instance Monad IO where
   ...bindings for return, (>>=), (>>)
   fail s = ioError (userError s)
```

The exceptions raised by the I/O functions in the Prelude are defined in Chapter 21.

JFP **13** (1): 103–124, January 2003. © 2003 Cambridge University Press
DOI: 10.1017/S0956796803001011 Printed in the United Kingdom

Chapter 8

Standard Prelude

In this chapter the entire Haskell Prelude is given. It constitutes a *specification* for the Prelude. Many of the definitions are written with clarity rather than efficiency in mind, and it is not required that the specification be implemented as shown here.

The default method definitions, given with `class` declarations, constitute a specification *only* of the default method. They do not constitute a specification of the meaning of the method in all instances. To take one particular example, the default method for `enumFrom` in class `Enum` will not work properly for types whose range exceeds that of `Int` (because `fromEnum` cannot map all values in the type to distinct `Int` values).

The Prelude shown here is organized into a root module, `Prelude`, and the three sub-modules `PreludeList`, `PreludeText`, and `PreludeIO`. This structure is purely presentational. An implementation is not required to use this organisation for the Prelude, nor are these three modules available for import separately. Only the exports of module `Prelude` are significant.

Some of these modules import Library modules, such as `Char`, `Monad`, `IO`, and `Numeric`. These modules are described fully in Part II. These imports are not, of course, part of the specification of the `Prelude`. That is, an implementation is free to import more, or less, of the Library modules, as it pleases.

Primitives that are not definable in Haskell, indicated by names starting with "`prim`", are defined in a system dependent manner in module `PreludeBuiltin` and are not shown here. Instance declarations that simply bind primitives to class methods are omitted. Some of the more verbose instances with obvious functionality have been left out for the sake of brevity.

Declarations for special types such as `Integer`, or `( )` are included in the Prelude for completeness even though the declaration may be incomplete or syntactically invalid. An ellipsis "`...`" is often used in places where the remainder of a definition cannot be given in Haskell.

To reduce the occurrence of unexpected ambiguity errors, and to improve efficiency, a number
of commonly-used functions over lists use the `Int` type rather than using a more general numeric type, such as `Integral a` or `Num a`. These functions are: `take`, `drop`, `!!`, `length`,
`splitAt`, and `replicate`. The more general versions are given in the `List` library, with the
prefix "`generic`"; for example `genericLength`.

8.1   Module `Prelude`

```
module Prelude (
    module PreludeList, module PreludeText, module PreludeIO,
    Bool(False, True),
    Maybe(Nothing, Just),
    Either(Left, Right),
    Ordering(LT, EQ, GT),
    Char, String, Int, Integer, Float, Double, Rational, IO,

--      These built-in types are defined in the Prelude, but
--      are denoted by built-in syntax, and cannot legally
--      appear in an export list.
--  List type: []((:), [])
--  Tuple types: (,)((,)), (,,)((,,)), etc.
--  Trivial type: ()(())
--  Functions: (->)

    Eq((==), (/=)),
    Ord(compare, (<), (<=), (>=), (>), max, min),
    Enum(succ, pred, toEnum, fromEnum, enumFrom, enumFromThen,
         enumFromTo, enumFromThenTo),
    Bounded(minBound, maxBound),
    Num((+), (-), (*), negate, abs, signum, fromInteger),
    Real(toRational),
    Integral(quot, rem, div, mod, quotRem, divMod, toInteger),
    Fractional((/), recip, fromRational),
    Floating(pi, exp, log, sqrt, (**), logBase, sin, cos, tan,
             asin, acos, atan, sinh, cosh, tanh, asinh, acosh, atanh),
    RealFrac(properFraction, truncate, round, ceiling, floor),
    RealFloat(floatRadix, floatDigits, floatRange, decodeFloat,
              encodeFloat, exponent, significand, scaleFloat, isNaN,
              isInfinite, isDenormalized, isIEEE, isNegativeZero, atan2),
    Monad((>>=), (>>), return, fail),
    Functor(fmap),
    mapM, mapM_, sequence, sequence_, (=<<),
    maybe, either,
    (&&), (||), not, otherwise,
    subtract, even, odd, gcd, lcm, (^), (^^),
    fromIntegral, realToFrac,
    fst, snd, curry, uncurry, id, const, (.), flip, ($), until,
    asTypeOf, error, undefined,
    seq, ($!)
  ) where
```

```
import PreludeBuiltin                         -- Contains all 'prim' values
import UnicodePrims( primUnicodeMaxChar )  -- Unicode primitives
import PreludeList
import PreludeText
import PreludeIO
import Ratio( Rational )

infixr 9  .
infixr 8  ^, ^^, **
infixl 7  *, /, 'quot', 'rem', 'div', 'mod'
infixl 6  +, -
-- The (:) operator is built-in syntax, and cannot legally be given
-- a fixity declaration; but its fixity is given by:
--    infixr 5  :
infix  4  ==, /=, <, <=, >=, >
infixr 3  &&
infixr 2  ||
infixl 1  >>, >>=
infixr 1  =<<
infixr 0  $, $!, 'seq'

-- Standard types, classes, instances and related functions
-- Equality and Ordered classes
class  Eq a  where
    (==), (/=) :: a -> a -> Bool
        -- Minimal complete definition:
        --      (==) or (/=)
    x /= y     =  not (x == y)
    x == y     =  not (x /= y)

class  (Eq a) => Ord a  where
    compare              :: a -> a -> Ordering
    (<), (<=), (>=), (>) :: a -> a -> Bool
    max, min             :: a -> a -> a
        -- Minimal complete definition:
        --      (<=) or compare
        -- Using compare can be more efficient for complex types.
    compare x y
        | x == y    =  EQ
        | x <= y    =  LT
        | otherwise =  GT

    x <= y           =  compare x y /= GT
    x <  y           =  compare x y == LT
    x >= y           =  compare x y /= LT
    x >  y           =  compare x y == GT

-- note that (min x y, max x y) = (x,y) or (y,x)
    max x y
        | x <= y    =  y
        | otherwise =  x
    min x y
        | x <= y    =  x
        | otherwise =  y
```

```
-- Enumeration and Bounded classes
class  Enum a   where
    succ, pred          :: a -> a
    toEnum              :: Int -> a
    fromEnum            :: a -> Int
    enumFrom            :: a -> [a]              -- [n..]
    enumFromThen        :: a -> a -> [a]         -- [n,n'..]
    enumFromTo          :: a -> a -> [a]         -- [n..m]
    enumFromThenTo      :: a -> a -> a -> [a]    -- [n,n'..m]
        -- Minimal complete definition:
        --        toEnum, fromEnum
        --
        -- NOTE: these default methods only make sense for types
        --       that map injectively into Int using fromEnum
        --       and toEnum.
    succ             = toEnum . (+1) . fromEnum
    pred             = toEnum . (subtract 1) . fromEnum
    enumFrom x       = map toEnum [fromEnum x ..]
    enumFromTo x y   = map toEnum [fromEnum x .. fromEnum y]
    enumFromThen x y = map toEnum [fromEnum x, fromEnum y ..]
    enumFromThenTo x y z =
                    map toEnum [fromEnum x, fromEnum y .. fromEnum z]

class  Bounded a   where
    minBound         :: a
    maxBound         :: a

-- Numeric classes
class  (Eq a, Show a) => Num a   where
    (+), (-), (*)    :: a -> a -> a
    negate           :: a -> a
    abs, signum      :: a -> a
    fromInteger      :: Integer -> a
        -- Minimal complete definition:
        --       All, except negate or (-)
    x - y            = x + negate y
    negate x         = 0 - x

class  (Num a, Ord a) => Real a   where
    toRational       ::  a -> Rational

class  (Real a, Enum a) => Integral a   where
    quot, rem        :: a -> a -> a
    div, mod         :: a -> a -> a
    quotRem, divMod  :: a -> a -> (a,a)
    toInteger        :: a -> Integer
        -- Minimal complete definition:
        --       quotRem, toInteger
    n 'quot' d       =  q  where (q,r) = quotRem n d
    n 'rem' d        =  r  where (q,r) = quotRem n d
    n 'div' d        =  q  where (q,r) = divMod n d
    n 'mod' d        =  r  where (q,r) = divMod n d
    divMod n d       =  if signum r == - signum d then (q-1, r+d) else qr
                        where qr@(q,r) = quotRem n d
```

```
class  (Num a) => Fractional a  where
    (/)              :: a -> a -> a
    recip            :: a -> a
    fromRational     :: Rational -> a

        -- Minimal complete definition:
        --       fromRational and (recip or (/))
    recip x          = 1 / x
    x / y            = x * recip y

class  (Fractional a) => Floating a  where
    pi                    :: a
    exp, log, sqrt        :: a -> a
    (**), logBase         :: a -> a -> a
    sin, cos, tan         :: a -> a
    asin, acos, atan      :: a -> a
    sinh, cosh, tanh      :: a -> a
    asinh, acosh, atanh :: a -> a

        -- Minimal complete definition:
        --       pi, exp, log, sin, cos, sinh, cosh
        --       asin, acos, atan
        --       asinh, acosh, atanh
    x ** y           = exp (log x * y)
    logBase x y      = log y / log x
    sqrt x           = x ** 0.5
    tan  x           = sin  x / cos  x
    tanh x           = sinh x / cosh x

class  (Real a, Fractional a) => RealFrac a  where
    properFraction   :: (Integral b) => a -> (b,a)
    truncate, round  :: (Integral b) => a -> b
    ceiling, floor   :: (Integral b) => a -> b

        -- Minimal complete definition:
        --       properFraction
    truncate x       = m  where (m,_) = properFraction x

    round x          = let (n,r) = properFraction x
                           m     = if r < 0 then n - 1 else n + 1
                       in case signum (abs r - 0.5) of
                               -1 -> n
                                0 -> if even n then n else m
                                1 -> m
    ceiling x        = if r > 0 then n + 1 else n
                       where (n,r) = properFraction x

    floor x          = if r < 0 then n - 1 else n
                       where (n,r) = properFraction x
```

```
class  (RealFrac a, Floating a) => RealFloat a  where
    floatRadix        :: a -> Integer
    floatDigits       :: a -> Int
    floatRange        :: a -> (Int,Int)
    decodeFloat       :: a -> (Integer,Int)
    encodeFloat       :: Integer -> Int -> a
    exponent          :: a -> Int
    significand       :: a -> a
    scaleFloat        :: Int -> a -> a
    isNaN, isInfinite, isDenormalized, isNegativeZero, isIEEE
                      :: a -> Bool
    atan2             :: a -> a -> a
        -- Minimal complete definition:
        --      All except exponent, significand,
        --              scaleFloat, atan2
    exponent x        = if m == 0 then 0 else n + floatDigits x
                        where (m,n) = decodeFloat x

    significand x     = encodeFloat m (- floatDigits x)
                        where (m,_) = decodeFloat x

    scaleFloat k x    = encodeFloat m (n+k)
                        where (m,n) = decodeFloat x

    atan2 y x
      | x>0                = atan (y/x)
      | x==0 && y>0        = pi/2
      | x<0  && y>0        = pi + atan (y/x)
      |(x<=0 && y<0)  ||
       (x<0 && isNegativeZero y) ||
       (isNegativeZero x && isNegativeZero y)
                           = -atan2 (-y) x
      | y==0 && (x<0  || isNegativeZero x)
                           = pi    -- must be after the previous test on zero y
      | x==0 && y==0  = y     -- must be after the other double zero tests
      | otherwise     = x + y -- x or y is a NaN, return a NaN (via +)

-- Numeric functions
subtract           :: (Num a) => a -> a -> a
subtract           = flip (-)

even, odd          :: (Integral a) => a -> Bool
even n             = n 'rem' 2 == 0
odd                = not . even

gcd                :: (Integral a) => a -> a -> a
gcd 0 0            = error "Prelude.gcd: gcd 0 0 is undefined"
gcd x y            = gcd' (abs x) (abs y)
                     where gcd' x 0  =  x
                           gcd' x y  =  gcd' y (x 'rem' y)

lcm                :: (Integral a) => a -> a -> a
lcm _ 0            = 0
lcm 0 _            = 0
lcm x y            = abs ((x 'quot' (gcd x y)) * y)
```

```
(^)                 :: (Num a, Integral b) => a -> b -> a
x ^ 0               = 1
x ^ n | n > 0       = f x (n-1) x
                      where f _ 0 y = y
                            f x n y = g x n  where
                                      g x n | even n  = g (x*x) (n 'quot' 2)
                                            | otherwise = f x (n-1) (x*y)
_   ^ _             = error "Prelude.^: negative exponent"

(^^)                :: (Fractional a, Integral b) => a -> b -> a
x ^^ n              = if n >= 0 then x^n else recip (x^(-n))

fromIntegral        :: (Integral a, Num b) => a -> b
fromIntegral        = fromInteger . toInteger

realToFrac          :: (Real a, Fractional b) => a -> b
realToFrac          = fromRational . toRational

-- Monadic classes
class  Functor f  where
    fmap                :: (a -> b) -> f a -> f b

class  Monad m  where
    (>>=)  :: m a -> (a -> m b) -> m b
    (>>)   :: m a -> m b -> m b
    return :: a -> m a
    fail   :: String -> m a

        -- Minimal complete definition:
        --      (>>=), return
    m >> k  =  m >>= \_ -> k
    fail s  = error s

sequence            :: Monad m => [m a] -> m [a]
sequence            = foldr mcons (return [])
                        where mcons p q = p >>= \x -> q >>= \y -> return (x:y)

sequence_           :: Monad m => [m a] -> m ()
sequence_           = foldr (>>) (return ())

-- The xxxM functions take list arguments, but lift the function or
-- list element to a monad type
mapM                :: Monad m => (a -> m b) -> [a] -> m [b]
mapM f as           = sequence (map f as)

mapM_               :: Monad m => (a -> m b) -> [a] -> m ()
mapM_ f as          = sequence_ (map f as)

(=<<)               :: Monad m => (a -> m b) -> m a -> m b
f =<< x             = x >>= f

-- Trivial type
data  ()  =  ()  deriving (Eq, Ord, Enum, Bounded)
        -- Not legal Haskell; for illustration only

-- Function type
-- identity function
id                  :: a -> a
id x                = x
```

```
-- constant function
const              :: a -> b -> a
const x _          = x

-- function composition
(.)                :: (b -> c) -> (a -> b) -> a -> c
f . g              = \ x -> f (g x)

-- flip f  takes its (first) two arguments in the reverse order of f.
flip               :: (a -> b -> c) -> b -> a -> c
flip f x y         = f y x

seq :: a -> b -> b
seq = ...           -- Primitive

-- right-associating infix application operators
-- (useful in continuation-passing style)
($), ($!) :: (a -> b) -> a -> b
f $  x     = f x
f $! x     = x 'seq' f x

-- Boolean type
data  Bool  = False | True      deriving (Eq, Ord, Enum, Read, Show, Bounded)

-- Boolean functions
(&&), (||)         :: Bool -> Bool -> Bool
True  && x         = x
False && _         = False
True  || _         = True
False || x         = x

not                :: Bool -> Bool
not True           = False
not False          = True

otherwise          :: Bool
otherwise          = True

-- Character type
data Char = ... 'a' | 'b' ... -- Unicode values

instance  Eq Char  where
    c == c'          =  fromEnum c == fromEnum c'

instance  Ord Char  where
    c <= c'          =  fromEnum c <= fromEnum c'

instance  Enum Char  where
    toEnum           = primIntToChar
    fromEnum         = primCharToInt
    enumFrom c       = map toEnum [fromEnum c .. fromEnum (maxBound::Char)]
    enumFromThen c c' = map toEnum [fromEnum c, fromEnum c' .. fromEnum lastChar]
                       where lastChar :: Char
                             lastChar | c' < c    = minBound
                                      | otherwise = maxBound

instance  Bounded Char  where
    minBound  =  '\0'
    maxBound  =  primUnicodeMaxChar
```

```
type   String = [Char]

-- Maybe type
data  Maybe a  =  Nothing | Just a       deriving (Eq, Ord, Read, Show)

maybe                :: b -> (a -> b) -> Maybe a -> b
maybe n f Nothing   =  n
maybe n f (Just x) =  f x

instance  Functor Maybe  where
    fmap f Nothing     =  Nothing
    fmap f (Just x)    =  Just (f x)

instance  Monad Maybe  where
    (Just x) >>= k   =  k x
    Nothing  >>= k   =  Nothing
    return           =  Just
    fail s           =  Nothing

-- Either type
data  Either a b  =  Left a | Right b   deriving (Eq, Ord, Read, Show)

either               :: (a -> c) -> (b -> c) -> Either a b -> c
either f g (Left x)  =  f x
either f g (Right y) =  g y

-- IO type
data IO a = ...           -- abstract

instance  Functor IO where
    fmap f x             =  x >>= (return . f)

instance Monad IO where
    (>>=)  = ...
    return = ...
    fail s = ioError (userError s)

-- Ordering type
data  Ordering  =  LT | EQ | GT
           deriving (Eq, Ord, Enum, Read, Show, Bounded)

-- Standard numeric types.  The data declarations for these types cannot
-- be expressed directly in Haskell since the constructor lists would be
-- far too large.
data  Int  =  minBound ... -1 | 0 | 1 ... maxBound
instance  Eq        Int  where ...
instance  Ord       Int  where ...
instance  Num       Int  where ...
instance  Real      Int  where ...
instance  Integral Int  where ...
instance  Enum      Int  where ...
instance  Bounded   Int  where ...
```

```
data  Integer  =  ... -1 | 0 | 1 ...
instance  Eq         Integer  where ...
instance  Ord        Integer  where ...
instance  Num        Integer  where ...
instance  Real       Integer  where ...
instance  Integral   Integer  where ...
instance  Enum       Integer  where ...

data  Float
instance  Eq           Float  where ...
instance  Ord          Float  where ...
instance  Num          Float  where ...
instance  Real         Float  where ...
instance  Fractional   Float  where ...
instance  Floating     Float  where ...
instance  RealFrac     Float  where ...
instance  RealFloat    Float  where ...

data  Double
instance  Eq           Double  where ...
instance  Ord          Double  where ...
instance  Num          Double  where ...
instance  Real         Double  where ...
instance  Fractional   Double  where ...
instance  Floating     Double  where ...
instance  RealFrac     Double  where ...
instance  RealFloat    Double  where ...

-- The Enum instances for Floats and Doubles are slightly unusual.
-- The 'toEnum' function truncates numbers to Int.  The definitions
-- of enumFrom and enumFromThen allow floats to be used in arithmetic
-- series: [0,0.1 .. 0.95].  However, roundoff errors make these somewhat
-- dubious.  This example may have either 10 or 11 elements, depending on
-- how 0.1 is represented.

instance  Enum Float  where
    succ x           = x+1
    pred x           = x-1
    toEnum           = fromIntegral
    fromEnum         = fromInteger . truncate   -- may overflow
    enumFrom         = numericEnumFrom
    enumFromThen     = numericEnumFromThen
    enumFromTo       = numericEnumFromTo
    enumFromThenTo   = numericEnumFromThenTo

instance  Enum Double  where
    succ x           = x+1
    pred x           = x-1
    toEnum           = fromIntegral
    fromEnum         = fromInteger . truncate   -- may overflow
    enumFrom         = numericEnumFrom
    enumFromThen     = numericEnumFromThen
    enumFromTo       = numericEnumFromTo
    enumFromThenTo   = numericEnumFromThenTo
```

```
numericEnumFrom          :: (Fractional a) => a -> [a]
numericEnumFromThen      :: (Fractional a) => a -> a -> [a]
numericEnumFromTo        :: (Fractional a, Ord a) => a -> a -> [a]
numericEnumFromThenTo    :: (Fractional a, Ord a) => a -> a -> a -> [a]
numericEnumFrom          = iterate (+1)
numericEnumFromThen n m  = iterate (+(m-n)) n
numericEnumFromTo n m     = takeWhile (<= m+1/2) (numericEnumFrom n)
numericEnumFromThenTo n n' m = takeWhile p (numericEnumFromThen n n')
                    where
                        p | n' >= n    = (<= m + (n'-n)/2)
                          | otherwise = (>= m + (n'-n)/2)

-- Lists
data  [a]  =  []  |  a : [a]  deriving (Eq, Ord)
        -- Not legal Haskell; for illustration only

instance Functor [] where
    fmap = map

instance  Monad []  where
    m >>= k          = concat (map k m)
    return x         = [x]
    fail s           = []

-- Tuples
data  (a,b)   =  (a,b)     deriving (Eq, Ord, Bounded)
data  (a,b,c) =  (a,b,c)   deriving (Eq, Ord, Bounded)
        -- Not legal Haskell; for illustration only

-- component projections for pairs:
-- (NB: not provided for triples, quadruples, etc.)
fst              :: (a,b) -> a
fst (x,y)        = x

snd              :: (a,b) -> b
snd (x,y)        = y

-- curry converts an uncurried function to a curried function;
-- uncurry converts a curried function to a function on pairs.
curry            :: ((a, b) -> c) -> a -> b -> c
curry f x y      = f (x, y)

uncurry          :: (a -> b -> c) -> ((a, b) -> c)
uncurry f p      = f (fst p) (snd p)

-- Misc functions
-- until p f  yields the result of applying f until p holds.
until            :: (a -> Bool) -> (a -> a) -> a -> a
until p f x
    | p x        = x
    | otherwise = until p f (f x)

-- asTypeOf is a type-restricted version of const.  It is usually used
-- as an infix operator, and its typing forces its first argument
-- (which is usually overloaded) to have the same type as the second.
asTypeOf         :: a -> a -> a
asTypeOf         = const
```

```
-- error stops execution and displays an error message
error             :: String -> a
error             = primError

-- It is expected that compilers will recognize this and insert error
-- messages that are more appropriate to the context in which undefined
-- appears.
undefined         :: a
undefined         = error "Prelude.undefined"
```

8.2   Module `PreludeList`

```
-- Standard list functions
module PreludeList (
    map, (++), filter, concat, concatMap,
    head, last, tail, init, null, length, (!!),
    foldl, foldl1, scanl, scanl1, foldr, foldr1, scanr, scanr1,
    iterate, repeat, replicate, cycle,
    take, drop, splitAt, takeWhile, dropWhile, span, break,
    lines, words, unlines, unwords, reverse, and, or,
    any, all, elem, notElem, lookup,
    sum, product, maximum, minimum,
    zip, zip3, zipWith, zipWith3, unzip, unzip3)
  where

import qualified Char(isSpace)

infixl 9  !!
infixr 5  ++
infix  4  'elem', 'notElem'

-- Map and append
map :: (a -> b) -> [a] -> [b]
map f []     = []
map f (x:xs) = f x : map f xs

(++) :: [a] -> [a] -> [a]
[]     ++ ys = ys
(x:xs) ++ ys = x : (xs ++ ys)

filter :: (a -> Bool) -> [a] -> [a]
filter p []              = []
filter p (x:xs) | p x        = x : filter p xs
                | otherwise = filter p xs

concat :: [[a]] -> [a]
concat xss = foldr (++) [] xss

concatMap :: (a -> [b]) -> [a] -> [b]
concatMap f = concat . map f
```

```
-- head and tail extract the first element and remaining elements,
-- respectively, of a list, which must be non-empty.  last and init
-- are the dual functions working from the end of a finite list,
-- rather than the beginning.
head                 :: [a] -> a
head (x:_)           = x
head []              = error "Prelude.head: empty list"

tail                 :: [a] -> [a]
tail (_:xs)          = xs
tail []              = error "Prelude.tail: empty list"

last                 :: [a] -> a
last [x]             = x
last (_:xs)          = last xs
last []              = error "Prelude.last: empty list"

init                 :: [a] -> [a]
init [x]             = []
init (x:xs)          = x : init xs
init []              = error "Prelude.init: empty list"

null                 :: [a] -> Bool
null []              = True
null (_:_)           = False

-- length returns the length of a finite list as an Int.
length               :: [a] -> Int
length []            = 0
length (_:l)         = 1 + length l

-- List index (subscript) operator, 0-origin
(!!)                     :: [a] -> Int -> a
xs     !! n | n < 0 =  error "Prelude.!!: negative index"
[]     !! _         =  error "Prelude.!!: index too large"
(x:_)  !! 0         =  x
(_:xs) !! n         =  xs !! (n-1)

-- foldl, applied to a binary operator, a starting value (typically the
-- left-identity of the operator), and a list, reduces the list using
-- the binary operator, from left to right:
--    foldl f z [x1, x2, ..., xn] == (...((z 'f' x1) 'f' x2) 'f'...) 'f' xn
-- foldl1 is a variant that has no starting value argument, and  thus must
-- be applied to non-empty lists.  scanl is similar to foldl, but returns
-- a list of successive reduced values from the left:
--      scanl f z [x1, x2, ...] == [z, z 'f' x1, (z 'f' x1) 'f' x2, ...]
-- Note that  last (scanl f z xs) == foldl f z xs.
-- scanl1 is similar, again without the starting element:
--      scanl1 f [x1, x2, ...] == [x1, x1 'f' x2, ...]
foldl                :: (a -> b -> a) -> a -> [b] -> a
foldl f z []         =  z
foldl f z (x:xs)     =  foldl f (f z x) xs

foldl1               :: (a -> a -> a) -> [a] -> a
foldl1 f (x:xs)      =  foldl f x xs
foldl1 _ []          =  error "Prelude.foldl1: empty list"
```

```
scanl            :: (a -> b -> a) -> a -> [b] -> [a]
scanl f q xs     = q : (case xs of
                             []    -> []
                             x:xs -> scanl f (f q x) xs)

scanl1           :: (a -> a -> a) -> [a] -> [a]
scanl1 f (x:xs)  = scanl f x xs
scanl1 _ []      = []
```

-- foldr, foldr1, scanr, and scanr1 are the right-to-left duals of the
-- above functions.

```
foldr            :: (a -> b -> b) -> b -> [a] -> b
foldr f z []     = z
foldr f z (x:xs) = f x (foldr f z xs)

foldr1           :: (a -> a -> a) -> [a] -> a
foldr1 f [x]     = x
foldr1 f (x:xs)  = f x (foldr1 f xs)
foldr1 _ []      = error "Prelude.foldr1: empty list"

scanr            :: (a -> b -> b) -> b -> [a] -> [b]
scanr f q0 []    = [q0]
scanr f q0 (x:xs) = f x q : qs
                    where qs@(q:_) = scanr f q0 xs

scanr1           :: (a -> a -> a) -> [a] -> [a]
scanr1 f []      = []
scanr1 f [x]     = [x]
scanr1 f (x:xs)  = f x q : qs
                    where qs@(q:_) = scanr1 f xs
```

-- iterate f x returns an infinite list of repeated applications of f to x:
-- iterate f x == [x, f x, f (f x), ...]
```
iterate          :: (a -> a) -> a -> [a]
iterate f x      = x : iterate f (f x)
```

-- repeat x is an infinite list, with x the value of every element.
```
repeat           :: a -> [a]
repeat x         = xs where xs = x:xs
```

-- replicate n x is a list of length n with x the value of every element
```
replicate        :: Int -> a -> [a]
replicate n x    = take n (repeat x)
```

-- cycle ties a finite list into a circular one, or equivalently,
-- the infinite repetition of the original list. It is the identity
-- on infinite lists.
```
cycle            :: [a] -> [a]
cycle []         = error "Prelude.cycle: empty list"
cycle xs         = xs' where xs' = xs ++ xs'
```

```
-- take n, applied to a list xs, returns the prefix of xs of length n,
-- or xs itself if n > length xs.  drop n xs returns the suffix of xs
-- after the first n elements, or [] if n > length xs.  splitAt n xs
-- is equivalent to (take n xs, drop n xs).
take                    :: Int -> [a] -> [a]
take n _     | n <= 0 =  []
take _ []             =  []
take n (x:xs)         =  x : take (n-1) xs

drop                    :: Int -> [a] -> [a]
drop n xs    | n <= 0 =  xs
drop _ []             =  []
drop n (_:xs)         =  drop (n-1) xs

splitAt                 :: Int -> [a] -> ([a],[a])
splitAt n xs          =  (take n xs, drop n xs)

-- takeWhile, applied to a predicate p and a list xs, returns the longest
-- prefix (possibly empty) of xs of elements that satisfy p.  dropWhile p xs
-- returns the remaining suffix.  span p xs is equivalent to
-- (takeWhile p xs, dropWhile p xs), while break p uses the negation of p.
takeWhile               :: (a -> Bool) -> [a] -> [a]
takeWhile p []        =  []
takeWhile p (x:xs)
           | p x      =  x : takeWhile p xs
           | otherwise =  []

dropWhile               :: (a -> Bool) -> [a] -> [a]
dropWhile p []        =  []
dropWhile p xs@(x:xs')
           | p x      =  dropWhile p xs'
           | otherwise =  xs

span, break             :: (a -> Bool) -> [a] -> ([a],[a])
span p []             =  ([],[])
span p xs@(x:xs')
           | p x      =  (x:ys,zs)
           | otherwise =  ([],xs)
                          where (ys,zs) = span p xs'

break p               =  span (not . p)

-- lines breaks a string up into a list of strings at newline characters.
-- The resulting strings do not contain newlines.  Similary, words
-- breaks a string up into a list of words, which were delimited by
-- white space.  unlines and unwords are the inverse operations.
-- unlines joins lines with terminating newlines, and unwords joins
-- words with separating spaces.
lines             :: String -> [String]
lines ""          =  []
lines s           =  let (l, s') = break (== '\n') s
                     in  l : case s' of
                                  []      -> []
                                  (_:s'') -> lines s''
```

```
words                 :: String -> [String]
words s               = case dropWhile Char.isSpace s of
                             "" -> []
                             s' -> w : words s''
                                  where (w, s'') = break Char.isSpace s'

unlines               :: [String] -> String
unlines               = concatMap (++ "\n")

unwords               :: [String] -> String
unwords []            = ""
unwords ws            = foldr1 (\w s -> w ++ ' ':s) ws
```

```
-- reverse xs returns the elements of xs in reverse order.  xs must be finite.
reverse               :: [a] -> [a]
reverse               = foldl (flip (:)) []
```

```
-- and returns the conjunction of a Boolean list.  For the result to be
-- True, the list must be finite; False, however, results from a False
-- value at a finite index of a finite or infinite list.  or is the
-- disjunctive dual of and.
and, or               :: [Bool] -> Bool
and                   = foldr (&&) True
or                    = foldr (||) False
```

```
-- Applied to a predicate and a list, any determines if any element
-- of the list satisfies the predicate.  Similarly, for all.
any, all              :: (a -> Bool) -> [a] -> Bool
any p                 = or . map p
all p                 = and . map p
```

```
-- elem is the list membership predicate, usually written in infix form,
-- e.g., x 'elem' xs.  notElem is the negation.
elem, notElem         :: (Eq a) => a -> [a] -> Bool
elem x                = any (== x)
notElem x             = all (/= x)
```

```
-- lookup key assocs looks up a key in an association list.
lookup                :: (Eq a) => a -> [(a,b)] -> Maybe b
lookup key []         = Nothing
lookup key ((x,y):xys)
      | key == x      = Just y
      | otherwise     = lookup key xys
```

```
-- sum and product compute the sum or product of a finite list of numbers.
sum, product          :: (Num a) => [a] -> a
sum                   = foldl (+) 0
product               = foldl (*) 1
```

```
-- maximum and minimum return the maximum or minimum value from a list,
-- which must be non-empty, finite, and of an ordered type.
maximum, minimum      :: (Ord a) => [a] -> a
maximum []            = error "Prelude.maximum: empty list"
maximum xs            = foldl1 max xs

minimum []            = error "Prelude.minimum: empty list"
minimum xs            = foldl1 min xs
```

```
-- zip takes two lists and returns a list of corresponding pairs.  If one
-- input list is short, excess elements of the longer list are discarded.
-- zip3 takes three lists and returns a list of triples.  Zips for larger
-- tuples are in the List library
zip               :: [a] -> [b] -> [(a,b)]
zip               = zipWith (,)

zip3              :: [a] -> [b] -> [c] -> [(a,b,c)]
zip3              = zipWith3 (,,)

-- The zipWith family generalises the zip family by zipping with the
-- function given as the first argument, instead of a tupling function.
-- For example, zipWith (+) is applied to two lists to produce the list
-- of corresponding sums.
zipWith           :: (a->b->c) -> [a]->[b]->[c]
zipWith z (a:as) (b:bs)
                  = z a b : zipWith z as bs
zipWith _ _ _     = []

zipWith3          :: (a->b->c->d) -> [a]->[b]->[c]->[d]
zipWith3 z (a:as) (b:bs) (c:cs)
                  = z a b c : zipWith3 z as bs cs
zipWith3 _ _ _ _  = []

-- unzip transforms a list of pairs into a pair of lists.
unzip             :: [(a,b)] -> ([a],[b])
unzip             = foldr (\(a,b) ~(as,bs) -> (a:as,b:bs)) ([],[])

unzip3            :: [(a,b,c)] -> ([a],[b],[c])
unzip3            = foldr (\(a,b,c) ~(as,bs,cs) -> (a:as,b:bs,c:cs))
                          ([],[],[])
```

8.3 Module PreludeText

```
module PreludeText (
    ReadS, ShowS,
    Read(readsPrec, readList),
    Show(showsPrec, show, showList),
    reads, shows, read, lex,
    showChar, showString, readParen, showParen ) where

-- The instances of Read and Show for
--      Bool, Maybe, Either, Ordering
-- are done via "deriving" clauses in Prelude.hs
import Char(isSpace, isAlpha, isDigit, isAlphaNum,
           showLitChar, readLitChar, lexLitChar)

import Numeric(showSigned, showInt, readSigned, readDec, showFloat,
               readFloat, lexDigits)

type  ReadS a  = String -> [(a,String)]
type  ShowS    = String -> String
```

```
class  Read a  where
    readsPrec          :: Int -> ReadS a
    readList           :: ReadS [a]

        -- Minimal complete definition:
        --        readsPrec
    readList           = readParen False (\r -> [pr |  ("[",s)   <- lex r,
                                                       pr        <- readl s])
                            where readl  s = [([],t)   | ("]",t)  <- lex s] ++
                                             [(x:xs,u) | (x,t)    <- reads s,
                                                         (xs,u)   <- readl' t]
                                  readl' s = [([],t)   | ("]",t)  <- lex s] ++
                                             [(x:xs,v) | (",",t)  <- lex s,
                                                         (x,u)    <- reads t,
                                                         (xs,v)   <- readl' u]

class  Show a  where
    showsPrec          :: Int -> a -> ShowS
    show               :: a -> String
    showList           :: [a] -> ShowS

        -- Mimimal complete definition:
        --        show or showsPrec
    showsPrec _ x s    = show x ++ s

    show x             = showsPrec 0 x ""

    showList []        = showString "[]"
    showList (x:xs)    = showChar '[' . shows x . showl xs
                            where showl [] = showChar ']'
                                  showl (x:xs) = showChar ',' . shows x .
                                                 showl xs

reads              :: (Read a) => ReadS a
reads              = readsPrec 0

shows              :: (Show a) => a -> ShowS
shows              = showsPrec 0

read               :: (Read a) => String -> a
read s             = case [x | (x,t) <- reads s, ("","") <- lex t] of
                          [x] -> x
                          []  -> error "Prelude.read: no parse"
                          _   -> error "Prelude.read: ambiguous parse"

showChar           :: Char -> ShowS
showChar           = (:)

showString         :: String -> ShowS
showString         = (++)

showParen          :: Bool -> ShowS -> ShowS
showParen b p      = if b then showChar '(' . p . showChar ')' else p

readParen          :: Bool -> ReadS a -> ReadS a
readParen b g      = if b then mandatory else optional
                        where optional r = g r ++ mandatory r
                              mandatory r = [(x,u) | ("(",s) <- lex r,
                                                     (x,t)   <- optional s,
                                                     (")",u) <- lex t    ]
```

```
-- This lexer is not completely faithful to the Haskell lexical syntax.
-- Current limitations:
--     Qualified names are not handled properly
--     Octal and hexadecimal numerics are not recognized as a single token
--     Comments are not treated properly
lex                   :: ReadS String
lex ""                =  [("","")]
lex (c:s)
   | isSpace c        =  lex (dropWhile isSpace s)
lex ('\'':s)          =  [('\'':ch++"'", t) | (ch,'\'':t)  <- lexLitChar s,
                                              ch /= "'" ]
lex ('"':s)           =  [('"':str, t)       | (str,t) <- lexString s]
                          where
                          lexString ('"':s) = [("\"",s)]
                          lexString s = [(ch++str, u)
                                             | (ch,t)  <- lexStrItem s,
                                               (str,u) <- lexString t  ]

                          lexStrItem ('\\':'&':s) =  [("\\&",s)]
                          lexStrItem ('\\':c:s) | isSpace c
                                             =  [("\\&",t) |
                                                 '\\':t <-
                                                  [dropWhile isSpace s]]
                          lexStrItem s             =  lexLitChar s

lex (c:s) | isSingle c = [([c],s)]
          | isSym c    = [(c:sym,t)          | (sym,t) <- [span isSym s]]
          | isAlpha c  = [(c:nam,t)          | (nam,t) <- [span isIdChar s]]
          | isDigit c  = [(c:ds++fe,t)       | (ds,s)  <- [span isDigit s],
                                               (fe,t)  <- lexFracExp s      ]
          | otherwise  = []      -- bad character
            where
            isSingle c = c 'elem' ",;()[]{}_'"
            isSym c    = c 'elem' "!@#$%&*+./<=>?\\^|:-~"
            isIdChar c = isAlphaNum c || c 'elem' "_'"
            lexFracExp ('.':c:cs) | isDigit c
                           = [('.':ds++e,u) | (ds,t) <- lexDigits (c:cs),
                                              (e,u)  <- lexExp t]
            lexFracExp s  = lexExp s
            lexExp (e:s) | e 'elem' "eE"
                      = [(e:c:ds,u) | (c:t)  <- [s], c 'elem' "+-",
                                      (ds,u) <- lexDigits t] ++
                        [(e:ds,t)   | (ds,t) <- lexDigits s]
            lexExp s = [("",s)]
instance  Show Int  where
    showsPrec n = showsPrec n . toInteger
        -- Converting to Integer avoids
        -- possible difficulty with minInt

instance  Read Int  where
  readsPrec p r = [(fromInteger i, t) | (i,t) <- readsPrec p r]
        -- Reading at the Integer type avoids
        -- possible difficulty with minInt

instance  Show Integer  where
    showsPrec            = showSigned showInt
```

```
instance  Read Integer  where
    readsPrec p        = readSigned readDec

instance  Show Float  where
    showsPrec p        = showFloat

instance  Read Float  where
    readsPrec p        = readSigned readFloat

instance  Show Double  where
    showsPrec p        = showFloat

instance  Read Double  where
    readsPrec p        = readSigned readFloat

instance  Show ()  where
    showsPrec p () = showString "()"

instance Read () where
    readsPrec p     = readParen False
                          (\r -> [((),t) | ("(",s) <- lex r,
                                           (")",t) <- lex s ] )
instance  Show Char  where
    showsPrec p '\'' = showString "'\\''"
    showsPrec p c    = showChar '\'' . showLitChar c . showChar '\''

    showList cs = showChar '"' . showl cs
                where showl ""        = showChar '"'
                      showl ('"':cs) = showString "\\\"" . showl cs
                      showl (c:cs)   = showLitChar c . showl cs

instance  Read Char  where
    readsPrec p     = readParen False
                          (\r -> [(c,t) | ('\'':s,t)<- lex r,
                                          (c,"\'")   <- readLitChar s])

    readList = readParen False (\r -> [(l,t) | ('"':s, t) <- lex r,
                                               (l,_)        <- readl s ])
          where readl ('"':s)      = [("",s)]
                readl ('\\':'&':s) = readl s
                readl s            = [(c:cs,u) | (c ,t) <- readLitChar s,
                                                 (cs,u) <- readl t        ]

instance  (Show a) => Show [a]  where
    showsPrec p      = showList

instance  (Read a) => Read [a]  where
    readsPrec p      = readList

-- Tuples
instance  (Show a, Show b) => Show (a,b)  where
    showsPrec p (x,y) = showChar '(' . shows x . showChar ',' .
                                       shows y . showChar ')'
```

```
instance  (Read a, Read b) => Read (a,b)  where
    readsPrec p      = readParen False
                       (\r -> [((x,y), w) | ("(",s) <- lex r,
                                            (x,t)   <- reads s,
                                            (",",u) <- lex t,
                                            (y,v)   <- reads u,
                                            (")",w) <- lex v ] )

-- Other tuples have similar Read and Show instances
```

8.4 Module PreludeIO

```
module PreludeIO (
    FilePath, IOError, ioError, userError, catch,
    putChar, putStr, putStrLn, print,
    getChar, getLine, getContents, interact,
    readFile, writeFile, appendFile, readIO, readLn
  ) where

import PreludeBuiltin

type  FilePath = String

data IOError     -- The internals of this type are system dependent

instance  Show IOError  where ...
instance  Eq IOError  where ...

ioError     ::  IOError -> IO a
ioError     =   primIOError

userError  ::  String -> IOError
userError  =   primUserError

catch       ::  IO a -> (IOError -> IO a) -> IO a
catch       =   primCatch

putChar     :: Char -> IO ()
putChar     =   primPutChar

putStr      :: String -> IO ()
putStr s    =   mapM_ putChar s

putStrLn    :: String -> IO ()
putStrLn s  =   do putStr s
                   putStr "\n"

print       :: Show a => a -> IO ()
print x     =   putStrLn (show x)

getChar     :: IO Char
getChar     =   primGetChar
```

```haskell
getLine    :: IO String
getLine    =  do c <- getChar
                 if c == '\n' then return "" else
                     do s <- getLine
                        return (c:s)

getContents :: IO String
getContents =  primGetContents

interact    ::  (String -> String) -> IO ()
-- The hSetBuffering ensures the expected interactive behaviour
interact f  =  do hSetBuffering stdin  NoBuffering
                  hSetBuffering stdout NoBuffering
                  s <- getContents
                  putStr (f s)

readFile   :: FilePath -> IO String
readFile   =  primReadFile

writeFile  :: FilePath -> String -> IO ()
writeFile  =  primWriteFile

appendFile :: FilePath -> String -> IO ()
appendFile =  primAppendFile
   -- raises an exception instead of an error
readIO    :: Read a => String -> IO a
readIO s =  case [x | (x,t) <- reads s, ("","") <- lex t] of
                [x] -> return x
                []  -> ioError (userError "Prelude.readIO: no parse")
                _   -> ioError (userError "Prelude.readIO: ambiguous parse")

readLn :: Read a => IO a
readLn =  do l <- getLine
             r <- readIO l
             return r
```

JFP **13** (1): 125–138, January 2003. © 2003 Cambridge University Press
DOI: 10.1017/S0956796803001114 Printed in the United Kingdom

Chapter 9

Syntax Reference

This chapter summarises the syntax of Haskell 98.

9.1 Notational Conventions

These notational conventions are used for presenting syntax:

$[pattern]$	optional
$\{pattern\}$	zero or more repetitions
$(pattern)$	grouping
$pat_1 \mid pat_2$	choice
$pat_{\langle pat' \rangle}$	difference – elements generated by pat
	except those generated by pat'
`fibonacci`	terminal syntax in typewriter font

BNF-like syntax is used throughout, with productions having the form:

$$nonterm \quad \rightarrow \quad alt_1 \mid alt_2 \mid \ldots \mid alt_n$$

There are some families of nonterminals indexed by precedence levels (written as a superscript). Similarly, the nonterminals op, $varop$, and $conop$ may have a double index: a letter l, r, or n for left-, right- or nonassociativity and a precedence level. A precedence-level variable i ranges from 0 to 9; an associativity variable a varies over $\{l, r, n\}$. Thus, for example

$$aexp \quad \rightarrow \quad (\ exp^{i+1} \ qop^{(a,i)} \ )$$

actually stands for 30 productions, with 10 substitutions for i and 3 for a.

In both the lexical and the context-free syntax, there are some ambiguities that are to be resolved by making grammatical phrases as long as possible, proceeding from left to right (in shift-reduce parsing, resolving shift/reduce conflicts by shifting). In the lexical syntax, this is the "maximal munch" rule. In the context-free syntax, this means that conditionals, let-expressions, and lambda abstractions extend to the right as far as possible.

9.2   Lexical Syntax

program	$\rightarrow$	$\{$ *lexeme* $\|$ *whitespace* $\}$
lexeme	$\rightarrow$	*qvarid* $\|$ *qconid* $\|$ *qvarsym* $\|$ *qconsym*
	$\|$	*literal* $\|$ *special* $\|$ *reservedop* $\|$ *reservedid*
literal	$\rightarrow$	*integer* $\|$ *float* $\|$ *char* $\|$ *string*
special	$\rightarrow$	$($ $\|$ $)$ $\|$ $,$ $\|$ $;$ $\|$ $[$ $\|$ $]$ $\|$ ` ` ` $\|$ $\{$ $\|$ $\}$
whitespace	$\rightarrow$	*whitestuff* $\{$ *whitestuff* $\}$
whitestuff	$\rightarrow$	*whitechar* $\|$ *comment* $\|$ *ncomment*
whitechar	$\rightarrow$	*newline* $\|$ *vertab* $\|$ *space* $\|$ *tab* $\|$ *uniWhite*
newline	$\rightarrow$	*return linefeed* $\|$ *return* $\|$ *linefeed* $\|$ *formfeed*
return	$\rightarrow$	a carriage return
linefeed	$\rightarrow$	a line feed
vertab	$\rightarrow$	a vertical tab
formfeed	$\rightarrow$	a form feed
space	$\rightarrow$	a space
tab	$\rightarrow$	a horizontal tab
uniWhite	$\rightarrow$	any Unicode character defined as whitespace
comment	$\rightarrow$	*dashes* $[$ *any*$_{\langle symbol \rangle}$ $\{$ *any* $\}$ $]$ *newline*
dashes	$\rightarrow$	$--$ $\{-\}$
opencom	$\rightarrow$	$\{-$
closecom	$\rightarrow$	$-\}$
ncomment	$\rightarrow$	*opencom ANYseq* $\{$ *ncomment ANYseq* $\}$ *closecom*
ANYseq	$\rightarrow$	$\{ANY\}_{\langle \{ANY\} \ (\ opencom \ \| \ closecom \ ) \ \{ANY\} \rangle}$
ANY	$\rightarrow$	*graphic* $\|$ *whitechar*
any	$\rightarrow$	*graphic* $\|$ *space* $\|$ *tab*
graphic	$\rightarrow$	*small* $\|$ *large* $\|$ *symbol* $\|$ *digit* $\|$ *special* $\|$ $:$ $\|$ $"$ $\|$ $'$
small	$\rightarrow$	*ascSmall* $\|$ *uniSmall* $\|$ $\_$
ascSmall	$\rightarrow$	a $\|$ b $\|$ $\ldots$ $\|$ z

uniSmall	$\rightarrow$	any Unicode lowercase letter
large	$\rightarrow$	*ascLarge* | *uniLarge*
ascLarge	$\rightarrow$	A | B | ... | Z
uniLarge	$\rightarrow$	any uppercase or titlecase Unicode letter
symbol	$\rightarrow$	*ascSymbol* | *uniSymbol*⟨ *special* | _ | : | " | ' ⟩
ascSymbol	$\rightarrow$	! | # | $ | % | & | * | + | . | / | < | = | > | ? | @
	|	\ | ^ | | | - | ~
uniSymbol	$\rightarrow$	any Unicode symbol or punctuation
digit	$\rightarrow$	*ascDigit* | *uniDigit*
ascDigit	$\rightarrow$	0 | 1 | ... | 9
uniDigit	$\rightarrow$	any Unicode decimal digit
octit	$\rightarrow$	0 | 1 | ... | 7
hexit	$\rightarrow$	*digit* | A | ... | F | a | ... | f

varid	$\rightarrow$	(*small* {*small* | *large* | *digit* | ' })⟨*reservedid*⟩
conid	$\rightarrow$	*large* {*small* | *large* | *digit* | ' }
reservedid	$\rightarrow$	case | class | data | default | deriving | do | else
	|	if | import | in | infix | infixl | infixr | instance
	|	let | module | newtype | of | then | type | where | _
varsym	$\rightarrow$	(*symbol* {*symbol* | : })⟨*reservedop* | *dashes*⟩
consym	$\rightarrow$	(: {*symbol* | : })⟨*reservedop*⟩
reservedop	$\rightarrow$	.. | : | :: | = | \ | | | <- | -> | @ | ~ | =>

varid			(variables)
conid			(constructors)
tyvar	$\rightarrow$	*varid*	(type variables)
tycon	$\rightarrow$	*conid*	(type constructors)
tycls	$\rightarrow$	*conid*	(type classes)
modid	$\rightarrow$	*conid*	(modules)

qvarid	$\rightarrow$	[*modid* .] *varid*
qconid	$\rightarrow$	[*modid* .] *conid*
qtycon	$\rightarrow$	[*modid* .] *tycon*
qtycls	$\rightarrow$	[*modid* .] *tycls*
qvarsym	$\rightarrow$	[*modid* .] *varsym*
qconsym	$\rightarrow$	[*modid* .] *consym*

decimal	$\rightarrow$	*digit*{*digit*}
octal	$\rightarrow$	*octit*{*octit*}
hexadecimal	$\rightarrow$	*hexit*{*hexit*}

integer	$\rightarrow$	*decimal*
	|	$\mathtt{0o}$ *octal* | $\mathtt{0O}$ *octal*
	|	$\mathtt{0x}$ *hexadecimal* | $\mathtt{0X}$ *hexadecimal*
float	$\rightarrow$	*decimal* $\mathtt{.}$ *decimal* [*exponent*]
	|	*decimal exponent*
exponent	$\rightarrow$	$(\mathtt{e} \mid \mathtt{E})$ [$+$ | $-$] *decimal*
char	$\rightarrow$	$\mathtt{'}$ (*graphic*$_{\langle \mathtt{'} \mid \backslash \rangle}$ | *space* | *escape*$_{\langle \backslash \mathtt{\&} \rangle}$) $\mathtt{'}$
string	$\rightarrow$	$\mathtt{"}$ {*graphic*$_{\langle \mathtt{"} \mid \backslash \rangle}$ | *space* | *escape* | *gap*} $\mathtt{"}$
escape	$\rightarrow$	$\backslash$ (*charesc* | *ascii* | *decimal* | $\mathtt{o}$ *octal* | $\mathtt{x}$ *hexadecimal*)
charesc	$\rightarrow$	$\mathtt{a} \mid \mathtt{b} \mid \mathtt{f} \mid \mathtt{n} \mid \mathtt{r} \mid \mathtt{t} \mid \mathtt{v} \mid \backslash \mid \mathtt{"} \mid \mathtt{'} \mid \mathtt{\&}$
ascii	$\rightarrow$	$\mathtt{\hat{}}$*cntrl* | $\mathtt{NUL}$ | $\mathtt{SOH}$ | $\mathtt{STX}$ | $\mathtt{ETX}$ | $\mathtt{EOT}$ | $\mathtt{ENQ}$ | $\mathtt{ACK}$
	|	$\mathtt{BEL}$ | $\mathtt{BS}$ | $\mathtt{HT}$ | $\mathtt{LF}$ | $\mathtt{VT}$ | $\mathtt{FF}$ | $\mathtt{CR}$ | $\mathtt{SO}$ | $\mathtt{SI}$ | $\mathtt{DLE}$
	|	$\mathtt{DC1}$ | $\mathtt{DC2}$ | $\mathtt{DC3}$ | $\mathtt{DC4}$ | $\mathtt{NAK}$ | $\mathtt{SYN}$ | $\mathtt{ETB}$ | $\mathtt{CAN}$
	|	$\mathtt{EM}$ | $\mathtt{SUB}$ | $\mathtt{ESC}$ | $\mathtt{FS}$ | $\mathtt{GS}$ | $\mathtt{RS}$ | $\mathtt{US}$ | $\mathtt{SP}$ | $\mathtt{DEL}$
cntrl	$\rightarrow$	*ascLarge* | $\mathtt{@}$ | $\mathtt{[}$ | $\backslash$ | $\mathtt{]}$ | $\mathtt{\hat{}}$ | $\_$
gap	$\rightarrow$	$\backslash$ *whitechar* {*whitechar*} $\backslash$

9.3   Layout

Section 2.7 gives an informal discussion of the layout rule. This section defines it more precisely.

The meaning of a Haskell program may depend on its *layout*. The effect of layout on its meaning can be completely described by adding braces and semicolons in places determined by the layout. The meaning of this augmented program is now layout insensitive.

The effect of layout is specified in this section by describing how to add braces and semicolons to a laid-out program. The specification takes the form of a function L that performs the translation. The input to L is:

- A stream of lexemes as specified by the lexical syntax in the Haskell report, with the following additional tokens:

  - If a **let**, **where**, **do**, or **of** keyword is not followed by the lexeme $\{$, the token $\{n\}$ is inserted after the keyword, where n is the indentation of the next lexeme if there is one, or *0* if the end of file has been reached.

  - If the first lexeme of a module is not $\{$ or **module**, then it is preceded by $\{n\}$ where n is the indentation of the lexeme.

  - Where the start of a lexeme is preceded only by white space on the same line, this lexeme is preceded by $< n >$ where n is the indentation of the lexeme, provided that it is not, as a consequence of the first two rules, preceded by $\{n\}$. (NB: a string literal may span multiple lines – Section 2.6. So in the fragment

```
f = ("Hello \
        \Bill", "Jake")
```

There is no $< n >$ inserted before the `\Bill`, because it is not the beginning of a complete lexeme; nor before the `,`, because it is not preceded only by white space.)

- A stack of "layout contexts", in which each element is either:

  - Zero, indicating that the enclosing context is explicit (i.e. the programmer supplied the opening brace. If the innermost context is 0, then no layout tokens will be inserted until either the enclosing context ends or a new context is pushed.

  - A positive integer, which is the indentation column of the enclosing layout context.

The "indentation" of a lexeme is the column number of the first character of that lexeme; the indentation of a line is the indentation of its leftmost lexeme. To determine the column number, assume a fixed-width font with the following conventions:

- The characters *newline*, *return*, *linefeed*, and *formfeed*, all start a new line.

- The first column is designated column 1, not 0.

- Tab stops are 8 characters apart.

- A tab character causes the insertion of enough spaces to align the current position with the next tab stop.

For the purposes of the layout rule, Unicode characters in a source program are considered to be of the same, fixed, width as an ASCII character. However, to avoid visual confusion, programmers should avoid writing programs in which the meaning of implicit layout depends on the width of non-space characters.

The application

$$L \; tokens \; []$$

delivers a layout-insensitive translation of *tokens*, where *tokens* is the result of lexically analysing a module and adding column-number indicators to it as described above. The definition of L is as follows, where we use ":" as a stream construction operator, and "[]" for the empty stream.

$$L\ (<n>:ts)\ (m:ms) \quad = \quad ;\ :\ (L\ ts\ (m:ms)) \qquad \text{if } m = n$$
$$= \quad \}\ :\ (L\ (<n>:ts)\ ms) \qquad \text{if } n < m$$
$$L\ (<n>:ts)\ ms \qquad = \quad L\ ts\ ms$$

$$L\ (\{n\}:ts)\ (m:ms) \quad = \quad \{\ :\ (L\ ts\ (n:m:ms)) \qquad \text{if } n > m\ (Note\ 1)$$
$$L\ (\{n\}:ts)\ [] \qquad = \quad \{\ :\ (L\ ts\ [n]) \qquad\qquad \text{if } n > 0\ (Note\ 1)$$
$$L\ (\{n\}:ts)\ ms \qquad = \quad \{\ :\ \}\ :\ (L\ (<n>:ts)\ ms) \quad (Note\ 2)$$

$$L\ (\}:ts)\ (0:ms) \qquad = \quad \}\ :\ (L\ ts\ ms) \qquad\qquad (Note\ 3)$$
$$L\ (\}:ts)\ ms \qquad = \quad \text{parse-error} \qquad\qquad (Note\ 3)$$

$$L\ (\{:ts)\ ms \qquad = \quad \{\ :\ (L\ ts\ (0:ms)) \qquad\qquad (Note\ 4)$$

$$L\ (t:ts)\ (m:ms) \qquad = \quad \}\ :\ (L\ (t:ts)\ ms) \qquad \text{if } m/= 0 \text{ and parse-error}(t)$$
$$(Note\ 5)$$
$$L\ (t:ts)\ ms \qquad = \quad t\ :\ (L\ ts\ ms)$$

$$L\ []\ [] \qquad = \quad []$$
$$L\ []\ (m:ms) \qquad = \quad \}\ :\ L\ []\ ms \qquad\qquad \text{if } m \neq 0\ (Note\ 6)$$

Note 1. A nested context must be further indented than the enclosing context ($n > m$). If not, L fails, and the compiler should indicate a layout error. An example is:

```
f x = let
            h y = let
      p z = z
                  in p
          in h
```

Here, the definition of p is indented less than the indentation of the enclosing context, which is set in this case by the definition of h.

Note 2. If the first token after a `where` (say) is not indented more than the enclosing layout context, then the block must be empty, so empty braces are inserted. The $\{n\}$ token is replaced by $<n>$, to mimic the situation if the empty braces had been explicit.

Note 3. By matching against 0 for the current layout context, we ensure that an explicit close brace can only match an explicit open brace. A parse error results if an explicit close brace matches an implicit open brace.

Note 4. This clause means that all brace pairs are treated as explicit layout contexts, including labelled construction and update (Section 3.15). This is a difference between this formulation and Haskell 1.4.

Note 5. The side condition parse-error(t) is to be interpreted as follows: if the tokens generated so far by L together with the next token t represent an invalid prefix of the Haskell grammar, and the tokens generated so far by L followed by the token "}" represent a valid prefix of the Haskell grammar, then parse-error(t) is true.

The test $m/ = 0$ checks that an implicitly-added closing brace would match an implicit open brace.

Note 6. At the end of the input, any pending close-braces are inserted. It is an error at this point to be within a non-layout context (i.e. $m = 0$).

If none of the rules given above matches, then the algorithm fails. It can fail for instance when the end of the input is reached, and a non-layout context is active, since the close brace is missing. Some error conditions are not detected by the algorithm, although they could be: for example `let }`.

Note 1 implements the feature that layout processing can be stopped prematurely by a parse error. For example

```
let x = e; y = x in e'
```

is valid, because it translates to

```
let { x = e; y = x } in e'
```

The close brace is inserted due to the parse error rule above. The parse-error rule is hard to implement in its full generality, because doing so involves fixities. For example, the expression

```
do a == b == c
```

has a single unambiguous (albeit probably type-incorrect) parse, namely

```
(do { a == b }) == c
```

because (`==`) is non-associative. Programmers are therefore advised to avoid writing code that requires the parser to insert a closing brace in such situations.

9.4 Literate Comments

The "literate comment" convention, first developed by Richard Bird and Philip Wadler for Orwell, and inspired in turn by Donald Knuth's "literate programming", is an alternative style for encoding Haskell source code. The literate style encourages comments by making them the default. A line in which ">" is the first character is treated as part of the program; all other lines are comment.

The program text is recovered by taking only those lines beginning with ">", and replacing the leading ">" with a space. Layout and comments apply exactly as described in Chapter 9 in the resulting text.

To capture some cases where one omits an ">" by mistake, it is an error for a program line to appear adjacent to a non-blank comment line, where a line is taken as blank if it consists only of whitespace.

By convention, the style of comment is indicated by the file extension, with ".hs" indicating a usual Haskell file and ".lhs" indicating a literate Haskell file. Using this style, a simple factorial program would be:

```
    This literate program prompts the user for a number
    and prints the factorial of that number:
> main :: IO ()
> main = do putStr "Enter a number: "
>           l <- readLine
>           putStr "n!= "
>           print (fact (read l))
    This is the factorial function.
> fact :: Integer -> Integer
> fact 0 = 1
> fact n = n * fact (n-1)
```

An alternative style of literate programming is particularly suitable for use with the LaTeX text processing system. In this convention, only those parts of the literate program that are entirely enclosed between \begin{code}...\end{code} delimiters are treated as program text; all other lines are comment. More precisely:

- Program code begins on the first line following a line that begins \begin{code}.

- Program code ends just before a subsequent line that begins \end{code} (ignoring string literals, of course).

It is not necessary to insert additional blank lines before or after these delimiters, though it may be stylistically desirable. For example,

```
\documentstyle{article}

\begin{document}

\section{Introduction}

This is a trivial program that prints the first 20 factorials.

\begin{code}
main :: IO ()
main =  print [ (n, product [1..n]) | n <- [1..20]]
\end{code}

\end{document}
```

This style uses the same file extension. It is not advisable to mix these two styles in the same file.

9.5 Context-Free Syntax

module	$\rightarrow$	**module** *modid* [*exports*] **where** *body*	
	|	*body*	
body	$\rightarrow$	{ *impdecls* ; *topdecls* }	
	|	{ *impdecls* }	
	|	{ *topdecls* }	

impdecls	$\rightarrow$	*impdecl$_1$* ; ... ; *impdecl$_n$*	$(n \geq 1)$

exports	$\rightarrow$	(*export$_1$* , ... , *export$_n$* [,])	$(n \geq 0)$

export	$\rightarrow$	*qvar*	
	|	*qtycon* [(..) | (*cname$_1$* , ... , *cname$_n$*)]	$(n \geq 0)$
	|	*qtycls* [(..) | (*qvar$_1$* , ... , *qvar$_n$*)]	$(n \geq 0)$
	|	**module** *modid*	

impdecl	$\rightarrow$	**import** [**qualified**] *modid* [**as** *modid*] [*impspec*]	
	|		(empty declaration)

impspec	$\rightarrow$	(*import$_1$* , ... , *import$_n$* [,])	$(n \geq 0)$
	|	**hiding** (*import$_1$* , ... , *import$_n$* [,])	$(n \geq 0)$

import	$\rightarrow$	*var*	
	|	*tycon* [(..) | (*cname$_1$* , ... , *cname$_n$*)]	$(n \geq 0)$
	|	*tycls* [(..) | (*var$_1$* , ... , *var$_n$*)]	$(n \geq 0)$
cname	$\rightarrow$	*var* | *con*	

topdecls	$\rightarrow$	*topdecl$_1$* ; ... ; *topdecl$_n$*	$(n \geq 0)$
topdecl	$\rightarrow$	**type** *simpletype* = *type*	
	|	**data** [*context* =>] *simpletype* = *constrs* [*deriving*]	
	|	**newtype** [*context* =>] *simpletype* = *newconstr* [*deriving*]	
	|	**class** [*scontext* =>] *tycls tyvar* [**where** *cdecls*]	
	|	**instance** [*scontext* =>] *qtycls inst* [**where** *idecls*]	
	|	**default** (*type$_1$* , ... , *type$_n$*)	$(n \geq 0)$
	|	*decl*	

decls	$\rightarrow$	{ *decl$_1$* ; ... ; *decl$_n$* }	$(n \geq 0)$
decl	$\rightarrow$	*gendecl*	

		(*funlhs* | *pat^0*) *rhs*	
cdecls	$\rightarrow$	{ *cdecl$_1$* ; ... ; *cdecl$_n$* }	($n \geq 0$)
cdecl	$\rightarrow$	*gendecl*	
	|	(*funlhs* | *var*) *rhs*	
idecls	$\rightarrow$	{ *idecl$_1$* ; ... ; *idecl$_n$* }	($n \geq 0$)
idecl	$\rightarrow$	(*funlhs* | *var*) *rhs*	
	|		(empty)
gendecl	$\rightarrow$	*vars* :: [*context* =>] *type*	(type signature)
	|	*fixity* [*integer*] *ops*	(fixity declaration)
	|		(empty declaration)
ops	$\rightarrow$	*op$_1$* , ... , *op$_n$*	($n \geq 1$)
vars	$\rightarrow$	*var$_1$* , ..., *var$_n$*	($n \geq 1$)
fixity	$\rightarrow$	`infixl` | `infixr` | `infix`	
type	$\rightarrow$	*btype* [`->` *type*]	(function type)
btype	$\rightarrow$	[*btype*] *atype*	(type application)
atype	$\rightarrow$	*gtycon*	
	|	*tyvar*	
	|	(*type$_1$* , ... , *type$_k$*)	(tuple type, $k \geq 2$)
	|	[*type*]	(list type)
	|	(*type*)	(parenthesized constructor)
gtycon	$\rightarrow$	*qtycon*	
	|	( )	(unit type)
	|	[ ]	(list constructor)
	|	(`->`)	(function constructor)
	|	(, { , })	(tupling constructors)
context	$\rightarrow$	*class*	
	|	(*class$_1$* , ... , *class$_n$*)	($n \geq 0$)
class	$\rightarrow$	*qtycls tyvar*	
	|	*qtycls* (*tyvar atype$_1$* ... *atype$_n$*)	($n \geq 1$)
scontext	$\rightarrow$	*simpleclass*	
	|	(*simpleclass$_1$* , ... , *simpleclass$_n$*)	($n \geq 0$)
simpleclass $\rightarrow$		*qtycls tyvar*	
simpletype $\rightarrow$		*tycon tyvar$_1$* ... *tyvar$_k$*	($k \geq 0$)

constrs	$\rightarrow$	$constr_1 \mid \ldots \mid constr_n$	$(n \geq 1)$
constr	$\rightarrow$	$con \; [\texttt{!}] \; atype_1 \; \ldots \; [\texttt{!}] \; atype_k$	(arity $con = k$, $k \geq 0$)
	$\mid$	$(btype \mid \texttt{!} \; atype) \; conop \; (btype \mid \texttt{!} \; atype)$	(infix *conop*)
	$\mid$	$con \; \{ \; fielddecl_1 \; , \; \ldots \; , \; fielddecl_n \; \}$	$(n \geq 0)$
newconstr	$\rightarrow$	$con \; atype$	
	$\mid$	$con \; \{ \; var \; \texttt{::} \; type \; \}$	
fielddecl	$\rightarrow$	$vars \; \texttt{::} \; (type \mid \texttt{!} \; atype)$	
deriving	$\rightarrow$	$\texttt{deriving} \; (dclass \mid (\; dclass_1 \; , \; \ldots \; , \; dclass_n \;))(n \geq 0)$	
dclass	$\rightarrow$	$qtycls$	
inst	$\rightarrow$	$gtycon$	
	$\mid$	$(\; gtycon \; tyvar_1 \; \ldots \; tyvar_k \;)$	$(k \geq 0$, *tyvars* distinct)
	$\mid$	$(\; tyvar_1 \; , \; \ldots \; , \; tyvar_k \;)$	$(k \geq 2$, *tyvars* distinct)
	$\mid$	$[\; tyvar \;]$	
	$\mid$	$(\; tyvar_1 \; \texttt{->} \; tyvar_2 \;)$	$tyvar_1$ and $tyvar_2$ distinct
funlhs	$\rightarrow$	$var \; apat \; \{ \; apat \; \}$	
	$\mid$	$pat^{i+1} \; varop^{(a,i)} \; pat^{i+1}$	
	$\mid$	$lpat^{i} \; varop^{(l,i)} \; pat^{i+1}$	
	$\mid$	$pat^{i+1} \; varop^{(r,i)} \; rpat^{i}$	
	$\mid$	$(\; funlhs \;) \; apat \; \{ \; apat \; \}$	
rhs	$\rightarrow$	$\texttt{=} \; exp \; [\texttt{where} \; decls]$	
	$\mid$	$gdrhs \; [\texttt{where} \; decls]$	
gdrhs	$\rightarrow$	$gd \; \texttt{=} \; exp \; [gdrhs]$	
gd	$\rightarrow$	$\mid \; exp^0$	
exp	$\rightarrow$	$exp^0 \; \texttt{::} \; [context \; \texttt{=>}] \; type$	(expression type signature)
	$\mid$	exp^0	
exp^i	$\rightarrow$	$exp^{i+1} \; [qop^{(n,i)} \; exp^{i+1}]$	
	$\mid$	$lexp^i$	
	$\mid$	$rexp^i$	
$lexp^i$	$\rightarrow$	$(lexp^i \mid exp^{i+1}) \; qop^{(l,i)} \; exp^{i+1}$	
$lexp^6$	$\rightarrow$	$\texttt{-} \; exp^7$	
$rexp^i$	$\rightarrow$	$exp^{i+1} \; qop^{(r,i)} \; (rexp^i \mid exp^{i+1})$	
exp^{10}	$\rightarrow$	$\texttt{\textbackslash} \; apat_1 \; \ldots \; apat_n \; \texttt{->} \; exp$	(lambda abstraction, $n \geq 1$)
	$\mid$	$\texttt{let} \; decls \; \texttt{in} \; exp$	(let expression)
	$\mid$	$\texttt{if} \; exp \; \texttt{then} \; exp \; \texttt{else} \; exp$	(conditional)
	$\mid$	$\texttt{case} \; exp \; \texttt{of} \; \{ \; alts \; \}$	(case expression)

			do { *stmts* }	(do expression)

$$
\begin{array}{lll}
 & \mid & \textit{fexp} \\
\textit{fexp} & \rightarrow & [\textit{fexp}]\ \textit{aexp} & \text{(function application)}
\end{array}
$$

$$
\begin{array}{lll}
\textit{aexp} & \rightarrow & \textit{qvar} & \text{(variable)} \\
 & \mid & \textit{gcon} & \text{(general constructor)} \\
 & \mid & \textit{literal} \\
 & \mid & (\ \textit{exp}\ ) & \text{(parenthesized expression)} \\
 & \mid & (\ \textit{exp}_1\ ,\ \ldots\ ,\ \textit{exp}_k\ ) & \text{(tuple, } k \geq 2) \\
 & \mid & [\ \textit{exp}_1\ ,\ \ldots\ ,\ \textit{exp}_k\ ] & \text{(list, } k \geq 1) \\
 & \mid & [\ \textit{exp}_1\ [,\ \textit{exp}_2]\ \textbf{..}\ [\textit{exp}_3]\ ] & \text{(arithmetic sequence)} \\
 & \mid & [\ \textit{exp}\ \mid\ \textit{qual}_1\ ,\ \ldots\ ,\ \textit{qual}_n\ ] & \text{(list comprehension, } n \geq 1) \\
 & \mid & (\ \textit{exp}^{i+1}\ \textit{qop}^{(a,i)}\ ) & \text{(left section)} \\
 & \mid & (\ \textit{lexp}^{i}\ \textit{qop}^{(l,i)}\ ) & \text{(left section)} \\
 & \mid & (\ \textit{qop}^{(a,i)}_{\langle -\rangle}\ \textit{exp}^{i+1}\ ) & \text{(right section)} \\
 & \mid & (\ \textit{qop}^{(r,i)}_{\langle -\rangle}\ \textit{rexp}^{i}\ ) & \text{(right section)} \\
 & \mid & \textit{qcon}\ \{\ \textit{fbind}_1\ ,\ \ldots\ ,\ \textit{fbind}_n\ \} & \text{(labeled construction, } n \geq 0) \\
 & \mid & \textit{aexp}_{\langle qcon\rangle}\ \{\ \textit{fbind}_1\ ,\ \ldots\ ,\ \textit{fbind}_n\ \} & \text{(labeled update, } n \geq 1)
\end{array}
$$

$$
\begin{array}{lll}
\textit{qual} & \rightarrow & \textit{pat}\ \textbf{<-}\ \textit{exp} & \text{(generator)} \\
 & \mid & \textbf{let}\ \textit{decls} & \text{(local declaration)} \\
 & \mid & \textit{exp} & \text{(guard)}
\end{array}
$$

$$
\begin{array}{lll}
\textit{alts} & \rightarrow & \textit{alt}_1\ \textbf{;}\ \ldots\ \textbf{;}\ \textit{alt}_n & (n \geq 1) \\
\textit{alt} & \rightarrow & \textit{pat}\ \textbf{->}\ \textit{exp}\ [\textbf{where}\ \textit{decls}] \\
 & \mid & \textit{pat}\ \textit{gdpat}\ [\textbf{where}\ \textit{decls}] \\
 & \mid & & \textit{(empty alternative)}
\end{array}
$$

$$
\begin{array}{lll}
\textit{gdpat} & \rightarrow & \textit{gd}\ \textbf{->}\ \textit{exp}\ [\ \textit{gdpat}\ ]
\end{array}
$$

$$
\begin{array}{lll}
\textit{stmts} & \rightarrow & \textit{stmt}_1\ \ldots\ \textit{stmt}_n\ \textit{exp}\ [\textbf{;}] & (n \geq 0) \\
\textit{stmt} & \rightarrow & \textit{exp}\ \textbf{;} \\
 & \mid & \textit{pat}\ \textbf{<-}\ \textit{exp}\ \textbf{;} \\
 & \mid & \textbf{let}\ \textit{decls}\ \textbf{;} \\
 & \mid & \textbf{;} & \textit{(empty statement)}
\end{array}
$$

$$
\begin{array}{lll}
\textit{fbind} & \rightarrow & \textit{qvar}\ \textbf{=}\ \textit{exp}
\end{array}
$$

$$
\begin{array}{lll}
\textit{pat} & \rightarrow & \textit{var}\ \textbf{+}\ \textit{integer} & \text{(successor pattern)}
\end{array}
$$

$$
\begin{array}{lll}
 & | & pat^0 \\
pat^i & \rightarrow & pat^{i+1} \; [qconop^{(n,i)} \; pat^{i+1}] \\
 & | & lpat^i \\
 & | & rpat^i \\
lpat^i & \rightarrow & (lpat^i \mid pat^{i+1}) \; qconop^{(l,i)} \; pat^{i+1} \\
lpat^6 & \rightarrow & - \; (integer \mid float) \\
rpat^i & \rightarrow & pat^{i+1} \; qconop^{(r,i)} \; (rpat^i \mid pat^{i+1}) \\
pat^{10} & \rightarrow & apat \\
 & | & gcon \; apat_1 \; \dots \; apat_k
\end{array}
$$

      (negative literal)

      (arity $gcon = k$, $k \geq 1$)

$$
\begin{array}{lll}
apat & \rightarrow & var \; [\, @ \; apat] \\
 & | & gcon \\
 & | & qcon \; \{ \; fpat_1 \; , \; \dots \; , \; fpat_k \; \} \\
 & | & literal \\
 & | & \_ \\
 & | & (\; pat \;) \\
 & | & (\; pat_1 \; , \; \dots \; , \; pat_k \;) \\
 & | & [\; pat_1 \; , \; \dots \; , \; pat_k \;] \\
 & | & {\sim} \; apat
\end{array}
$$

      (as pattern)
      (arity $gcon = 0$)
      (labeled pattern, $k \geq 0$)

      (wildcard)
      (parenthesized pattern)
      (tuple pattern, $k \geq 2$)
      (list pattern, $k \geq 1$)
      (irrefutable pattern)

$$
\begin{array}{lll}
fpat & \rightarrow & qvar = pat
\end{array}
$$

$$
\begin{array}{lll}
gcon & \rightarrow & (\,) \\
 & | & [\,] \\
 & | & (\,,\{,\}) \\
 & | & qcon
\end{array}
$$

$$
\begin{array}{lll}
var & \rightarrow & varid \mid (\; varsym \;) \\
qvar & \rightarrow & qvarid \mid (\; qvarsym \;) \\
con & \rightarrow & conid \mid (\; consym \;) \\
qcon & \rightarrow & qconid \mid (\; gconsym \;) \\
varop & \rightarrow & varsym \mid {`} varid {`} \\
qvarop & \rightarrow & qvarsym \mid {`} qvarid {`} \\
conop & \rightarrow & consym \mid {`} conid {`} \\
qconop & \rightarrow & gconsym \mid {`} qconid {`} \\
op & \rightarrow & varop \mid conop \\
qop & \rightarrow & qvarop \mid qconop \\
gconsym & \rightarrow & : \mid qconsym
\end{array}
$$

      (variable)
      (qualified variable)
      (constructor)
      (qualified constructor)
      (variable operator)
      (qualified variable operator)
      (constructor operator)
      (qualified constructor operator)
      (operator)
      (qualified operator)

JFP **13** (1): 139–144, January 2003. © 2003 Cambridge University Press
DOI: 10.1017/S0956796803001217 Printed in the United Kingdom

Chapter 10

Specification of Derived Instances

A *derived instance* is an instance declaration that is generated automatically in conjunction with a `data` or `newtype` declaration. The body of a derived instance declaration is derived syntactically from the definition of the associated type. Derived instances are possible only for classes known to the compiler: those defined in either the Prelude or a standard library. In this appendix, we describe the derivation of classes defined by the Prelude.

If T is an algebraic datatype declared by:

$$\texttt{data } cx \texttt{ => } T \; u_1 \; \ldots \; u_k \;\; = \;\; K_1 \; t_{11} \; \ldots \; t_{1k_1} \; | \; \cdots \; | \; K_n \; t_{n1} \; \ldots \; t_{nk_n}$$
$$\texttt{deriving } (\, C_1 , \; \ldots , \; C_m \,)$$

(where $m \geq 0$ and the parentheses may be omitted if $m = 1$) then a derived instance declaration is possible for a class C if these conditions hold:

1. C is one of `Eq`, `Ord`, `Enum`, `Bounded`, `Show`, or `Read`.

2. There is a context cx' such that $cx' \Rightarrow C \; t_{ij}$ holds for each of the constituent types t_{ij}.

3. If C is `Bounded`, the type must be either an enumeration (all constructors must be nullary) or have only one constructor.

4. If C is `Enum`, the type must be an enumeration.

5. There must be no explicit instance declaration elsewhere in the program that makes $T \; u_1 \; \ldots \; u_k$ an instance of C.

For the purposes of derived instances, a `newtype` declaration is treated as a `data` declaration with a single constructor.

If the `deriving` form is present, an instance declaration is automatically generated for $T\ u_1\ \dots\ u_k$ over each class C_i. If the derived instance declaration is impossible for any of the C_i then a static error results. If no derived instances are required, the `deriving` form may be omitted or the form `deriving ()` may be used.

Each derived instance declaration will have the form:

$$\texttt{instance}\ (cx,\ \ cx')\ \texttt{=>}\ C_i\ (T\ u_1\ \dots\ u_k)\ \texttt{where}\ \{\ d\ \}$$

where d is derived automatically depending on C_i and the data type declaration for T (as will be described in the remainder of this chapter).

The context cx' is the smallest context satisfying point (2) above. For mutually recusive data types, the compiler may need to perform a fixpoint calculation to compute it.

The remaining details of the derived instances for each of the derivable Prelude classes are now given. Free variables and constructors used in these translations always refer to entities defined by the `Prelude`.

10.1 Derived Instances of `Eq` and `Ord`

The class methods automatically introduced by derived instances of `Eq` and `Ord` are `(==)`, `(/=)`, `compare`, `(<)`, `(<=)`, `(>)`, `(>=)`, `max`, and `min`. The latter seven operators are defined so as to compare their arguments lexicographically with respect to the constructor set given, with earlier constructors in the datatype declaration counting as smaller than later ones. For example, for the `Bool` datatype, we have that `(True > False) == True`.

Derived comparisons always traverse constructors from left to right. These examples illustrate this property:

```
(1,undefined)  ==  (2,undefined)  ⇒    False
(undefined,1)  ==  (undefined,2)  ⇒     ⊥
```

All derived operations of class `Eq` and `Ord` are strict in both arguments. For example, `False <= ⊥` is ⊥, even though `False` is the first constructor of the `Bool` type.

10.2 Derived Instances of `Enum`

Derived instance declarations for the class `Enum` are only possible for enumerations (data types with only nullary constructors).

The nullary constructors are assumed to be numbered left-to-right with the indices 0 through $n - 1$. The succ and pred operators give the successor and predecessor respectively of a value, under this numbering scheme. It is an error to apply succ to the maximum element, or pred to the minimum element.

The toEnum and fromEnum operators map enumerated values to and from the Int type; toEnum raises a runtime error if the Int argument is not the index of one of the constructors.

The definitions of the remaining methods are

```
enumFrom x            = enumFromTo x lastCon
enumFromThen x y      = enumFromThenTo x y bound
                        where
                           bound | fromEnum y >= fromEnum x = lastCon
                                 | otherwise                = firstCon
enumFromTo x y        = map toEnum [fromEnum x .. fromEnum y]
enumFromThenTo x y z  = map toEnum [fromEnum x, fromEnum y .. fromEnum z]
```

where firstCon and lastCon are, respectively, the first and last constructors listed in the data declaration. For example, given the datatype:

```
data  Color = Red | Orange | Yellow | Green  deriving (Enum)
```

we would have:

```
[Orange ..]            ==  [Orange, Yellow, Green]
fromEnum Yellow        ==  2
```

10.3   Derived Instances of Bounded

The Bounded class introduces the class methods minBound and maxBound, which define the minimal and maximal elements of the type. For an enumeration, the first and last constructors listed in the data declaration are the bounds. For a type with a single constructor, the constructor is applied to the bounds for the constituent types. For example, the following datatype:

```
data  Pair a b = Pair a b deriving Bounded
```

would generate the following Bounded instance:

```
instance (Bounded a, Bounded b) => Bounded (Pair a b) where
   minBound = Pair minBound minBound
   maxBound = Pair maxBound maxBound
```

10.4   Derived Instances of `Read` and `Show`

The class methods automatically introduced by derived instances of `Read` and `Show` are `showsPrec`, `readsPrec`, `showList`, and `readList`. They are used to coerce values into strings and parse strings into values.

The function `showsPrec d x r` accepts a precedence level d (a number from 0 to 11), a value x, and a string r. It returns a string representing x concatenated to r. `showsPrec` satisfies the law:

$$\texttt{showsPrec d x r ++ s == showsPrec d x (r ++ s)}$$

The representation will be enclosed in parentheses if the precedence of the top-level constructor in x is less than d. Thus, if d is 0 then the result is never surrounded in parentheses; if d is 11 it is always surrounded in parentheses, unless it is an atomic expression. (Recall that function application has precedence 10.) The extra parameter r is essential if tree-like structures are to be printed in linear time rather than time quadratic in the size of the tree.

The function `readsPrec d s` accepts a precedence level d (a number from 0 to 10) and a string s, and attempts to parse a value from the front of the string, returning a list of (parsed value, remaining string) pairs. If there is no successful parse, the returned list is empty. Parsing of an unparenthesised infix operator application succeeds only if the precedence of the operator is greater than or equal to d.

It should be the case that

$$\texttt{(x, "")   is an element of   (readsPrec d (showsPrec d x ""))}$$

That is, `readsPrec` should be able to parse the string produced by `showsPrec`, and should deliver the value that `showsPrec` started with.

`showList` and `readList` allow lists of objects to be represented using non-standard denotations. This is especially useful for strings (lists of `Char`).

`readsPrec` will parse any valid representation of the standard types apart from strings, for which only quoted strings are accepted, and other lists, for which only the bracketed form [...] is accepted. See Chapter 8 for full details.

The result of `show` is a syntactically correct Haskell expression containing only constants, given the fixity declarations in force at the point where the type is declared. It contains only the constructor names defined in the data type, parentheses, and spaces. When labelled constructor fields are used, braces, commas, field names, and equal signs are also used. Parentheses are only added where needed, *ignoring associativity*. No line breaks are added. The result of `show` is readable by `read` if all component types are readable. (This is true for all instances defined in the Prelude but may not be true for user-defined instances.)

Derived instances of `Read` make the following assumptions, which derived instances of `Show` obey:

- If the constructor is defined to be an infix operator, then the derived `Read` instance will parse only infix applications of the constructor (not the prefix form).

- Associativity is not used to reduce the occurrence of parentheses, although precedence may be. For example, given

```
infixr 4 :$
data T = Int :$ T  |  NT
```

then:

- `show (1 :$ 2 :$ NT)` produces the string `"1 :$ (2 :$ NT)"`.
- `read "1 :$ (2 :$ NT)"` succeeds, with the obvious result.
- `read "1 :$ 2 :$ NT"` fails.

- If the constructor is defined using record syntax, the derived `Read` will parse only the record-syntax form, and furthermore, the fields must be given in the same order as the original declaration.

- The derived `Read` instance allows arbitrary Haskell whitespace between tokens of the input string. Extra parentheses are also allowed.

The derived `Read` and `Show` instances may be unsuitable for some uses. Some problems include:

- Circular structures cannot be printed or read by these instances.

- The printer loses shared substructure; the printed representation of an object may be much larger than necessary.

- The parsing techniques used by the reader are very inefficient; reading a large structure may be quite slow.

- There is no user control over the printing of types defined in the Prelude. For example, there is no way to change the formatting of floating point numbers.

10.5 An Example

As a complete example, consider a tree datatype:

```
data Tree a = Leaf a | Tree a :^: Tree a
       deriving (Eq, Ord, Read, Show)
```

Automatic derivation of instance declarations for `Bounded` and `Enum` are not possible, as `Tree` is not an enumeration or single-constructor datatype. The complete instance declarations for `Tree` are shown in Figure 10.1, Note the implicit use of default class method definitions – for example, only `<=` is defined for `Ord`, with the other class methods (`<`, `>`, `>=`, `max`, and `min`) being defined by the defaults given in the class declaration shown in Figure 6.1 (page 85).

```
infixr 5 :^:
data Tree a =  Leaf a   |   Tree a :^: Tree a
instance (Eq a) => Eq (Tree a) where
        Leaf m == Leaf n  =   m==n
        u:^:v   == x:^:y   =   u==x && v==y
             _  ==  _      =   False
instance (Ord a) => Ord (Tree a) where
        Leaf m <= Leaf n  =   m<=n
        Leaf m <= x:^:y   =   True
        u:^:v  <= Leaf n  =   False
        u:^:v  <= x:^:y   =   u<x || u==x && v<=y
instance (Show a) => Show (Tree a) where
        showsPrec d (Leaf m) = showParen (d > app_prec) showStr
          where
             showStr = showString "Leaf " . showsPrec (app_prec+1) m
        showsPrec d (u :^: v) = showParen (d > up_prec) showStr
          where
             showStr = showsPrec (up_prec+1) u .
                         showString " :^: "             .
                         showsPrec (up_prec+1) v
             -- Note: right-associativity of :^: ignored
instance (Read a) => Read (Tree a) where
        readsPrec d r =  readParen (d > up_prec)
                            (\r -> [(u:^:v,w) |
                                    (u,s) <- readsPrec (up_prec+1) r,
                                    (":^:",t) <- lex s,
                                    (v,w) <- readsPrec (up_prec+1) t]) r
                      ++ readParen (d > app_prec)
                            (\r -> [(Leaf m,t) |
                                    ("Leaf",s) <- lex r,
                                    (m,t) <- readsPrec (app_prec+1) s]) r
up_prec  = 5    -- Precedence of :^:
app_prec = 10   -- Application has precedence one more than
                -- the most tightly-binding operator
```

Figure 10.1: Example of Derived Instances

JFP **13** (1): 145–146, January 2003. © 2003 Cambridge University Press
DOI: 10.1017/S095679680300131X Printed in the United Kingdom

Chapter 11

Compiler Pragmas

Some compiler implementations support compiler *pragmas*, which are used to give additional instructions or hints to the compiler, but which do not form part of the Haskell language proper and do not change a program's semantics. This chapter summarizes this existing practice. An implementation is not required to respect any pragma, but the pragma should be ignored if an implementation is not prepared to handle it. Lexically, pragmas appear as comments, except that the enclosing syntax is {-# #-}.

11.1 Inlining

$$
\begin{array}{lll}
decl & \rightarrow & \texttt{\{-\# INLINE } qvars \texttt{ \#-\}} \\
decl & \rightarrow & \texttt{\{-\# NOINLINE } qvars \texttt{ \#-\}}
\end{array}
$$

The INLINE pragma instructs the compiler to inline the specified variables at their use sites. Compilers will often automatically inline simple expressions. This may be prevented by the NOINLINE pragma.

11.2 Specialization

$$
\begin{array}{llll}
decl & \rightarrow & \texttt{\{-\# SPECIALIZE } spec_1 \texttt{ , } \ldots \texttt{ , } spec_k \texttt{ \#-\}} & (k \geq 1) \\
spec & \rightarrow & vars :: type &
\end{array}
$$

Specialization is used to avoid inefficiencies involved in dispatching overloaded functions. For example, in

```
factorial :: Num a => a -> a
factorial 0 = 0
factorial n = n * factorial (n-1)
{-# SPECIALIZE factorial :: Int -> Int,
                factorial :: Integer -> Integer #-}
```

calls to `factorial` in which the compiler can detect that the parameter is either `Int` or `Integer` will use specialized versions of `factorial` which do not involve overloaded numeric operations.

Part II

The Haskell 98 Libraries

JFP **13** (1): 149–152, January 2003. © 2003 Cambridge University Press
DOI: 10.1017/S0956796803001412   Printed in the United Kingdom

Chapter 12

Rational Numbers

```
module  Ratio (
    Ratio, Rational, (%), numerator, denominator, approxRational ) where

infixl 7  %
data  (Integral a)       => Ratio a = ...
type  Rational           = Ratio Integer
(%)                      :: (Integral a) => a -> a -> Ratio a
numerator, denominator   :: (Integral a) => Ratio a -> a
approxRational           :: (RealFrac a) => a -> a -> Rational
instance  (Integral a)   => Eq         (Ratio a)  where ...
instance  (Integral a)   => Ord        (Ratio a)  where ...
instance  (Integral a)   => Num        (Ratio a)  where ...
instance  (Integral a)   => Real       (Ratio a)  where ...
instance  (Integral a)   => Fractional (Ratio a)  where ...
instance  (Integral a)   => RealFrac   (Ratio a)  where ...
instance  (Integral a)   => Enum       (Ratio a)  where ...
instance  (Read a,Integral a) => Read  (Ratio a)  where ...
instance  (Integral a)   => Show       (Ratio a)  where ...
```

For each `Integral` type t, there is a type `Ratio` t of rational pairs with components of type t. The type name `Rational` is a synonym for `Ratio Integer`.

`Ratio` is an instance of classes `Eq, Ord, Num, Real, Fractional, RealFrac, Enum, Read,` and `Show`. In each case, the instance for `Ratio` t simply "lifts" the corresponding operations over t. If t is a bounded type, the results may be unpredictable; for example `Ratio Int` may give rise to integer overflow even for rational numbers of small absolute size.

The operator (%) forms the ratio of two integral numbers, reducing the fraction to terms with no common factor and such that the denominator is positive. The functions numerator and denominator extract the components of a ratio; these are in reduced form with a positive denominator. Ratio is an abstract type. For example, 12 % 8 is reduced to 3/2 and 12 % (-8) is reduced to (-3)/2.

The approxRational function, applied to two real fractional numbers x and epsilon, returns the simplest rational number within the open interval $(x - \text{epsilon}, x + \text{epsilon})$. A rational number n/d in reduced form is said to be simpler than another n'/d' if $|n| \leq |n'|$ and $d \leq d'$. Note that it can be proved that any real interval contains a unique simplest rational.

12.1 Library Ratio

```
-- Standard functions on rational numbers
module  Ratio (
    Ratio, Rational, (%), numerator, denominator, approxRational ) where

infixl 7  %

ratPrec = 7 :: Int

data  (Integral a)      => Ratio a = !a :% !a  deriving (Eq)
type   Rational         =  Ratio Integer

(%)                     :: (Integral a) => a -> a -> Ratio a
numerator, denominator  :: (Integral a) => Ratio a -> a
approxRational          :: (RealFrac a) => a -> a -> Rational

-- "reduce" is a subsidiary function used only in this module.
-- It normalises a ratio by dividing both numerator
-- and denominator by their greatest common divisor.
--
-- E.g., 12 'reduce' 8     ==  3 :%   2
--       12 'reduce' (-8) ==  3 :% (-2)
reduce _ 0              =  error "Ratio.% : zero denominator"
reduce x y              =  (x 'quot' d) :% (y 'quot' d)
                              where d = gcd x y

x % y                   =  reduce (x * signum y) (abs y)

numerator (x :% _)      =  x

denominator (_ :% y)    =  y

instance  (Integral a)  => Ord (Ratio a)   where
    (x:%y) <= (x':%y')  =  x * y' <= x' * y
    (x:%y) <  (x':%y')  =  x * y' <  x' * y
```

```
instance  (Integral a)  => Num (Ratio a)  where
    (x:%y) + (x':%y')   =  reduce (x*y' + x'*y) (y*y')
    (x:%y) * (x':%y')   =  reduce (x * x') (y * y')
    negate (x:%y)       =  (-x) :% y
    abs (x:%y)          =  abs x :% y
    signum (x:%y)       =  signum x :% 1
    fromInteger x       =  fromInteger x :% 1

instance  (Integral a)  => Real (Ratio a)  where
    toRational (x:%y)   =  toInteger x :% toInteger y

instance  (Integral a)  => Fractional (Ratio a)  where
    (x:%y) / (x':%y')   =  (x*y') % (y*x')
    recip (x:%y)        =  y % x
    fromRational (x:%y) =  fromInteger x :% fromInteger y

instance  (Integral a)  => RealFrac (Ratio a)  where
    properFraction (x:%y) = (fromIntegral q, r:%y)
                          where (q,r) = quotRem x y

instance  (Integral a)  => Enum (Ratio a)  where
    succ x          =  x+1
    pred x          =  x-1
    toEnum          =  fromIntegral
    fromEnum        =  fromInteger . truncate -- May overflow
    enumFrom        =  numericEnumFrom        -- These numericEnumXXX functions
    enumFromThen    =  numericEnumFromThen    -- are as defined in Prelude.hs
    enumFromTo      =  numericEnumFromTo      -- but not exported from it!
    enumFromThenTo  =  numericEnumFromThenTo

instance  (Read a, Integral a)  => Read (Ratio a)  where
    readsPrec p  =  readParen (p > ratPrec)
                              (\r -> [(x%y,u) | (x,s)  <- readsPrec
                                                            (ratPrec+1) r,
                                                ("%",t) <- lex s,
                                                (y,u)   <- readsPrec
                                                            (ratPrec+1) t ]

instance  (Integral a)  => Show (Ratio a)  where
    showsPrec p (x:%y)  =  showParen (p > ratPrec)
                              (showsPrec (ratPrec+1) x .
                               showString " % " .
                               showsPrec (ratPrec+1) y)
```

```
approxRational x eps    =  simplest (x-eps) (x+eps)
        where simplest x y | y < x        =  simplest y x
                           | x == y     =  xr
                           | x > 0      =  simplest' n d n' d'
                           | y < 0      =  - simplest' (-n') d' (-n) d
                           | otherwise  =  0 :% 1
                                where xr@(n:%d) = toRational x
                                      (n':%d')  = toRational y

        simplest' n d n' d'        -- assumes 0 < n%d < n'%d'
                | r == 0     =  q :% 1
                | q /= q'    =  (q+1) :% 1
                | otherwise  =  (q*n''+d'') :% n''
                        where (q,r)       =  quotRem n d
                              (q',r')     =  quotRem n' d'
                              (n'':%d'')  =  simplest' d' r' d r
```

JFP **13** (1): 153–156, January 2003. © 2003 Cambridge University Press

DOI: 10.1017/S0956796803001515 Printed in the United Kingdom

Chapter 13

Complex Numbers

```
module  Complex (
    Complex((:+)), realPart, imagPart, conjugate,
    mkPolar, cis, polar, magnitude, phase ) where

infix  6  :+

data  (RealFloat a)       => Complex a = !a :+ !a

realPart, imagPart      :: (RealFloat a) => Complex a -> a
conjugate               :: (RealFloat a) => Complex a -> Complex a
mkPolar                 :: (RealFloat a) => a -> a -> Complex a
cis                     :: (RealFloat a) => a -> Complex a
polar                   :: (RealFloat a) => Complex a -> (a,a)
magnitude, phase        :: (RealFloat a) => Complex a -> a

instance   (RealFloat a) => Eq         (Complex a)   where ...
instance   (RealFloat a) => Read       (Complex a)   where ...
instance   (RealFloat a) => Show       (Complex a)   where ...
instance   (RealFloat a) => Num        (Complex a)   where ...
instance   (RealFloat a) => Fractional (Complex a)   where ...
instance   (RealFloat a) => Floating   (Complex a)   where ...
```

Complex numbers are an algebraic type. The constructor (:+) forms a complex number from its real and imaginary rectangular components. This constructor is strict: if either the real part or the imaginary part of the number is ⊥, the entire number is ⊥. A complex number may also be formed from polar components of magnitude and phase by the function mkPolar. The function

153

`cis` produces a complex number from an angle t. Put another way, `cis` t is a complex value with magnitude 1 and phase t (modulo 2π).

The function `polar` takes a complex number and returns a (magnitude, phase) pair in canonical form: The magnitude is nonnegative, and the phase, in the range $(-\pi, \pi]$; if the magnitude is zero, then so is the phase.

The functions `realPart` and `imagPart` extract the rectangular components of a complex number and the functions `magnitude` and `phase` extract the polar components of a complex number. The function `conjugate` computes the conjugate of a complex number in the usual way.

The magnitude and sign of a complex number are defined as follows:

```
abs z              =   magnitude z :+ 0
signum 0           =   0
signum z@(x:+y)    =   x/r :+ y/r   where r = magnitude z
```

That is, `abs` z is a number with the magnitude of z, but oriented in the positive real direction, whereas `signum` z has the phase of z, but unit magnitude.

13.1 Library `Complex`

```
module Complex(Complex((:+)), realPart, imagPart, conjugate, mkPolar,
               cis, polar, magnitude, phase)  where

infix  6  :+

data  (RealFloat a)     => Complex a = !a :+ !a  deriving (Eq,Read,Show)

realPart, imagPart :: (RealFloat a) => Complex a -> a
realPart (x:+y)  =   x
imagPart (x:+y)  =   y

conjugate          ::  (RealFloat a) => Complex a -> Complex a
conjugate (x:+y) =   x :+ (-y)

mkPolar            ::  (RealFloat a) => a -> a -> Complex a
mkPolar r theta  =   r * cos theta :+ r * sin theta

cis                ::  (RealFloat a) => a -> Complex a
cis theta        =   cos theta :+ sin theta

polar              ::  (RealFloat a) => Complex a -> (a,a)
polar z          =   (magnitude z, phase z)

magnitude :: (RealFloat a) => Complex a -> a
magnitude (x:+y) =   scaleFloat k
                     (sqrt ((scaleFloat mk x)^2 + (scaleFloat mk y)^2))
                   where k  = max (exponent x) (exponent y)
                         mk = - k
```

```
phase :: (RealFloat a) => Complex a -> a
phase (0 :+ 0) = 0
phase (x :+ y) = atan2 y x

instance  (RealFloat a) => Num (Complex a)  where
    (x:+y) + (x':+y')     =   (x+x')  :+ (y+y')
    (x:+y) - (x':+y')     =   (x-x')  :+ (y-y')
    (x:+y) * (x':+y')     =   (x*x'-y*y') :+ (x*y'+y*x')
    negate (x:+y)         =   negate x :+ negate y
    abs z                 =   magnitude z :+ 0
    signum 0              =   0
    signum z@(x:+y)       =   x/r :+ y/r  where r = magnitude z
    fromInteger n         =   fromInteger n :+ 0

instance  (RealFloat a) => Fractional (Complex a)  where
    (x:+y) / (x':+y')     =   (x*x''+y*y'') / d :+ (y*x''-x*y'') / d
                              where x'' = scaleFloat k x'
                                    y'' = scaleFloat k y'
                                    k   = - max (exponent x') (exponent y')
                                    d   = x'*x'' + y'*y''

    fromRational a        =   fromRational a :+ 0
```

```
instance   (RealFloat a) => Floating (Complex a) where
    pi                 =   pi :+ 0
    exp (x:+y)         =   expx * cos y :+ expx * sin y
                           where expx = exp x
    log z              =   log (magnitude z) :+ phase z
    sqrt 0             =   0
    sqrt z@(x:+y)      =   u :+ (if y < 0 then -v else v)
                           where (u,v) = if x < 0 then (v',u') else (u',v')
                                 v'    = abs y / (u'*2)
                                 u'    = sqrt ((magnitude z + abs x) / 2)
    sin (x:+y)         =   sin x * cosh y :+ cos x * sinh y
    cos (x:+y)         =   cos x * cosh y :+ (- sin x * sinh y)
    tan (x:+y)         =   (sinx*coshy:+cosx*sinhy)/(cosx*coshy:+(-sinx*sinhy))
                           where sinx  = sin x
                                 cosx  = cos x
                                 sinhy = sinh y
                                 coshy = cosh y
    sinh (x:+y)        =   cos y * sinh x :+ sin  y * cosh x
    cosh (x:+y)        =   cos y * cosh x :+ sin y * sinh x
    tanh (x:+y)        =   (cosy*sinhx:+siny*coshx)/(cosy*coshx:+siny*sinhx)
                           where siny  = sin y
                                 cosy  = cos y
                                 sinhx = sinh x
                                 coshx = cosh x
    asin z@(x:+y)      =   y':+(-x')
                           where  (x':+y') = log (((-y):+x) + sqrt (1 - z*z))
    acos z@(x:+y)      =   y'':+(-x'')
                           where (x'':+y'') = log (z + ((-y'):+x'))
                                 (x':+y')   = sqrt (1 - z*z)
    atan z@(x:+y)      =   y':+(-x')
                           where (x':+y') = log (((1-y):+x) / sqrt (1+z*z))
    asinh z            =   log (z + sqrt (1+z*z))
    acosh z            =   log (z + (z+1) * sqrt ((z-1)/(z+1)))
    atanh z            =   log ((1+z) / sqrt (1-z*z))
```

JFP **13** (1): 157–168, January 2003. © 2003 Cambridge University Press
DOI: 10.1017/S0956796803001618 Printed in the United Kingdom

Chapter 14

Numeric Functions

```
module Numeric(fromRat,
               showSigned, showIntAtBase,
               showInt, showOct, showHex,
               readSigned, readInt,
               readDec, readOct, readHex,
               floatToDigits,
               showEFloat, showFFloat, showGFloat, showFloat,
               readFloat, lexDigits) where

fromRat        :: (RealFloat a) => Rational -> a

showSigned     :: (Real a) => (a -> ShowS) -> Int -> a -> ShowS
showIntAtBase  :: Integral a => a -> (Int -> Char) -> a -> ShowS
showInt        :: Integral a => a -> ShowS
showOct        :: Integral a => a -> ShowS
showHex        :: Integral a => a -> ShowS

readSigned     :: (Real a) => ReadS a -> ReadS a
readInt        :: (Integral a) =>
                     a -> (Char -> Bool) -> (Char -> Int) -> ReadS a
readDec        :: (Integral a) => ReadS a
readOct        :: (Integral a) => ReadS a
readHex        :: (Integral a) => ReadS a
```

```
showEFloat       :: (RealFloat a) => Maybe Int -> a -> ShowS
showFFloat       :: (RealFloat a) => Maybe Int -> a -> ShowS
showGFloat       :: (RealFloat a) => Maybe Int -> a -> ShowS
showFloat        :: (RealFloat a) => a -> ShowS

floatToDigits    :: (RealFloat a) => Integer -> a -> ([Int], Int)

readFloat        :: (RealFrac a) => ReadS a
lexDigits        :: ReadS String
```

This library contains assorted numeric functions, many of which are used in the standard Prelude.

In what follows, recall the following type definitions from the `Prelude`:

```
type ShowS = String -> String
type ReadS = String -> [(a,String)]
```

14.1   Showing Functions

- `showSigned :: (Real a) => (a -> ShowS) -> Int -> a -> ShowS`
  converts a possibly-negative `Real` value of type `a` into a string. In the call (`showSigned` *show prec val*), *val* is the value to show, *prec* is the precedence of the enclosing context, and *show* is a function that can show unsigned values.

- `showIntAtBase :: Integral a => a -> (Int -> Char) -> a -> ShowS`
  shows a *non-negative* `Integral` number using the base specified by the first argument, and the character representation specified by the second.

- `showInt, showOct, showHex :: Integral a => a -> ShowS`
  show *non-negative* `Integral` numbers in base 10, 8 and 16, respectively.

- `showFFloat, showEFloat, showGFloat`
       `:: (RealFloat a) => Maybe Int -> a -> ShowS` These three functions all show signed `RealFloat` values:

  - `showFFloat` uses standard decimal notation (e.g. `245000`, `0.0015`).
  - `showEFloat` uses scientific (exponential) notation (e.g. `2.45e2`, `1.5e-3`).
  - `showGFloat` uses standard decimal notation for arguments whose absolute value lies between `0.1` and `9,999,999`, and scientific notation otherwise.

  In the call (`showEFloat` *digs val*), if *digs* is `Nothing`, the value is shown to full precision; if *digs* is `Just d`, then at most *d* digits after the decimal point are shown. Exactly the same applies to the *digs* argument of the other two functions.

- `floatToDigits :: (RealFloat a) => Integer -> a -> ([Int], Int)`
  converts a base and a value to the representation of the value in digits, plus an exponent. More specifically, if

$$\text{floatToDigits } b\, r = (\,[d_1, d_2, ...d_n]\,,\ e\,)$$

then the following properties hold:

  - $r = 0.d_1 d_2 ..., d_n\, *\, b^e$
  - $n \geq 0$
  - $d_1 \neq 0$ (when $n > 0$)
  - $0 \leq d_i \leq b - 1$

14.2 Reading Functions

- `readSigned :: (Real a) => ReadS a -> ReadS a`
  reads a *signed* `Real` value, given a reader for an unsigned value.

- `readInt :: (Integral a) => a -> (Char->Bool) -> (Char->Int) -> ReadS a` reads an *unsigned* `Integral` value in an arbitrary base. In the (`readInt base isdig d2i`) call, *base* is the base, *isdig* is a predicate distinguishing valid digits in this base, and *d2i* converts a valid digit character to an `Int`.

- `readFloat :: (RealFrac a) => ReadS a`
  reads an *unsigned* `RealFrac` value, expressed in decimal scientific notation.

- `readDec, readOct, readHex :: (Integral a) => ReadS a`
  each read an unsigned number, in decimal, octal, and hexadecimal notation, respectively. In the hexadecimal case, both upper or lower case letters are allowed.

- `lexDigits :: ReadS String` reads a non-empty string of decimal digits.

(NB: `readInt` is the "dual" of `showIntAtBase`, and `readDec` is the "dual" of `showInt`. The inconsistent naming is a historical accident.)

14.3 Miscellaneous

- `fromRat :: (RealFloat a) => Rational -> a` converts a `Rational` value into any type in class `RealFloat`.

14.4   Library `Numeric`

```
module Numeric(fromRat,
               showSigned, showIntAtBase,
               showInt, showOct, showHex,
               readSigned, readInt,
               readDec, readOct, readHex,
               floatToDigits,
               showEFloat, showFFloat, showGFloat, showFloat,
               readFloat, lexDigits) where

import Char   ( isDigit, isOctDigit, isHexDigit
             , digitToInt, intToDigit )
import Ratio  ( (%), numerator, denominator )
import Array  ( (!), Array, array )

-- This converts a rational to a floating.  This should be used in the
-- Fractional instances of Float and Double.
fromRat :: (RealFloat a) => Rational -> a
fromRat x =
    if x == 0 then encodeFloat 0 0          -- Handle exceptional cases
    else if x < 0 then - fromRat' (-x)      -- first.
    else fromRat' x

-- Conversion process:
-- Scale the rational number by the RealFloat base until
-- it lies in the range of the mantissa (as used by decodeFloat/encodeFloat).
-- Then round the rational to an Integer and encode it with the exponent
-- that we got from the scaling.
-- To speed up the scaling process we compute the log2 of the number to get
-- a first guess of the exponent.
fromRat' :: (RealFloat a) => Rational -> a
fromRat' x = r
  where b = floatRadix r
        p = floatDigits r
        (minExp0, _) = floatRange r
        minExp = minExp0 - p            -- the real minimum exponent
        xMin = toRational (expt b (p-1))
        xMax = toRational (expt b p)
        p0 = (integerLogBase b (numerator x) -
             integerLogBase b (denominator x) - p) `max` minExp
        f = if p0 < 0 then 1 % expt b (-p0) else expt b p0 % 1
        (x', p') = scaleRat (toRational b) minExp xMin xMax p0 (x / f)
        r = encodeFloat (round x') p'
```

```
-- Scale x until xMin <= x < xMax, or p (the exponent) <= minExp.
scaleRat :: Rational -> Int -> Rational -> Rational ->
            Int -> Rational -> (Rational, Int)
scaleRat b minExp xMin xMax p x =
    if p <= minExp then
        (x, p)
    else if x >= xMax then
        scaleRat b minExp xMin xMax (p+1) (x/b)
    else if x < xMin  then
        scaleRat b minExp xMin xMax (p-1) (x*b)
    else
        (x, p)

-- Exponentiation with a cache for the most common numbers.
minExpt = 0::Int
maxExpt = 1100::Int
expt :: Integer -> Int -> Integer
expt base n =
    if base == 2 && n >= minExpt && n <= maxExpt then
        expts!n
    else
        base^n

expts :: Array Int Integer
expts = array (minExpt,maxExpt) [(n,2^n) | n <- [minExpt .. maxExpt]]

-- Compute the (floor of the) log of i in base b.
-- Simplest way would be just divide i by b until it's smaller then b,
-- but that would be very slow!  We are just slightly more clever.
integerLogBase :: Integer -> Integer -> Int
integerLogBase b i =
    if i < b then
        0
    else
        -- Try squaring the base first to cut down the number of divisions.
        let l = 2 * integerLogBase (b*b) i
            doDiv :: Integer -> Int -> Int
            doDiv i l = if i < b then l else doDiv (i 'div' b) (l+1)
        in  doDiv (i 'div' (b^l)) l

-- Misc utilities to show integers and floats
showSigned :: Real a => (a -> ShowS) -> Int -> a -> ShowS
showSigned showPos p x
  | x < 0      = showParen (p > 6) (showChar '-' . showPos (-x))
  | otherwise = showPos x

-- showInt, showOct, showHex are used for positive numbers only
showInt, showOct, showHex :: Integral a => a -> ShowS
showOct = showIntAtBase  8 intToDigit
showInt = showIntAtBase 10 intToDigit
showHex = showIntAtBase 16 intToDigit
```

```
showIntAtBase :: Integral a
               => a                  -- base
               -> (Int -> Char)      -- digit to char
               -> a                  -- number to show
               -> ShowS
showIntAtBase base intToDig n rest
  | n < 0     = error "Numeric.showIntAtBase: can't show negative numbers"
  | n' == 0   = rest'
  | otherwise = showIntAtBase base intToDig n' rest'
  where
    (n',d) = quotRem n base
    rest'  = intToDig (fromIntegral d) : rest

readSigned :: (Real a) => ReadS a -> ReadS a
readSigned readPos = readParen False read'
                  where read' r  = read'' r ++
                                   [(-x,t) | ("-",s) <- lex r,
                                             (x,t)   <- read'' s]
                        read'' r = [(n,s)  | (str,s) <- lex r,
                                             (n,"")  <- readPos str]

-- readInt reads a string of digits using an arbitrary base.
-- Leading minus signs must be handled elsewhere.
readInt :: (Integral a) => a -> (Char -> Bool) -> (Char -> Int) -> ReadS a
readInt radix isDig digToInt s =
   [(foldl1 (\n d -> n * radix + d) (map (fromIntegral . digToInt) ds), r)
          | (ds,r) <- nonnull isDig s ]

-- Unsigned readers for various bases
readDec, readOct, readHex :: (Integral a) => ReadS a
readDec = readInt 10 isDigit    digitToInt
readOct = readInt  8 isOctDigit digitToInt
readHex = readInt 16 isHexDigit digitToInt

showEFloat      :: (RealFloat a) => Maybe Int -> a -> ShowS
showFFloat      :: (RealFloat a) => Maybe Int -> a -> ShowS
showGFloat      :: (RealFloat a) => Maybe Int -> a -> ShowS
showFloat       :: (RealFloat a) => a -> ShowS

showEFloat d x =  showString (formatRealFloat FFExponent d x)
showFFloat d x =  showString (formatRealFloat FFFixed d x)
showGFloat d x =  showString (formatRealFloat FFGeneric d x)
showFloat      =  showGFloat Nothing

-- These are the format types.  This type is not exported.
data FFFormat = FFExponent | FFFixed | FFGeneric
```

```
formatRealFloat :: (RealFloat a) => FFFormat -> Maybe Int -> a -> String
formatRealFloat fmt decs x
  = s
  where
    base = 10
    s = if isNaN x then
          "NaN"
        else if isInfinite x then
          if x < 0 then "-Infinity" else "Infinity"
        else if x < 0 || isNegativeZero x then
          '-' : doFmt fmt (floatToDigits (toInteger base) (-x))
        else
          doFmt fmt (floatToDigits (toInteger base) x)
    doFmt fmt (is, e)
      = let
          ds = map intToDigit is
        in
        case fmt of
          FFGeneric ->
            doFmt (if e < 0 || e > 7 then FFExponent else FFFixed)
                  (is, e)
          FFExponent ->
            case decs of
              Nothing ->
                case ds of
                  []     -> "0.0e0"
                  [d]    -> d : ".0e" ++ show (e-1)
                  d:ds   -> d : '.' : ds ++ 'e':show (e-1)
              Just dec ->
                let dec' = max dec 1 in
                case is of
                  [] -> '0':'.':take dec' (repeat '0') ++ "e0"
                  _ ->
                    let (ei, is') = roundTo base (dec'+1) is
                        d:ds = map intToDigit
                                    (if ei > 0 then init is' else is')
                    in d:'.':ds  ++ "e" ++ show (e-1+ei)
```

```
        FFFixed ->
         case decs of
            Nothing   -- Always prints a decimal point
              | e > 0       -> take e (ds ++ repeat '0')

                           ++ '.' : mk0 (drop e ds)
              | otherwise -> "0." ++ mk0 (replicate (-e) '0' ++ ds)
            Just dec ->   -- Print decimal point iff dec > 0
              let dec' = max dec 0 in
              if e >= 0 then
                let (ei, is') = roundTo base (dec' + e) is
                    (ls, rs)  = splitAt (e+ei)
                                          (map intToDigit is')
                in   mk0 ls ++ mkdot0 rs
              else
                let (ei, is') = roundTo base dec'
                                      (replicate (-e) 0 ++ is)
                    d : ds = map intToDigit
                                  (if ei > 0 then is' else 0:is')
                in   d : mkdot0 ds
           where
             mk0 "" = "0"          -- Print 0.34, not .34
             mk0 s  = s

             mkdot0 "" = ""        -- Print 34, not 34.
             mkdot0 s  = '.' : s   -- when the format specifies no
                                   -- digits after the decimal point

roundTo :: Int -> Int -> [Int] -> (Int, [Int])
roundTo base d is = case f d is of
                (0, is) -> (0, is)
                (1, is) -> (1, 1 : is)
  where b2 = base 'div' 2
        f n [] = (0, replicate n 0)
        f 0 (i:_) = (if i >= b2 then 1 else 0, [])
        f d (i:is) =
           let (c, ds) = f (d-1) is
               i' = c + i
           in  if i' == base then (1, 0:ds) else (0, i':ds)
```

```
-- Based on "Printing Floating-Point Numbers Quickly and Accurately"
-- by R.G. Burger and R. K. Dybvig, in PLDI 96.
-- The version here uses a much slower logarithm estimator.
-- It should be improved.
-- This function returns a non-empty list of digits (Ints in [0..base-1])
-- and an exponent.  In general, if
--       floatToDigits r = ([a, b, ... z], e)
-- then
--       r = 0.ab..z * base^e
--
floatToDigits :: (RealFloat a) => Integer -> a -> ([Int], Int)
floatToDigits _ 0 = ([], 0)
floatToDigits base x =
    let (f0, e0) = decodeFloat x
        (minExp0, _) = floatRange x
        p = floatDigits x
        b = floatRadix x
        minExp = minExp0 - p              -- the real minimum exponent

        -- Haskell requires that f be adjusted so denormalized numbers
        -- will have an impossibly low exponent.  Adjust for this.
        f :: Integer
        e :: Int
        (f, e) = let n = minExp - e0
                 in  if n > 0 then (f0 'div' (b^n), e0+n) else (f0, e0)

        (r, s, mUp, mDn) =
           if e >= 0 then
               let be = b^e in
               if f == b^(p-1) then
                   (f*be*b*2, 2*b, be*b, b)
               else
                   (f*be*2, 2, be, be)
           else
               if e > minExp && f == b^(p-1) then
                   (f*b*2, b^(-e+1)*2, b, 1)
               else
                   (f*2, b^(-e)*2, 1, 1)
```

```haskell
      k = let k0 =
                if b==2 && base==10 then
                     -- logBase 10 2 is slightly bigger than 3/10 so
                     -- the following will err on the low side.  Ignoring
                     -- the fraction will make it err even more.
                     -- Haskell promises that p-1 <= logBase b f < p.
                     (p - 1 + e0) * 3 'div' 10
                else
                     ceiling ((log (fromInteger (f+1)) +
                               fromIntegral e * log (fromInteger b)) /
                              log (fromInteger base))
          fixup n =
              if n >= 0 then
                  if r + mUp <= expt base n * s then n else fixup (n+1)
              else
                  if expt base (-n) * (r + mUp) <= s then n
                                                    else fixup (n+1)
          in  fixup k0
      gen ds rn sN mUpN mDnN =
          let (dn, rn') = (rn * base) 'divMod' sN
              mUpN' = mUpN * base
              mDnN' = mDnN * base
          in  case (rn' < mDnN', rn' + mUpN' > sN) of
              (True,  False) -> dn : ds
              (False, True)  -> dn+1 : ds
              (True,  True)  -> if rn' * 2 < sN then dn : ds else dn+1 : ds
              (False, False) -> gen (dn:ds) rn' sN mUpN' mDnN'
      rds =
          if k >= 0 then
              gen [] r (s * expt base k) mUp mDn
          else
              let bk = expt base (-k)
              in  gen [] (r * bk) s (mUp * bk) (mDn * bk)
  in  (map fromIntegral (reverse rds), k)
```

```
-- This floating point reader uses a less restrictive syntax for floating
-- point than the Haskell lexer.  The '.' is optional.
readFloat      :: (RealFrac a) => ReadS a
readFloat r    = [(fromRational ((n%1)*10^^(k-d)),t) | (n,d,s) <- readFix r,
                                             (k,t)   <- readExp s] ++
                 [ (0/0, t) | ("NaN",t)      <- lex r] ++
                 [ (1/0, t) | ("Infinity",t) <- lex r]
                 where
                 readFix r = [(read (ds++ds'), length ds', t)
                                  | (ds,d) <- lexDigits r,
                                    (ds',t) <- lexFrac d ]

                 lexFrac ('.':ds) = lexDigits ds
                 lexFrac s        = [("",s)]

                 readExp (e:s) | e 'elem' "eE" = readExp' s
                 readExp s                     = [(0,s)]

                 readExp' ('-':s) = [(-k,t) | (k,t) <- readDec s]
                 readExp' ('+':s) = readDec s
                 readExp' s       = readDec s

lexDigits      :: ReadS String
lexDigits      =  nonnull isDigit

nonnull        :: (Char -> Bool) -> ReadS String
nonnull p s    =  [(cs,t) | (cs@(_:_),t) <- [span p s]]
```

JFP **13** (1): 169–172, January 2003. © 2003 Cambridge University Press
DOI: 10.1017/S0956796803001710 Printed in the United Kingdom

Chapter 15

Indexing Operations

```
module Ix ( Ix(range, index, inRange, rangeSize) ) where

class  Ord a => Ix a  where
    range        :: (a,a) -> [a]
    index        :: (a,a) -> a -> Int
    inRange      :: (a,a) -> a -> Bool
    rangeSize    :: (a,a) -> Int

instance                       Ix Char      where ...
instance                       Ix Int       where ...
instance                       Ix Integer   where ...
instance  (Ix a, Ix b)  => Ix (a,b)         where ...
-- et cetera
instance                       Ix Bool      where ...
instance                       Ix Ordering  where ...
```

The `Ix` class is used to map a contiguous subrange of values in a type onto integers. It is used primarily for array indexing (see Chapter 16). The `Ix` class contains the methods `range`, `index`, and `inRange`. The `index` operation maps a bounding pair, which defines the lower and upper bounds of the range, and a subscript, to an integer. The `range` operation enumerates all subscripts; the `inRange` operation tells whether a particular subscript lies in the range defined by a bounding pair.

An implementation is entitled to assume the following laws about these operations:

```
instance  (Ix a, Ix b)   => Ix (a,b) where
        range ((l,l'),(u,u'))
                  = [(i,i')  |  i <- range (l,u), i' <- range (l',u')]
        index ((l,l'),(u,u'))  (i,i')
                  =  index (l,u) i * rangeSize (l',u') + index (l',u') i'
        inRange ((l,l'),(u,u'))  (i,i')
                  = inRange (l,u) i && inRange (l',u') i'
-- Instances for other tuples are obtained from this scheme:
--
--   instance  (Ix a1, Ix a2, ... , Ix ak) => Ix (a1,a2,...,ak)   where
--        range ((l1,l2,...,lk),(u1,u2,...,uk)) =
--            [(i1,i2,...,ik)  |  i1 <- range (l1,u1),
--                                i2 <- range (l2,u2),
--                                ...
--                                ik <- range (lk,uk)]
--
--        index ((l1,l2,...,lk),(u1,u2,...,uk))  (i1,i2,...,ik) =
--          index (lk,uk) ik + rangeSize (lk,uk) * (
--           index (lk-1,uk-1) ik-1 + rangeSize (lk-1,uk-1) * (
--            ...
--             index (l1,u1)))
--
--        inRange ((l1,l2,...lk),(u1,u2,...,uk))  (i1,i2,...,ik) =
--            inRange (l1,u1) i1 && inRange (l2,u2) i2 &&
--                ... && inRange (lk,uk) ik
```

Figure 15.1: Derivation of Ix instances

```
range (l,u) !! index (l,u) i == i    -- when i is in range
inRange (l,u) i                == i 'elem' range (l,u)
map index (range (l,u))        == [0..rangeSize (l,u)]
```

15.1 Deriving Instances of `Ix`

It is possible to derive an instance of `Ix` automatically, using a `deriving` clause on a `data` declaration (Section 4.3.3 of the Language Report). Such derived instance declarations for the class `Ix` are only possible for enumerations (i.e. datatypes having only nullary constructors) and single-constructor datatypes, whose constituent types are instances of `Ix`. A Haskell implementation must provide `Ix` instances for tuples up to at least size 15.

- For an *enumeration*, the nullary constructors are assumed to be numbered left-to-right with the indices being 0 to $n - 1$ inclusive. This is the same numbering defined by the `Enum` class. For example, given the datatype:

  ```
  data Colour = Red | Orange | Yellow | Green
              | Blue | Indigo | Violet
  ```

we would have:

```
range    (Yellow,Blue)          ==   [Yellow,Green,Blue]
index    (Yellow,Blue) Green    ==   1
inRange  (Yellow,Blue) Red      ==   False
```

- For *single-constructor datatypes*, the derived instance declarations are as shown for tuples in Figure 15.1.

15.2 Library Ix

```
module Ix ( Ix(range, index, inRange, rangeSize) ) where

class  Ord a => Ix a   where
    range     :: (a,a) -> [a]
    index     :: (a,a) -> a -> Int
    inRange   :: (a,a) -> a -> Bool
    rangeSize :: (a,a) -> Int

    rangeSize b@(l,h) | null (range b) = 0
                      | otherwise      = index b h + 1
        -- NB: replacing "null (range b)" by  "not (l <= h)"
        -- fails if the bounds are tuples.  For example,
        --      (1,2) <= (2,1)
        -- but the range is nevertheless empty
        --      range ((1,2),(2,1)) = []

instance  Ix Char   where
    range (m,n)        = [m..n]
    index b@(c,c') ci
        | inRange b ci  =  fromEnum ci - fromEnum c
        | otherwise     =  error "Ix.index: Index out of range."
    inRange (c,c') i    =  c <= i && i <= c'

instance  Ix Int   where
    range (m,n)        = [m..n]
    index b@(m,n) i
        | inRange b i   =  i - m
        | otherwise     =  error "Ix.index: Index out of range."
    inRange (m,n) i     =  m <= i && i <= n

instance  Ix Integer   where
    range (m,n)        = [m..n]
    index b@(m,n) i
        | inRange b i   =  fromInteger (i - m)
        | otherwise     =  error "Ix.index: Index out of range."
    inRange (m,n) i     =  m <= i && i <= n

instance (Ix a,Ix b) => Ix (a, b) -- as derived, for all tuples
instance Ix Bool                  -- as derived
instance Ix Ordering              -- as derived
instance Ix ()                    -- as derived
```

JFP **13** (1): 173–178, January 2003. © 2003 Cambridge University Press
DOI: 10.1017/S0956796803001813 Printed in the United Kingdom

Chapter 16

Arrays

```
module  Array (
        module Ix,  -- export all of Ix for convenience
        Array, array, listArray, (!), bounds, indices, elems, assocs,
        accumArray, (//), accum, ixmap ) where

import Ix

infixl 9  !, //

data  (Ix a)     => Array a b = ...        -- Abstract

array          :: (Ix a) => (a,a) -> [(a,b)] -> Array a b
listArray      :: (Ix a) => (a,a) -> [b] -> Array a b
(!)            :: (Ix a) => Array a b -> a -> b
bounds         :: (Ix a) => Array a b -> (a,a)
indices        :: (Ix a) => Array a b -> [a]
elems          :: (Ix a) => Array a b -> [b]
assocs         :: (Ix a) => Array a b -> [(a,b)]
accumArray     :: (Ix a) => (b -> c -> b) -> b -> (a,a) -> [(a,c)]
                          -> Array a b
(//)           :: (Ix a) => Array a b -> [(a,b)] -> Array a b
accum          :: (Ix a) => (b -> c -> b) -> Array a b -> [(a,c)]
                          -> Array a b
ixmap          :: (Ix a, Ix b) => (a,a) -> (a -> b) -> Array b c
                          -> Array a c
```

```
instance                                Functor (Array a) where ...
instance (Ix a, Eq b)           => Eq   (Array a b) where ...
instance (Ix a, Ord b)          => Ord  (Array a b) where ...
instance (Ix a, Show a, Show b) => Show (Array a b) where ...
instance (Ix a, Read a, Read b) => Read (Array a b) where ...
```

Haskell provides indexable *arrays*, which may be thought of as functions whose domains are isomorphic to contiguous subsets of the integers. Functions restricted in this way can be implemented efficiently; in particular, a programmer may reasonably expect rapid access to the components. To ensure the possibility of such an implementation, arrays are treated as data, not as general functions.

Since most array functions involve the class `Ix`, this module is exported from `Array` so that modules need not import both `Array` and `Ix`.

16.1 Array Construction

If `a` is an index type and `b` is any type, the type of arrays with indices in `a` and elements in `b` is written `Array a b`. An array may be created by the function `array`. The first argument of `array` is a pair of *bounds*, each of the index type of the array. These bounds are the lowest and highest indices in the array, in that order. For example, a one-origin vector of length 10 has bounds `(1,10)`, and a one-origin 10 by 10 matrix has bounds `((1,1),(10,10))`.

The second argument of `array` is a list of *associations* of the form (*index*, *value*). Typically, this list will be expressed as a comprehension. An association (`i`, `x`) defines the value of the array at index `i` to be `x`. The array is undefined (i.e. $\perp$) if any index in the list is out of bounds. If any two associations in the list have the same index, the value at that index is undefined (i.e. $\perp$). Because the indices must be checked for these errors, `array` is strict in the bounds argument and in the indices of the association list, but nonstrict in the values. Thus, recurrences such as the following are possible:

```
a = array (1,100) ((1,1) : [(i, i * a!(i-1)) | i <- [2..100]])
```

Not every index within the bounds of the array need appear in the association list, but the values associated with indices that do not appear will be undefined (i.e. $\perp$). Figure 16.1 shows some examples that use the `array` constructor.

The (`!`) operator denotes array subscripting. The `bounds` function applied to an array returns its bounds. The functions `indices`, `elems`, and `assocs`, when applied to an array, return lists of the indices, elements, or associations, respectively, in index order. An array may be constructed from a pair of bounds and a list of values in index order using the function `listArray`.

If, in any dimension, the lower bound is greater than the upper bound, then the array is legal, but empty. Indexing an empty array always gives an array-bounds error, but `bounds` still yields the bounds with which the array was constructed.

```
-- Scaling an array of numbers by a given number:
scale :: (Num a, Ix b) => a -> Array b a -> Array b a
scale x a = array b [(i, a!i * x) | i <- range b]
            where b = bounds a
-- Inverting an array that holds a permutation of its indices
invPerm :: (Ix a) => Array a a -> Array a a
invPerm a = array b [(a!i, i) | i <- range b]
            where b = bounds a
-- The inner product of two vectors
inner :: (Ix a, Num b) => Array a b -> Array a b -> b
inner v w = if b == bounds w
               then sum [v!i * w!i | i <- range b]
               else error "inconformable arrays for inner product"
            where b = bounds v
```

Figure 16.1: Array examples

16.1.1 Accumulated Arrays

Another array creation function, `accumArray`, relaxes the restriction that a given index may appear at most once in the association list, using an *accumulating function* which combines the values of associations with the same index. The first argument of `accumArray` is the accumulating function; the second is an initial value; the remaining two arguments are a bounds pair and an association list, as for the `array` function. For example, given a list of values of some index type, `hist` produces a histogram of the number of occurrences of each index within a specified range:

```
hist :: (Ix a, Num b) => (a,a) -> [a] -> Array a b
hist bnds is = accumArray (+) 0 bnds [(i, 1) | i<-is, inRange bnds i]
```

If the accumulating function is strict, then `accumArray` is strict in the values, as well as the indices, in the association list. Thus, unlike ordinary arrays, accumulated arrays should not in general be recursive.

16.2 Incremental Array Updates

The operator (`//`) takes an array and a list of pairs and returns an array identical to the left argument except that it has been updated by the associations in the right argument. (As with the `array` function, the indices in the association list must be unique for the updated elements to be defined.) For example, if m is a 1-origin, n by n matrix, then `m//[((i,i), 0) | i <- [1..n]]` is the same matrix, except with the diagonal zeroed.

accum *f* takes an array and an association list and accumulates pairs from the list into the array with the accumulating function *f*. Thus `accumArray` can be defined using `accum`:

```
accumArray f z b = accum f (array b [(i, z) | i <- range b])
```

```
-- A rectangular subarray
subArray :: (Ix a) => (a,a) -> Array a b -> Array a b
subArray bnds = ixmap bnds (\i->i)

-- A row of a matrix
row :: (Ix a, Ix b) => a -> Array (a,b) c -> Array b c
row i x = ixmap (l',u') (\j->(i,j)) x where ((_,l'),(_,u')) = bounds x

-- Diagonal of a matrix (assumed to be square)
diag :: (Ix a) => Array (a,a) b -> Array a b
diag x = ixmap (l,u) (\i->(i,i)) x
         where
             ((l,_),(u,_)) = bounds x

-- Projection of first components of an array of pairs
firstArray :: (Ix a) => Array a (b,c) -> Array a b
firstArray = fmap (\(x,y)->x)
```

Figure 16.2: Derived array examples

16.3   Derived Arrays

The two functions `fmap` and `ixmap` derive new arrays from existing ones; they may be thought
of as providing function composition on the left and right, respectively, with the mapping that the
original array embodies. The `fmap` function transforms the array values while `ixmap` allows for
transformations on array indices. Figure 16.2 shows some examples.

16.4   Library `Array`

```
module  Array (
    module Ix,   -- export all of Ix
    Array, array, listArray, (!), bounds, indices, elems, assocs,
    accumArray, (//), accum, ixmap ) where

import Ix
import List( (\\) )

infixl 9  !, //

data (Ix a) => Array a b = MkArray (a,a) (a -> b) deriving ()
```

```
array          :: (Ix a) => (a,a) -> [(a,b)] -> Array a b
array b ivs =
    if and [inRange b i | (i,_) <- ivs]
        then MkArray b
                    (\j -> case [v | (i,v) <- ivs, i == j] of
                        [v]    -> v
                        []     -> error "Array.!: \
                                        \undefined array element"
                        _      -> error "Array.!: \
                                        \multiply defined array element")
        else error "Array.array: out-of-range array association"

listArray              :: (Ix a) => (a,a) -> [b] -> Array a b
listArray b vs         = array b (zipWith (\ a b -> (a,b)) (range b) vs)

(!)                    :: (Ix a) => Array a b -> a -> b
(!) (MkArray _ f)      = f

bounds                 :: (Ix a) => Array a b -> (a,a)
bounds (MkArray b _)   = b

indices                :: (Ix a) => Array a b -> [a]
indices                = range . bounds

elems                  :: (Ix a) => Array a b -> [b]
elems a                = [a!i | i <- indices a]

assocs                 :: (Ix a) => Array a b -> [(a,b)]
assocs a               = [(i, a!i) | i <- indices a]

(//)                   :: (Ix a) => Array a b -> [(a,b)] -> Array a b
a // new_ivs           = array (bounds a) (old_ivs ++ new_ivs)
                        where
                            old_ivs = [(i,a!i) | i <- indices a,
                                                 i 'notElem' new_is]
                            new_is  = [i | (i,_) <- new_ivs]

accum                  :: (Ix a) => (b -> c -> b) -> Array a b -> [(a,c)]
                                    -> Array a b
accum f                = foldl (\a (i,v) -> a // [(i,f (a!i) v)])

accumArray             :: (Ix a) => (b -> c -> b) -> b -> (a,a) -> [(a,c)]
                                    -> Array a b
accumArray f z b       = accum f (array b [(i,z) | i <- range b])

ixmap                  :: (Ix a, Ix b) => (a,a) -> (a -> b) -> Array b c
                                          -> Array a c
ixmap b f a            = array b [(i, a ! f i) | i <- range b]

instance  (Ix a)         => Functor (Array a) where
    fmap fn (MkArray b f) =  MkArray b (fn . f)

instance  (Ix a, Eq b)  => Eq (Array a b)  where
    a == a' =  assocs a == assocs a'

instance  (Ix a, Ord b) => Ord (Array a b)  where
    a <= a' =  assocs a <= assocs a'
```

```
instance  (Ix a, Show a, Show b) => Show (Array a b)   where
    showsPrec p a = showParen (p > arrPrec) (
                    showString "array " .
                    showsPrec (arrPrec+1) (bounds a) . showChar ' ' .
                    showsPrec (arrPrec+1) (assocs a)                     )

instance  (Ix a, Read a, Read b) => Read (Array a b)   where
    readsPrec p = readParen (p > arrPrec)
          (\r -> [ (array b as, u)
                 | ("array",s) <- lex r,
                   (b,t)       <- readsPrec (arrPrec+1) s,
                   (as,u)      <- readsPrec (arrPrec+1) t ])

-- Precedence of the 'array' function is that of application itself
arrPrec = 10
```

JFP **13** (1): 179–190, January 2003. © 2003 Cambridge University Press
DOI: 10.1017/S0956796803001916 Printed in the United Kingdom

Chapter 17

List Utilities

```
module List (
    elemIndex, elemIndices,
    find, findIndex, findIndices,
    nub, nubBy, delete, deleteBy, (\\), deleteFirstsBy,
    union, unionBy, intersect, intersectBy,
    intersperse, transpose, partition, group, groupBy,
    inits, tails, isPrefixOf, isSuffixOf,
    mapAccumL, mapAccumR,
    sort, sortBy, insert, insertBy, maximumBy, minimumBy,
    genericLength, genericTake, genericDrop,
    genericSplitAt, genericIndex, genericReplicate,
    zip4, zip5, zip6, zip7,
    zipWith4, zipWith5, zipWith6, zipWith7,
    unzip4, unzip5, unzip6, unzip7, unfoldr,

    -- ...and what the Prelude exports
    -- ](((:), []),    -- This is built-in syntax
    map, (++), concat, filter,
    head, last, tail, init, null, length, (!!),
    foldl, foldl1, scanl, scanl1, foldr, foldr1, scanr, scanr1,
    iterate, repeat, replicate, cycle,
    take, drop, splitAt, takeWhile, dropWhile, span, break,
    lines, words, unlines, unwords, reverse, and, or,
    any, all, elem, notElem, lookup,
    sum, product, maximum, minimum, concatMap,
    zip, zip3, zipWith, zipWith3, unzip, unzip3
    ) where

infix 5 \\
```

```
elemIndex           :: Eq a => a -> [a] -> Maybe Int
elemIndices         :: Eq a => a -> [a] -> [Int]
find                :: (a -> Bool) -> [a] -> Maybe a
findIndex           :: (a -> Bool) -> [a] -> Maybe Int
findIndices         :: (a -> Bool) -> [a] -> [Int]
nub                 :: Eq a => [a] -> [a]
nubBy               :: (a -> a -> Bool) -> [a] -> [a]
delete              :: Eq a => a -> [a] -> [a]
deleteBy            :: (a -> a -> Bool) -> a -> [a] -> [a]
(\\)                :: Eq a => [a] -> [a] -> [a]
deleteFirstsBy      :: (a -> a -> Bool) -> [a] -> [a] -> [a]
union               :: Eq a => [a] -> [a] -> [a]
unionBy             :: (a -> a -> Bool) -> [a] -> [a] -> [a]

intersect           :: Eq a => [a] -> [a] -> [a]
intersectBy         :: (a -> a -> Bool) -> [a] -> [a] -> [a]
intersperse         :: a -> [a] -> [a]
transpose           :: [[a]] -> [[a]]
partition           :: (a -> Bool) -> [a] -> ([a],[a])
group               :: Eq a => [a] -> [[a]]
groupBy             :: (a -> a -> Bool) -> [a] -> [[a]]
inits               :: [a] -> [[a]]
tails               :: [a] -> [[a]]
isPrefixOf          :: Eq a => [a] -> [a] -> Bool
isSuffixOf          :: Eq a => [a] -> [a] -> Bool
mapAccumL           :: (a -> b -> (a, c)) -> a -> [b] -> (a, [c])
mapAccumR           :: (a -> b -> (a, c)) -> a -> [b] -> (a, [c])
unfoldr             :: (b -> Maybe (a,b)) -> b -> [a]
sort                :: Ord a => [a] -> [a]
sortBy              :: (a -> a -> Ordering) -> [a] -> [a]
insert              :: Ord a => a -> [a] -> [a]
insertBy            :: (a -> a -> Ordering) -> a -> [a] -> [a]
maximumBy           :: (a -> a -> Ordering) -> [a] -> a
minimumBy           :: (a -> a -> Ordering) -> [a] -> a
genericLength       :: Integral a => [b] -> a
genericTake         :: Integral a => a -> [b] -> [b]
genericDrop         :: Integral a => a -> [b] -> [b]
genericSplitAt      :: Integral a => a -> [b] -> ([b],[b])
genericIndex        :: Integral a => [b] -> a -> b
genericReplicate    :: Integral a => a -> b -> [b]

zip4                :: [a] -> [b] -> [c] -> [d] -> [(a,b,c,d)]
zip5                :: [a] -> [b] -> [c] -> [d] -> [e] -> [(a,b,c,d,e)]
zip6                :: [a] -> [b] -> [c] -> [d] -> [e] -> [f]
                         -> [(a,b,c,d,e,f)]
zip7                :: [a] -> [b] -> [c] -> [d] -> [e] -> [f] -> [g]
                         -> [(a,b,c,d,e,f,g)]
zipWith4            :: (a->b->c->d->e) -> [a]->[b]->[c]->[d]->[e]
zipWith5            :: (a->b->c->d->e->f) ->
                         [a]->[b]->[c]->[d]->[e]->[f]
zipWith6            :: (a->b->c->d->e->f->g) ->
                         [a]->[b]->[c]->[d]->[e]->[f]->[g]
zipWith7            :: (a->b->c->d->e->f->g->h) ->
                         [a]->[b]->[c]->[d]->[e]->[f]->[g]->[h]
unzip4              :: [(a,b,c,d)] -> ([a],[b],[c],[d])
unzip5              :: [(a,b,c,d,e)] -> ([a],[b],[c],[d],[e])
unzip6              :: [(a,b,c,d,e,f)] -> ([a],[b],[c],[d],[e],[f])
unzip7              :: [(a,b,c,d,e,f,g)] -> ([a],[b],[c],[d],[e],[f],[g])
```

This library defines some lesser-used operations over lists.

17.1   Indexing Lists

- `elemIndex val list` returns the index of the first occurrence, if any, of `val` in `list` as `Just index`. `Nothing` is returned if `not (val 'elem' list)`.

- `elemIndices val list` returns an in-order list of indices, giving the occurrences of `val` in `list`.

- `find` returns the first element of a list that satisfies a predicate, or Nothing, if there is no such element. `findIndex` returns the corresponding index. `findIndices` returns a list of all such indices.

17.2   "Set" Operations

There are a number of "set" operations defined over the `List` type. `nub` (meaning "essence") removes duplicates elements from a list. `delete`, `(\\)`, `union` and `intersect` (and their By variants) preserve the invariant that their result does not contain duplicates, provided that their first argument contains no duplicates.

- `nub` removes duplicate elements from a list. For example:
    ```
    nub [1,3,1,4,3,3] = [1,3,4]
    ```

- `delete x` removes the first occurrence of `x` from its list argument, e.g.
    ```
    delete 'a' "banana" == "bnana"
    ```

- `(\\)` is list difference (non-associative). In the result of `xs \\ ys`, the first occurrence of each element of `ys` in turn (if any) has been removed from `xs`. Thus,
    ```
    (xs ++ ys) \\ xs == ys.
    ```

- `union` is list union, e.g.
    ```
    "dog" 'union' "cow" == "dogcw"
    ```

- `intersect` is list intersection, e.g.
    ```
    [1,2,3,4] 'intersect' [2,4,6,8] == [2,4]
    ```

17.3   List Transformations

- `intersperse` `sep` inserts `sep` between the elements of its list argument, e.g.

    `intersperse ',' "abcde" == "a,b,c,d,e"`

- `transpose` transposes the rows and columns of its argument, e.g.

    `transpose [[1,2,3],[4,5,6]] == [[1,4],[2,5],[3,6]]`

- `partition` takes a predicate and a list and returns a pair of lists: those elements of the argument list that do and do not satisfy the predicate, respectively; i.e.

    `partition p xs == (filter p xs, filter (not . p) xs)`

- `sort` implement a stable sorting algorithm, here specified in terms of the `insertBy` function, which inserts objects into a list according to the specified ordering relation.

- `insert` inserts a new element into an *ordered* list (arranged in increasing order).

- `group` splits its list argument into a list of lists of equal, adjacent elements. For example

    `group "Mississippi" == ["M","i","ss","i","ss","i","pp","i"]`

- `inits` returns the list of initial segments of its argument list, shortest first.

    `inits "abc" == ["","a","ab","abc"]`

- `tails` returns the list of all final segments of its argument list, longest first.

    `tails "abc" == ["abc", "bc", "c",""]`

- `mapAccumL` `f` `s` `l` applies `f` to an accumulating "state" parameter `s` and to each element of `l` in turn.

- `mapAccumR` is similar to `mapAccumL` except that the list is processed from right-to-left rather than left-to-right.

17.4   `unfoldr`

The `unfoldr` function is a "dual" to `foldr`: while `foldr` reduces a list to a summary value, `unfoldr` builds a list from a seed value. For example:

```
iterate f == unfoldr (\x -> Just (x, f x))
```

In some cases, `unfoldr` can undo a `foldr` operation:

```
unfoldr f' (foldr f z xs) == xs
```

if the following holds:

```
f' (f x y) = Just (x,y)
f' z       = Nothing
```

17.5 Predicates

`isPrefixOf` and `isSuffixOf` check whether the first argument is a prefix (resp. suffix) of the second argument.

17.6 The "`By`" Operations

By convention, overloaded functions have a non-overloaded counterpart whose name is suffixed with "`By`". For example, the function `nub` could be defined as follows:

```
nub            :: (Eq a) => [a] -> [a]
nub []         =  []
nub (x:xs)     =  x : nub (filter (\y -> not (x == y)) xs)
```

However, the equality method may not be appropriate in all situations. The function:

```
nubBy           :: (a -> a -> Bool) -> [a] -> [a]
nubBy eq []      = []
nubBy eq (x:xs)  = x : nubBy eq (filter (\y -> not (eq x y)) xs)
```

allows the programmer to supply their own equality test. When the "`By`" function replaces an `Eq` context by a binary predicate, the predicate is assumed to define an equivalence; when the "`By`" function replaces an `Ord` context by a binary predicate, the predicate is assumed to define a total ordering.

The "`By`" variants are as follows: `nubBy`, `deleteBy`, `deleteFirstsBy` (the By variant of `\\`), `unionBy`, `intersectBy`, `groupBy`, `sortBy`, `insertBy`, `maximumBy`, `minimumBy`.

The library does not provide `elemBy`, because `any (eq x)` does the same job as `elemBy eq x` would. A handful of overloaded functions (`elemIndex`, `elemIndices`, `isPrefixOf`, `isSuffixOf`) were not considered important enough to have "`By`" variants.

17.7   The "`generic`" Operations

The prefix "`generic`" indicates an overloaded function that is a generalised version of a `Prelude` function. For example,

```
genericLength        :: Integral a => [b] -> a
```

is a generalised version of `length`.

The "`generic`" operations are as follows: `genericLength`, `genericTake`, `genericDrop`, `genericSplitAt`, `genericIndex` (the generic version of `!!`), `genericReplicate`.

17.8   Further "`zip`" Operations

The Prelude provides `zip`, `zip3`, `unzip`, `unzip3`, `zipWith`, and `zipWith3`. The List library provides these same three operations for 4, 5, 6, and 7 arguments.

17.9   Library `List`

```
module List (
    elemIndex, elemIndices,
    find, findIndex, findIndices,
    nub, nubBy, delete, deleteBy, (\\), deleteFirstsBy,
    union, unionBy, intersect, intersectBy,
    intersperse, transpose, partition, group, groupBy,
    inits, tails, isPrefixOf, isSuffixOf,
    mapAccumL, mapAccumR,
    sort, sortBy, insert, insertBy, maximumBy, minimumBy,
    genericLength, genericTake, genericDrop,
    genericSplitAt, genericIndex, genericReplicate,
    zip4, zip5, zip6, zip7,
    zipWith4, zipWith5, zipWith6, zipWith7,
    unzip4, unzip5, unzip6, unzip7, unfoldr,

    -- ...and what the Prelude exports
    -- [](:), []),      -- This is built-in syntax
    map, (++), concat, filter,
    head, last, tail, init, null, length, (!!),
    foldl, foldl1, scanl, scanl1, foldr, foldr1, scanr, scanr1,
    iterate, repeat, replicate, cycle,
    take, drop, splitAt, takeWhile, dropWhile, span, break,
    lines, words, unlines, unwords, reverse, and, or,
    any, all, elem, notElem, lookup,
    sum, product, maximum, minimum, concatMap,
    zip, zip3, zipWith, zipWith3, unzip, unzip3
    ) where

import Maybe( listToMaybe )
```

```
infix 5 \\

elemIndex               :: Eq a => a -> [a] -> Maybe Int
elemIndex x             = findIndex (x ==)

elemIndices             :: Eq a => a -> [a] -> [Int]
elemIndices x           = findIndices (x ==)

find                    :: (a -> Bool) -> [a] -> Maybe a
find p                  = listToMaybe . filter p

findIndex               :: (a -> Bool) -> [a] -> Maybe Int
findIndex p             = listToMaybe . findIndices p

findIndices             :: (a -> Bool) -> [a] -> [Int]
findIndices p xs        = [ i | (x,i) <- zip xs [0..], p x ]

nub                     :: Eq a => [a] -> [a]
nub                     = nubBy (==)

nubBy                   :: (a -> a -> Bool) -> [a] -> [a]
nubBy eq []             = []
nubBy eq (x:xs)         = x : nubBy eq (filter (\y -> not (eq x y)) xs

delete                  :: Eq a => a -> [a] -> [a]
delete                  = deleteBy (==)

deleteBy                :: (a -> a -> Bool) -> a -> [a] -> [a]
deleteBy eq x []        = []
deleteBy eq x (y:ys)    = if x 'eq' y then ys else y : deleteBy eq x ys

(\\)                    :: Eq a => [a] -> [a] -> [a]
(\\)                    = foldl (flip delete)

deleteFirstsBy          :: (a -> a -> Bool) -> [a] -> [a] -> [a]
deleteFirstsBy eq       = foldl (flip (deleteBy eq))

union                   :: Eq a => [a] -> [a] -> [a]
union                   = unionBy (==)

unionBy                 :: (a -> a -> Bool) -> [a] -> [a] -> [a]
unionBy eq xs ys        = xs ++ deleteFirstsBy eq (nubBy eq ys) xs

intersect               :: Eq a => [a] -> [a] -> [a]
intersect               = intersectBy (==)

intersectBy             :: (a -> a -> Bool) -> [a] -> [a] -> [a]
intersectBy eq xs ys    = [x | x <- xs, any (eq x) ys]

intersperse             :: a -> [a] -> [a]
intersperse sep []      = []
intersperse sep [x]     = [x]
intersperse sep (x:xs)  = x : sep : intersperse sep xs
```

```
-- transpose is lazy in both rows and columns,
--        and works for non-rectangular 'matrices'
-- For example, transpose [[1,2],[3,4,5],[]]  =  [[1,3],[2,4],[5]]
-- Note that [h | (h:t) <- xss] is not the same as (map head xss)
--        because the former discards empty sublists inside xss
transpose                  :: [[a]] -> [[a]]
transpose []               = []
transpose ([]    : xss) = transpose xss
transpose ((x:xs) : xss) = (x : [h | (h:t) <- xss]) :
                          transpose (xs : [t | (h:t) <- xss])

partition                  :: (a -> Bool) -> [a] -> ([a],[a])
partition p xs             = (filter p xs, filter (not . p) xs)

-- group splits its list argument into a list of lists of equal, adjacent
-- elements.  e.g.,
-- group "Mississippi" == ["M","i","ss","i","ss","i","pp","i"]
group                      :: Eq a => [a] -> [[a]]
group                      = groupBy (==)

groupBy                    :: (a -> a -> Bool) -> [a] -> [[a]]
groupBy eq []              = []
groupBy eq (x:xs)          = (x:ys) : groupBy eq zs
                             where (ys,zs) = span (eq x) xs

-- inits xs returns the list of initial segments of xs, shortest first.
-- e.g., inits "abc" == ["","a","ab","abc"]
inits                      :: [a] -> [[a]]
inits []                   = [[]]
inits (x:xs)               = [[]] ++ map (x:) (inits xs)

-- tails xs returns the list of all final segments of xs, longest first.
-- e.g., tails "abc" == ["abc", "bc", "c",""]
tails                      :: [a] -> [[a]]
tails []                   = [[]]
tails xxs@(_:xs)           = xxs : tails xs

isPrefixOf                 :: Eq a => [a] -> [a] -> Bool
isPrefixOf []         _    = True
isPrefixOf _         []    = False
isPrefixOf (x:xs) (y:ys) = x == y && isPrefixOf xs ys

isSuffixOf                 :: Eq a => [a] -> [a] -> Bool
isSuffixOf x y             = reverse x 'isPrefixOf' reverse y

mapAccumL                  :: (a -> b -> (a, c)) -> a -> [b] -> (a, [c])
mapAccumL f s []           = (s, [])
mapAccumL f s (x:xs)       = (s'',y:ys)
                             where (s', y ) = f s x
                                   (s'',ys) = mapAccumL f s' xs

mapAccumR                  :: (a -> b -> (a, c)) -> a -> [b] -> (a, [c])
mapAccumR f s []           = (s, [])
mapAccumR f s (x:xs)       = (s'', y:ys)
                             where (s'',y ) = f s' x
                                   (s', ys) = mapAccumR f s xs
```

```
unfoldr                    :: (b -> Maybe (a,b)) -> b -> [a]
unfoldr f b                = case f b of
                                   Nothing   -> []
                                   Just (a,b) -> a : unfoldr f b

sort                       :: (Ord a) => [a] -> [a]
sort                       =  sortBy compare

sortBy                     :: (a -> a -> Ordering) -> [a] -> [a]
sortBy cmp                 =  foldr (insertBy cmp) []

insert                     :: (Ord a) => a -> [a] -> [a]
insert                     = insertBy compare

insertBy                   :: (a -> a -> Ordering) -> a -> [a] -> [a]
insertBy cmp x []          =  [x]
insertBy cmp x ys@(y:ys')
                           =  case cmp x y of
                                   GT -> y : insertBy cmp x ys'
                                   _  -> x : ys

maximumBy                  :: (a -> a -> Ordering) -> [a] -> a
maximumBy cmp []           =  error "List.maximumBy: empty list"
maximumBy cmp xs           =  foldl1 max xs
                           where
                              max x y = case cmp x y of
                                             GT -> x
                                             _  -> y

minimumBy                  :: (a -> a -> Ordering) -> [a] -> a
minimumBy cmp []           =  error "List.minimumBy: empty list"
minimumBy cmp xs           =  foldl1 min xs
                           where
                              min x y = case cmp x y of
                                             GT -> y
                                             _  -> x

genericLength              :: (Integral a) => [b] -> a
genericLength []           =  0
genericLength (x:xs)       =  1 + genericLength xs

genericTake                :: (Integral a) => a -> [b] -> [b]
genericTake _ []           =  []
genericTake 0 _            =  []
genericTake n (x:xs)
     | n > 0               =  x : genericTake (n-1) xs
     | otherwise           =  error "List.genericTake: negative argument"

genericDrop                :: (Integral a) => a -> [b] -> [b]
genericDrop 0 xs           =  xs
genericDrop _ []           =  []
genericDrop n (_:xs)
     | n > 0               =  genericDrop (n-1) xs
     | otherwise           =  error "List.genericDrop: negative argument"
```

```haskell
genericSplitAt         :: (Integral a) => a -> [b] -> ([b],[b])
genericSplitAt 0 xs    = ([],xs)
genericSplitAt _ []    = ([],[])
genericSplitAt n (x:xs)
    | n > 0            = (x:xs',xs'')
    | otherwise        = error "List.genericSplitAt: negative argument"
        where (xs',xs'') = genericSplitAt (n-1) xs

genericIndex           :: (Integral a) => [b] -> a -> b
genericIndex (x:_)  0  = x
genericIndex (_:xs) n
        | n > 0        = genericIndex xs (n-1)
        | otherwise    = error "List.genericIndex: negative argument"
genericIndex _ _       = error "List.genericIndex: index too large"

genericReplicate       :: (Integral a) => a -> b -> [b]
genericReplicate n x   = genericTake n (repeat x)

zip4                   :: [a] -> [b] -> [c] -> [d] -> [(a,b,c,d)]
zip4                   = zipWith4 (,,,)

zip5                   :: [a] -> [b] -> [c] -> [d] -> [e] -> [(a,b,c,d,e)]
zip5                   = zipWith5 (,,,,)

zip6                   :: [a] -> [b] -> [c] -> [d] -> [e] -> [f] ->
                             [(a,b,c,d,e,f)]
zip6                   = zipWith6 (,,,,,)

zip7                   :: [a] -> [b] -> [c] -> [d] -> [e] -> [f] ->
                             [g] -> [(a,b,c,d,e,f,g)]
zip7                   = zipWith7 (,,,,,,)

zipWith4               :: (a->b->c->d->e) -> [a]->[b]->[c]->[d]->[e]
zipWith4 z (a:as) (b:bs) (c:cs) (d:ds)
                       = z a b c d : zipWith4 z as bs cs ds
zipWith4 _ _ _ _ _     = []

zipWith5               :: (a->b->c->d->e->f) ->
                             [a]->[b]->[c]->[d]->[e]->[f]
zipWith5 z (a:as) (b:bs) (c:cs) (d:ds) (e:es)
                       = z a b c d e : zipWith5 z as bs cs ds es
zipWith5 _ _ _ _ _ _   = []

zipWith6               :: (a->b->c->d->e->f->g) ->
                             [a]->[b]->[c]->[d]->[e]->[f]->[g]
zipWith6 z (a:as) (b:bs) (c:cs) (d:ds) (e:es) (f:fs)
                       = z a b c d e f : zipWith6 z as bs cs ds es fs
zipWith6 _ _ _ _ _ _ _ = []

zipWith7               :: (a->b->c->d->e->f->g->h) ->
                             [a]->[b]->[c]->[d]->[e]->[f]->[g]->[h]
zipWith7 z (a:as) (b:bs) (c:cs) (d:ds) (e:es) (f:fs) (g:gs)
                 = z a b c d e f g : zipWith7 z as bs cs ds es fs gs
zipWith7 _ _ _ _ _ _ _ _ = []

unzip4                 :: [(a,b,c,d)] -> ([a],[b],[c],[d])
unzip4                 = foldr (\(a,b,c,d) ~(as,bs,cs,ds) ->
                                    (a:as,b:bs,c:cs,d:ds))
                             ([],[],[],[])
```

```
unzip5        :: [(a,b,c,d,e)] -> ([a],[b],[c],[d],[e])
unzip5        =  foldr (\(a,b,c,d,e) ~(as,bs,cs,ds,es) ->
                         (a:as,b:bs,c:cs,d:ds,e:es))
                        ([],[],[],[],[])

unzip6        :: [(a,b,c,d,e,f)] -> ([a],[b],[c],[d],[e],[f])
unzip6        =  foldr (\(a,b,c,d,e,f) ~(as,bs,cs,ds,es,fs) ->
                         (a:as,b:bs,c:cs,d:ds,e:es,f:fs))
                        ([],[],[],[],[],[])

unzip7        :: [(a,b,c,d,e,f,g)] -> ([a],[b],[c],[d],[e],[f],[g])
unzip7        =  foldr (\(a,b,c,d,e,f,g) ~(as,bs,cs,ds,es,fs,gs) ->
                         (a:as,b:bs,c:cs,d:ds,e:es,f:fs,g:gs))
                        ([],[],[],[],[],[],[])
```

JFP **13** (1): 191–192, January 2003. © 2003 Cambridge University Press
DOI: 10.1017/S0956796803002016 Printed in the United Kingdom

Chapter 18

Maybe Utilities

```
module Maybe(
    isJust, isNothing,
    fromJust, fromMaybe, listToMaybe, maybeToList,
    catMaybes, mapMaybe,

    -- ...and what the Prelude exports
    Maybe(Nothing, Just),
    maybe
  ) where

isJust, isNothing     :: Maybe a -> Bool
fromJust              :: Maybe a -> a
fromMaybe             :: a -> Maybe a -> a
listToMaybe           :: [a] -> Maybe a
maybeToList           :: Maybe a -> [a]
catMaybes             :: [Maybe a] -> [a]
mapMaybe              :: (a -> Maybe b) -> [a] -> [b]
```

The type constructor `Maybe` is defined in `Prelude` as

```
data Maybe a = Nothing | Just a
```

The purpose of the `Maybe` type is to provide a method of dealing with illegal or optional values without terminating the program, as would happen if `error` were used, and without using

IOError from the IO monad, which would cause the expression to become monadic. A correct result is encapsulated by wrapping it in Just; an incorrect result is returned as Nothing.

Other operations on Maybe are provided as part of the monadic classes in the Prelude.

18.1   Library Maybe

```
module Maybe(
    isJust, isNothing,
    fromJust, fromMaybe, listToMaybe, maybeToList,
    catMaybes, mapMaybe,

    -- ...and what the Prelude exports
    Maybe(Nothing, Just),
    maybe
  ) where

isJust                      :: Maybe a -> Bool
isJust (Just a)             =  True
isJust Nothing              =  False

isNothing                   :: Maybe a -> Bool
isNothing                   =  not . isJust

fromJust                    :: Maybe a -> a
fromJust (Just a)           =  a
fromJust Nothing            =  error "Maybe.fromJust: Nothing"

fromMaybe                   :: a -> Maybe a -> a
fromMaybe d Nothing         =  d
fromMaybe d (Just a)        =  a

maybeToList                 :: Maybe a -> [a]
maybeToList Nothing         =  []
maybeToList (Just a)        =  [a]

listToMaybe                 :: [a] -> Maybe a
listToMaybe []              =  Nothing
listToMaybe (a:_)           =  Just a

catMaybes                   :: [Maybe a] -> [a]
catMaybes ms                =  [ m | Just m <- ms ]

mapMaybe                    :: (a -> Maybe b) -> [a] -> [b]
mapMaybe f                  =  catMaybes . map f
```

JFP **13** (1): 193–198, January 2003. © 2003 Cambridge University Press
DOI: 10.1017/S0956796803002119 Printed in the United Kingdom

Chapter 19

Character Utilities

```
module Char (
    isAscii, isLatin1, isControl, isPrint, isSpace, isUpper, isLower,
    isAlpha, isDigit, isOctDigit, isHexDigit, isAlphaNum,
    digitToInt, intToDigit,
    toUpper, toLower,
    ord, chr,
    readLitChar, showLitChar, lexLitChar,
        -- ...and what the Prelude exports
    Char, String
    ) where

isAscii, isLatin1, isControl, isPrint, isSpace, isUpper, isLower,
 isAlpha, isDigit, isOctDigit, isHexDigit, isAlphaNum :: Char -> Bool

toUpper, toLower          :: Char -> Char

digitToInt :: Char -> Int
intToDigit :: Int -> Char

ord        :: Char -> Int
chr        :: Int  -> Char

lexLitChar  :: ReadS String
readLitChar :: ReadS Char
showLitChar :: Char -> ShowS
```

This library provides a limited set of operations on the Unicode character set. The first 128 entries of this character set are identical to the ASCII set; with the next 128 entries comes the remainder of the Latin-1 character set. This module offers only a limited view of the full Unicode character set; the full set of Unicode character attributes is not accessible in this library.

Unicode characters may be divided into five general categories: non-printing, lower case alphabetic, other alphabetic, numeric digits, and other printable characters. For the purposes of Haskell, any alphabetic character which is not lower case is treated as upper case (Unicode actually has three cases: upper, lower, and title). Numeric digits may be part of identifiers but digits outside the ASCII range are not used by the reader to represent numbers.

For each sort of Unicode character, here are the predicates which return `True`:

Character Type	Predicates			
Lower Case Alphabetic	`isPrint`	`isAlphaNum`	`isAlpha`	`isLower`
Other Alphabetic	`isPrint`	`isAlphaNum`	`isAlpha`	`isUpper`
Digits	`isPrint`	`isAlphaNum`		
Other Printable	`isPrint`			
Non-printing				

The `isDigit`, `isOctDigit`, and `isHexDigit` functions select only ASCII characters. `intToDigit` and `digitToInt` convert between a single digit `Char` and the corresponding `Int`. `digitToInt` operates fails unless its argument satisfies `isHexDigit`, but recognises both upper and lower-case hexadecimal digits (i.e. `'0'..'9'`, `'a'..'f'`, `'A'..'F'`). `intToDigit` fails unless its argument is in the range 0..15, and generates lower-case hexadecimal digits.

The `isSpace` function recognizes only white characters in the Latin-1 range.

The function `showLitChar` converts a character to a string using only printable characters, using Haskell source-language escape conventions. The function `lexLitChar` does the reverse, returning the sequence of characters that encode the character. The function `readLitChar` does the same, but in addition converts the to the character that it encodes. For example:

```
showLitChar '\n' s      =  "\\n" ++ s
lexLitChar  "\\nHello"  =  [("\\n", "Hello")]
readLitChar "\\nHello"  =  [('\n', "Hello")]
```

Function `toUpper` converts a letter to the corresponding upper-case letter, leaving any other character unchanged. Any Unicode letter which has an upper-case equivalent is transformed. Similarly, `toLower` converts a letter to the corresponding lower-case letter, leaving any other character unchanged.

The `ord` and `chr` functions are `fromEnum` and `toEnum` restricted to the type `Char`.

19.1 Library Char

```
module Char (
    isAscii, isLatin1, isControl, isPrint, isSpace, isUpper, isLower,
    isAlpha, isDigit, isOctDigit, isHexDigit, isAlphaNum,
    digitToInt, intToDigit,
    toUpper, toLower,
    ord, chr,
    readLitChar, showLitChar, lexLitChar,
        -- ...and what the Prelude exports
    Char, String
    ) where

import Array          -- Used for character name table.
import Numeric (readDec, readOct, lexDigits, readHex)
import UnicodePrims   -- Source of primitive Unicode functions.

-- Character-testing operations
isAscii, isLatin1, isControl, isPrint, isSpace, isUpper, isLower,
 isAlpha, isDigit, isOctDigit, isHexDigit, isAlphaNum :: Char -> Bool

isAscii c               = c < '\x80'

isLatin1 c              = c <= '\xff'

isControl c             = c < ' ' || c >= '\DEL' && c <= '\x9f'

isPrint                 = primUnicodeIsPrint

isSpace c               = c 'elem' " \t\n\r\f\v\xA0"
        -- Only Latin-1 spaces recognized

isUpper                 = primUnicodeIsUpper   -- 'A'..'Z'

isLower                 = primUnicodeIsLower   -- 'a'..'z'

isAlpha c               = isUpper c || isLower c

isDigit c               = c >= '0' && c <= '9'

isOctDigit c            = c >= '0' && c <= '7'

isHexDigit c            = isDigit c || c >= 'A' && c <= 'F' ||
                                       c >= 'a' && c <= 'f'

isAlphaNum              = primUnicodeIsAlphaNum

-- Digit conversion operations
digitToInt :: Char -> Int
digitToInt c
    | isDigit c               = fromEnum c - fromEnum '0'
    | c >= 'a' && c <= 'f' = fromEnum c - fromEnum 'a' + 10
    | c >= 'A' && c <= 'F' = fromEnum c - fromEnum 'A' + 10
    | otherwise               = error "Char.digitToInt: not a digit"
```

```haskell
intToDigit :: Int -> Char
intToDigit i
  | i >= 0  && i <= 9    = toEnum (fromEnum '0' + i)
  | i >= 10 && i <= 15   = toEnum (fromEnum 'a' + i - 10)
  | otherwise            = error "Char.intToDigit: not a digit"

-- Case-changing operations
toUpper :: Char -> Char
toUpper = primUnicodeToUpper

toLower :: Char -> Char
toLower = primUnicodeToLower

-- Character code functions
ord  :: Char -> Int
ord  = fromEnum

chr  :: Int  -> Char
chr  = toEnum

-- Text functions
readLitChar            :: ReadS Char
readLitChar ('\\':s) =  readEsc s
readLitChar (c:s)     = [(c,s)]

readEsc            :: ReadS Char
readEsc ('a':s)  = [('\a',s)]
readEsc ('b':s)  = [('\b',s)]
readEsc ('f':s)  = [('\f',s)]
readEsc ('n':s)  = [('\n',s)]
readEsc ('r':s)  = [('\r',s)]
readEsc ('t':s)  = [('\t',s)]
readEsc ('v':s)  = [('\v',s)]
readEsc ('\\':s) = [('\\',s)]
readEsc ('"':s)  = [('"',s)]
readEsc ('\'':s) = [('\'',s)]
readEsc ('^':c:s) | c >= '@' && c <= '_'
                 = [(chr (ord c - ord '@'), s)]
readEsc s@(d:_) | isDigit d
                 = [(chr n, t) | (n,t) <- readDec s]
readEsc ('o':s)  = [(chr n, t) | (n,t) <- readOct s]
readEsc ('x':s)  = [(chr n, t) | (n,t) <- readHex s]
readEsc s@(c:_) | isUpper c
                 = let table = ('\DEL', "DEL") : assocs asciiTab
                   in case [(c,s') | (c, mne) <- table,
                                     ([],s') <- [match mne s]]
                      of (pr:_) -> [pr]
                         []     -> []
readEsc _        = []

match                      :: (Eq a) => [a] -> [a] -> ([a],[a])
match (x:xs) (y:ys) | x == y  =  match xs ys
match xs     ys          =  (xs,ys)
```

```
showLitChar                   :: Char -> ShowS
showLitChar c | c > '\DEL' =   showChar '\\' .
                                protectEsc isDigit (shows (ord c))
showLitChar '\DEL'        =   showString "\\DEL"
showLitChar '\\'          =   showString "\\\\"
showLitChar c | c >= ' '  =   showChar c
showLitChar '\a'          =   showString "\\a"
showLitChar '\b'          =   showString "\\b"
showLitChar '\f'          =   showString "\\f"
showLitChar '\n'          =   showString "\\n"
showLitChar '\r'          =   showString "\\r"
showLitChar '\t'          =   showString "\\t"
showLitChar '\v'          =   showString "\\v"
showLitChar '\SO'         =   protectEsc (== 'H') (showString "\\SO")
showLitChar c             =   showString ('\\' : asciiTab!c)

protectEsc p f            = f . cont
                           where cont s@(c:_) | p c = "\\&" ++ s
                                 cont s             = s
asciiTab = listArray ('\NUL', ' ')
           ["NUL", "SOH", "STX", "ETX", "EOT", "ENQ", "ACK", "BEL",
            "BS",  "HT",  "LF",  "VT",  "FF",  "CR",  "SO",  "SI",
            "DLE", "DC1", "DC2", "DC3", "DC4", "NAK", "SYN", "ETB",
            "CAN", "EM",  "SUB", "ESC", "FS",  "GS",  "RS",  "US",
            "SP"]

lexLitChar          :: ReadS String
lexLitChar ('\\':s) =  map (prefix '\\') (lexEsc s)
        where
            lexEsc (c:s)    | c 'elem' "abfnrtv\\\"'" = [([c],s)]
            lexEsc ('^':c:s) | c >= '@' && c <= '_'   = [(['^',c],s)]

            -- Numeric escapes
            lexEsc ('o':s)              = [prefix 'o' (span isOctDigit s)]
            lexEsc ('x':s)              = [prefix 'x' (span isHexDigit s)]
            lexEsc s@(d:_)  | isDigit d = [span isDigit s]

            -- Very crude approximation to \XYZ.
            lexEsc s@(c:_)  | isUpper c = [span isCharName s]
            lexEsc _                    = []

            isCharName c  = isUpper c || isDigit c
            prefix c (t,s) = (c:t, s)

lexLitChar (c:s)   =  [([c],s)]
lexLitChar ""      =  []
```

JFP **13** (1): 199–204, January 2003. © 2003 Cambridge University Press
DOI: 10.1017/S0956796803002211   Printed in the United Kingdom

Chapter 20

Monad Utilities

```
module Monad (
    MonadPlus(mzero, mplus),
    join, guard, when, unless, ap,
    msum,
    filterM, mapAndUnzipM, zipWithM, zipWithM_, foldM,
    liftM, liftM2, liftM3, liftM4, liftM5,

    -- ...and what the Prelude exports
    Monad((>>=), (>>), return, fail),
    Functor(fmap),
    mapM, mapM_, sequence, sequence_, (=<<),
    ) where

class  Monad m => MonadPlus m  where
    mzero   :: m a
    mplus   :: m a -> m a -> m a

join            :: Monad m => m (m a) -> m a
guard           :: MonadPlus m => Bool -> m ()
when            :: Monad m => Bool -> m () -> m ()
unless          :: Monad m => Bool -> m () -> m ()
ap              :: Monad m => m (a -> b) -> m a -> m b

mapAndUnzipM    :: Monad m => (a -> m (b,c)) -> [a] -> m ([b], [c])
zipWithM        :: Monad m => (a -> b -> m c) -> [a] -> [b] -> m [c]
zipWithM_       :: Monad m => (a -> b -> m c) -> [a] -> [b] -> m ()
foldM           :: Monad m => (a -> b -> m a) -> a -> [b] -> m a
filterM         :: Monad m => (a -> m Bool) -> [a] -> m [a]
```

```
msum              :: MonadPlus m => [m a] -> m a

liftM             :: Monad m => (a -> b) -> (m a -> m b)
liftM2            :: Monad m => (a -> b -> c) -> (m a -> m b -> m c)
liftM3            :: Monad m => (a -> b -> c -> d) ->
                                (m a -> m b -> m c -> m d)
liftM4            :: Monad m => (a -> b -> c -> d -> e) ->
                                (m a -> m b -> m c -> m d -> m e)
liftM5            :: Monad m => (a -> b -> c -> d -> e -> f) ->
                                (m a -> m b -> m c -> m d -> m e -> m f)
```

The Monad library defines the MonadPlus class, and provides some useful operations on monads.

20.1   Naming Conventions

The functions in this library use the following naming conventions:

- A postfix "M" always stands for a function in the Kleisli category: m is added to function results (modulo currying) and nowhere else. So, for example,

```
filter  ::                 (a ->    Bool) -> [a] ->    [a]
filterM :: Monad m => (a -> m Bool) -> [a] -> m [a]
```

- A postfix "_" changes the result type from (m a) to (m ()). Thus (in the Prelude):

```
sequence   :: Monad m => [m a] -> m [a]
sequence_  :: Monad m => [m a] -> m ()
```

- A prefix "m" generalises an existing function to a monadic form. Thus, for example:

```
sum  :: Num a         => [a]    -> a
msum :: MonadPlus m => [m a] -> m a
```


20.2   Class MonadPlus

The MonadPlus class is defined as follows:

```
class  Monad m => MonadPlus m   where
    mzero  :: m a
    mplus  :: m a -> m a -> m a
```

The class methods mzero and mplus are the zero and plus of the monad.

Lists and the `Maybe` type are instances of `MonadPlus`, thus:

```
instance  MonadPlus Maybe  where
    mzero                 = Nothing
    Nothing 'mplus' ys    = ys
    xs      'mplus' ys    = xs

instance  MonadPlus []  where
    mzero = []
    mplus = (++)
```

20.3 Functions

The `join` function is the conventional monad join operator. It is used to remove one level of monadic structure, projecting its bound argument into the outer level.

The `mapAndUnzipM` function maps its first argument over a list, returning the result as a pair of lists. This function is mainly used with complicated data structures or a state-transforming monad.

The `zipWithM` function generalises `zipWith` to arbitrary monads. For instance the following function displays a file, prefixing each line with its line number,

```
listFile :: String -> IO ()
listFile nm =
  do cts <- readFile nm
     zipWithM_ (\i line -> do putStr (show i); putStr ": "; putStrLn line)
               [1..]
               (lines cts)
```

The `foldM` function is analogous to `foldl`, except that its result is encapsulated in a monad. Note that `foldM` works from left-to-right over the list arguments. This could be an issue where (`>>`) and the "folded function" are not commutative.

```
      foldM f a1 [x1, x2, ..., xm ]
==
      do
        a2 <- f a1 x1
        a3 <- f a2 x2
        ...
        f am xm
```

If right-to-left evaluation is required, the input list should be reversed.

The `when` and `unless` functions provide conditional execution of monadic expressions. For example,

```
when debug (putStr "Debugging\n")
```

will output the string "Debugging\n" if the Boolean value debug is True, and otherwise do nothing.

The monadic lifting operators promote a function to a monad. The function arguments are scanned left to right. For example,

```
liftM2 (+) [0,1] [0,2] = [0,2,1,3]
liftM2 (+) (Just 1) Nothing = Nothing
```

In many situations, the liftM operations can be replaced by uses of ap, which promotes function application.

```
return f 'ap' x1 'ap' ... 'ap' xn
```

is equivalent to

```
liftMn f x1 x2 ... xn
```

20.4   Library Monad

```
module Monad (
    MonadPlus(mzero, mplus),
    join, guard, when, unless, ap,
    msum,
    filterM, mapAndUnzipM, zipWithM, zipWithM_, foldM,
    liftM, liftM2, liftM3, liftM4, liftM5,
    -- ...and what the Prelude exports
    Monad((>>=), (>>), return, fail),
    Functor(fmap),
    mapM, mapM_, sequence, sequence_, (=<<),
    ) where

-- The MonadPlus class definition
class  (Monad m) => MonadPlus m  where
    mzero  :: m a
    mplus  :: m a -> m a -> m a

-- Instances of MonadPlus
instance  MonadPlus Maybe  where
    mzero                = Nothing
    Nothing 'mplus' ys   = ys
    xs      'mplus' ys   = xs

instance  MonadPlus []  where
    mzero = []
    mplus = (++)
```

```
-- Functions

msum                :: MonadPlus m => [m a] -> m a
msum xs             = foldr mplus mzero xs

join                :: (Monad m) => m (m a) -> m a
join x              = x >>= id

when                :: (Monad m) => Bool -> m () -> m ()
when p s            = if p then s else return ()

unless              :: (Monad m) => Bool -> m () -> m ()
unless p s          = when (not p) s

ap                  :: (Monad m) => m (a -> b) -> m a -> m b
ap                  = liftM2 ($)

guard               :: MonadPlus m => Bool -> m ()
guard p             = if p then return () else mzero

mapAndUnzipM        :: (Monad m) => (a -> m (b,c)) -> [a] -> m ([b], [c])
mapAndUnzipM f xs   = sequence (map f xs) >>= return . unzip

zipWithM            :: (Monad m) => (a -> b -> m c) -> [a] -> [b] -> m [c]
zipWithM f xs ys    = sequence (zipWith f xs ys)

zipWithM_           :: (Monad m) => (a -> b -> m c) -> [a] -> [b] -> m ()
zipWithM_ f xs ys   = sequence_ (zipWith f xs ys)

foldM               :: (Monad m) => (a -> b -> m a) -> a -> [b] -> m a
foldM f a []        = return a
foldM f a (x:xs)    = f a x >>= \ y -> foldM f y xs

filterM :: Monad m => (a -> m Bool) -> [a] -> m [a]
filterM p []        = return []
filterM p (x:xs)    = do { b  <- p x;
                           ys <- filterM p xs;
                           return (if b then (x:ys) else ys)
                         }

liftM               :: (Monad m) => (a -> b) -> (m a -> m b)
liftM f             = \a -> do { a' <- a; return (f a') }

liftM2              :: (Monad m) => (a -> b -> c) -> (m a -> m b -> m c)
liftM2 f            = \a b -> do { a' <- a; b' <- b; return (f a' b') }

liftM3              :: (Monad m) => (a -> b -> c -> d) ->
                                    (m a -> m b -> m c -> m d)
liftM3 f            = \a b c -> do { a' <- a; b' <- b; c' <- c;
                                     return (f a' b' c') }

liftM4              :: (Monad m) => (a -> b -> c -> d -> e) ->
                                    (m a -> m b -> m c -> m d -> m e)
liftM4 f            = \a b c d -> do { a' <- a; b' <- b; c' <- c; d' <- d;
                                       return (f a' b' c' d') }

liftM5              :: (Monad m) => (a -> b -> c -> d -> e -> f) ->
                                    (m a -> m b -> m c -> m d -> m e -> m f)
liftM5 f            = \a b c d e -> do { a' <- a; b' <- b; c' <- c; d' <- d;
                                         e' <- e; return (f a' b' c' d' e') }
```

JFP **13** (1): 205–218, January 2003. © 2003 Cambridge University Press
DOI: 10.1017/S0956796803002314   Printed in the United Kingdom

Chapter 21

Input/Output

```
module IO (
    Handle, HandlePosn,
    IOMode(ReadMode,WriteMode,AppendMode,ReadWriteMode),
    BufferMode(NoBuffering,LineBuffering,BlockBuffering),
    SeekMode(AbsoluteSeek,RelativeSeek,SeekFromEnd),
    stdin, stdout, stderr,
    openFile, hClose, hFileSize, hIsEOF, isEOF,
    hSetBuffering, hGetBuffering, hFlush,
    hGetPosn, hSetPosn, hSeek,
    hWaitForInput, hReady, hGetChar, hGetLine, hLookAhead, hGetContents,
    hPutChar, hPutStr, hPutStrLn, hPrint,
    hIsOpen, hIsClosed, hIsReadable, hIsWritable, hIsSeekable,
    isAlreadyExistsError, isDoesNotExistError, isAlreadyInUseError,
    isFullError, isEOFError,
    isIllegalOperation, isPermissionError, isUserError,
    ioeGetErrorString, ioeGetHandle, ioeGetFileName,
    try, bracket, bracket_,

    -- ...and what the Prelude exports
    IO, FilePath, IOError, ioError, userError, catch, interact,
    putChar, putStr, putStrLn, print, getChar, getLine, getContents,
    readFile, writeFile, appendFile, readIO, readLn
    ) where

import Ix(Ix)
```

```
data Handle = ...                       -- implementation-dependent
instance Eq Handle where ...
instance Show Handle where ..           -- implementation-dependent

data HandlePosn = ...                   -- implementation-dependent
instance Eq HandlePosn where ...
instance Show HandlePosn where ---      -- implementation-dependent

data IOMode      = ReadMode | WriteMode | AppendMode | ReadWriteMode
                   deriving (Eq, Ord, Ix, Bounded, Enum, Read, Show)
data BufferMode  = NoBuffering | LineBuffering
                 | BlockBuffering (Maybe Int)
                   deriving (Eq, Ord, Read, Show)
data SeekMode    = AbsoluteSeek | RelativeSeek | SeekFromEnd
                   deriving (Eq, Ord, Ix, Bounded, Enum, Read, Show)

stdin, stdout, stderr :: Handle

openFile           :: FilePath -> IOMode -> IO Handle
hClose             :: Handle -> IO ()

hFileSize          :: Handle -> IO Integer
hIsEOF             :: Handle -> IO Bool
isEOF              :: IO Bool
isEOF              = hIsEOF stdin

hSetBuffering      :: Handle  -> BufferMode -> IO ()
hGetBuffering      :: Handle  -> IO BufferMode
hFlush             :: Handle -> IO ()
hGetPosn           :: Handle -> IO HandlePosn
hSetPosn           :: HandlePosn -> IO ()
hSeek              :: Handle -> SeekMode -> Integer -> IO ()

hWaitForInput      :: Handle -> Int -> IO Bool
hReady             :: Handle -> IO Bool
hReady h           = hWaitForInput h 0
hGetChar           :: Handle -> IO Char
hGetLine           :: Handle -> IO String
hLookAhead         :: Handle -> IO Char
hGetContents       :: Handle -> IO String
hPutChar           :: Handle -> Char -> IO ()
hPutStr            :: Handle -> String -> IO ()
hPutStrLn          :: Handle -> String -> IO ()
hPrint             :: Show a => Handle -> a -> IO ()
```

```
hIsOpen                 :: Handle -> IO Bool
hIsClosed               :: Handle -> IO Bool
hIsReadable             :: Handle -> IO Bool
hIsWritable             :: Handle -> IO Bool
hIsSeekable             :: Handle -> IO Bool

isAlreadyExistsError    :: IOError -> Bool
isDoesNotExistError     :: IOError -> Bool
isAlreadyInUseError     :: IOError -> Bool
isFullError             :: IOError -> Bool
isEOFError              :: IOError -> Bool
isIllegalOperation      :: IOError -> Bool
isPermissionError       :: IOError -> Bool
isUserError             :: IOError -> Bool

ioeGetErrorString       :: IOError -> String
ioeGetHandle            :: IOError -> Maybe Handle
ioeGetFileName          :: IOError -> Maybe FilePath

try                     :: IO a -> IO (Either IOError a)
bracket                 :: IO a -> (a -> IO b) -> (a -> IO c) -> IO c
bracket_                :: IO a -> (a -> IO b) -> IO c -> IO c
```

The monadic I/O system used in Haskell is described by the Haskell language report. Commonly used I/O functions such as `print` are part of the standard prelude and need not be explicitly imported. This library contain more advanced I/O features. Some related operations on file systems are contained in the `Directory` library.

21.1 I/O Errors

Errors of type `IOError` are used by the I/O monad. This is an abstract type; the library provides functions to interrogate and construct values in `IOError`:

- `isAlreadyExistsError` – the operation failed because one of its arguments already exists.

- `isDoesNotExistError` – the operation failed because one of its arguments does not exist.

- `isAlreadyInUseError` – the operation failed because one of its arguments is a single-use resource, which is already being used (for example, opening the same file twice for writing might give this error).

- `isFullError` – the operation failed because the device is full.

- `isEOFError` – the operation failed because the end of file has been reached.

- `isIllegalOperation` – the operation is not possible.

- `isPermissionError` – the operation failed because the user does not have sufficient operating system privilege to perform that operation.

- `isUserError` – a programmer-defined error value has been raised using `fail`.

All these functions return a `Bool`, which is `True` if its argument is the corresponding kind of error, and `False` otherwise.

Any computation which returns an `IO` result may fail with `isIllegalOperation`. Additional errors which could be raised by an implementation are listed after the corresponding operation. In some cases, an implementation will not be able to distinguish between the possible error causes. In this case it should return `isIllegalOperation`.

Three additional functions are provided to obtain information about an error value. These are `ioeGetHandle` which returns `Just` *hdl* if the error value refers to handle *hdl* and `Nothing` otherwise; `ioeGetFileName` which returns `Just` *name* if the error value refers to file *name*, and `Nothing` otherwise; and `ioeGetErrorString` which returns a string. For "user" errors (those which are raised using `fail`), the string returned by `ioeGetErrorString` is the argument that was passed to `fail`; for all other errors, the string is implementation-dependent.

The `try` function returns an error in a computation explicitly using the `Either` type.

The `bracket` function captures a common allocate, compute, deallocate idiom in which the deallocation step must occur even in the case of an error during computation. This is similar to try-catch-finally in Java.

21.2   Files and Handles

Haskell interfaces to the external world through an abstract *file system*. This file system is a collection of named *file system objects*, which may be organised in *directories* (see `Directory`). In some implementations, directories may themselves be file system objects and could be entries in other directories. For simplicity, any non-directory file system object is termed a *file*, although it could in fact be a communication channel, or any other object recognised by the operating system. *Physical files* are persistent, ordered files, and normally reside on disk.

File and directory names are values of type `String`, whose precise meaning is operating system dependent. Files can be opened, yielding a handle which can then be used to operate on the contents of that file.

Haskell defines operations to read and write characters from and to files, represented by values of type `Handle`. Each value of this type is a *handle*: a record used by the Haskell run-time system to *manage* I/O with file system objects. A handle has at least the following properties:

- whether it manages input or output or both;

- whether it is *open*, *closed* or *semi-closed*;

- whether the object is seekable;

- whether buffering is disabled, or enabled on a line or block basis;

- a buffer (whose length may be zero).

Most handles will also have a current I/O position indicating where the next input or output operation will occur. A handle is *readable* if it manages only input or both input and output; likewise, it is *writable* if it manages only output or both input and output. A handle is *open* when first allocated. Once it is closed it can no longer be used for either input or output, though an implementation cannot re-use its storage while references remain to it. Handles are in the Show and Eq classes. The string produced by showing a handle is system dependent; it should include enough information to identify the handle for debugging. A handle is equal according to == only to itself; no attempt is made to compare the internal state of different handles for equality.

21.2.1 Standard Handles

Three handles are allocated during program initialisation. The first two (stdin and stdout) manage input or output from the Haskell program's standard input or output channel respectively. The third (stderr) manages output to the standard error channel. These handles are initially open.

21.2.2 Semi-Closed Handles

The operation hGetContents *hdl* (Section 21.9.4) puts a handle *hdl* into an intermediate state, *semi-closed*. In this state, *hdl* is effectively closed, but items are read from *hdl* on demand and accumulated in a special list returned by hGetContents *hdl*.

Any operation that fails because a handle is closed, also fails if a handle is semi-closed. The only exception is hClose. A semi-closed handle becomes closed:

- if hClose is applied to it;

- if an I/O error occurs when reading an item from the handle;

- or once the entire contents of the handle has been read.

Once a semi-closed handle becomes closed, the contents of the associated list becomes fixed. The contents of this final list is only partially specified: it will contain at least all the items of the stream that were evaluated prior to the handle becoming closed.

Any I/O errors encountered while a handle is semi-closed are simply discarded.

21.2.3 File Locking

Implementations should enforce as far as possible, at least locally to the Haskell process, multiple-reader single-writer locking on files. That is, *there may either be many handles on the same file which manage input, or just one handle on the file which manages output*. If any open or semi-closed handle is managing a file for output, no new handle can be allocated for that file. If any open or semi-closed handle is managing a file for input, new handles can only be allocated if they do not manage output. Whether two files are the same is implementation-dependent, but they should normally be the same if they have the same absolute path name and neither has been renamed, for example.

Warning: the readFile operation (Section 7.1 of the Haskell Language Report) holds a semi-closed handle on the file until the entire contents of the file have been consumed. It follows that an attempt to write to a file (using writeFile, for example) that was earlier opened by readFile will usually result in failure with isAlreadyInUseError.

21.3 Opening and Closing Files

21.3.1 Opening Files

Computation openFile *file mode* allocates and returns a new, open handle to manage the file *file*. It manages input if *mode* is ReadMode, output if *mode* is WriteMode or AppendMode, and both input and output if mode is ReadWriteMode.

If the file does not exist and it is opened for output, it should be created as a new file. If *mode* is WriteMode and the file already exists, then it should be truncated to zero length. Some operating systems delete empty files, so there is no guarantee that the file will exist following an openFile with *mode* WriteMode unless it is subsequently written to successfully. The handle is positioned at the end of the file if *mode* is AppendMode, and otherwise at the beginning (in which case its internal I/O position is 0). The initial buffer mode is implementation-dependent.

If openFile fails on a file opened for output, the file may still have been created if it did not already exist.

Error reporting: the openFile computation may fail with isAlreadyInUseError if the file is already open and cannot be reopened; isDoesNotExistError if the file does not exist; or isPermissionError if the user does not have permission to open the file.

21.3.2 Closing Files

Computation hClose *hdl* makes handle *hdl* closed. Before the computation finishes, if *hdl* is writable its buffer is flushed as for hFlush. Performing hClose on a handle that has already been closed has no effect; doing so not an error. All other operations on a closed handle will fail. If hClose fails for any reason, any further operations (apart from hClose) on the handle will still fail as if *hdl* had been successfully closed.

21.4   Determining the Size of a File

For a handle *hdl* which is attached to a physical file, hFileSize *hdl* returns the size of that file in 8-bit bytes (≥ 0).

21.5   Detecting the End of Input

For a readable handle *hdl*, computation hIsEOF *hdl* returns True if no further input can be taken from *hdl*; for a handle attached to a physical file this means that the current I/O position is equal to the length of the file. Otherwise, it returns False. The computation isEOF is identical, except that it works only on stdin.

21.6   Buffering Operations

Three kinds of buffering are supported: line-buffering, block-buffering or no-buffering. These modes have the following effects. For output, items are written out, or *flushed*, from the internal buffer according to the buffer mode:

- **line-buffering:** the entire buffer is flushed whenever a newline is output, the buffer overflows, a hFlush is issued, or the handle is closed.

- **block-buffering:** the entire buffer is written out whenever it overflows, a hFlush is issued, or the handle is closed.

- **no-buffering:** output is written immediately, and never stored in the buffer.

An implementation is free to flush the buffer more frequently, but not less frequently, than specified above. The buffer is emptied as soon as it has been written out.

Similarly, input occurs according to the buffer mode for handle *hdl*.

- **line-buffering:** when the buffer for *hdl* is not empty, the next item is obtained from the buffer; otherwise, when the buffer is empty, characters are read into the buffer until the next newline character is encountered or the buffer is full. No characters are available until the newline character is available or the buffer is full.

- **block-buffering:** when the buffer for *hdl* becomes empty, the next block of data is read into the buffer.

- **no-buffering:** the next input item is read and returned. The `hLookAhead` operation (Section 21.9.3) implies that even a no-buffered handle may require a one-character buffer.

For most implementations, physical files will normally be block-buffered and terminals will normally be line-buffered.

Computation `hSetBuffering` *hdl mode* sets the mode of buffering for handle *hdl* on subsequent reads and writes.

- If *mode* is `LineBuffering`, line-buffering is enabled if possible.

- If *mode* is `BlockBuffering` *size*, then block-buffering is enabled if possible. The size of the buffer is *n* items if *size* is `Just` *n* and is otherwise implementation-dependent.

- If *mode* is `NoBuffering`, then buffering is disabled if possible.

If the buffer mode is changed from `BlockBuffering` or `LineBuffering` to `NoBuffering`, then

- if *hdl* is writable, the buffer is flushed as for `hFlush`;

- if *hdl* is not writable, the contents of the buffer is discarded.

Error reporting: the `hSetBuffering` computation may fail with `isPermissionError` if the handle has already been used for reading or writing and the implementation does not allow the buffering mode to be changed.

Computation `hGetBuffering` *hdl* returns the current buffering mode for *hdl*.

The default buffering mode when a handle is opened is implementation-dependent and may depend on the file system object which is attached to that handle.

21.6.1   Flushing Buffers

Computation `hFlush` *hdl* causes any items buffered for output in handle *hdl* to be sent immediately to the operating system.

Error reporting: the `hFlush` computation may fail with: `isFullError` if the device is full; `isPermissionError` if a system resource limit would be exceeded. It is unspecified whether the characters in the buffer are discarded or retained under these circumstances.

21.7 Repositioning Handles

21.7.1 Revisiting an I/O Position

Computation `hGetPosn` *hdl* returns the current I/O position of *hdl* as a value of the abstract type `HandlePosn`. If a call to `hGetPosn` *h* returns a position *p*, then computation `hSetPosn` *p* sets the position of *h* to the position it held at the time of the call to `hGetPosn`.

Error reporting: the `hSetPosn` computation may fail with: `isPermissionError` if a system resource limit would be exceeded.

21.7.2 Seeking to a New Position

Computation `hSeek` *hdl mode i* sets the position of handle *hdl* depending on *mode*. If *mode* is:

- `AbsoluteSeek`: the position of *hdl* is set to *i*.
- `RelativeSeek`: the position of *hdl* is set to offset *i* from the current position.
- `SeekFromEnd`: the position of *hdl* is set to offset *i* from the end of the file.

The offset is given in terms of 8-bit bytes.

If *hdl* is block- or line-buffered, then seeking to a position which is not in the current buffer will first cause any items in the output buffer to be written to the device, and then cause the input buffer to be discarded. Some handles may not be seekable (see `hIsSeekable`), or only support a subset of the possible positioning operations (for instance, it may only be possible to seek to the end of a tape, or to a positive offset from the beginning or current position). It is not possible to set a negative I/O position, or for a physical file, an I/O position beyond the current end-of-file.

Error reporting: the `hSeek` computation may fail with: `isPermissionError` if a system resource limit would be exceeded.

21.8 Handle Properties

The functions `hIsOpen`, `hIsClosed`, `hIsReadable`, `hIsWritable` and `hIsSeekable` return information about the properties of a handle. Each of these returns `True` if the handle has the specified property, and `False` otherwise.

21.9   Text Input and Output

Here we define a standard set of input operations for reading characters and strings from text files, using handles. Many of these functions are generalizations of Prelude functions. I/O in the Prelude generally uses `stdin` and `stdout`; here, handles are explicitly specified by the I/O operation.

21.9.1   Checking for Input

Computation `hWaitForInput` *hdl* *t* waits until input is available on handle *hdl*. It returns `True` as soon as input is available on *hdl*, or `False` if no input is available within *t* milliseconds.

Computation `hReady` *hdl* indicates whether at least one item is available for input from handle *hdl*.

Error reporting. The `hWaitForInput` and `hReady` computations fail with `isEOFError` if the end of file has been reached.

21.9.2   Reading Input

Computation `hGetChar` *hdl* reads a character from the file or channel managed by *hdl*.

Computation `hGetLine` *hdl* reads a line from the file or channel managed by *hdl*. The Prelude's `getLine` is a shorthand for `hGetLine stdin`.

Error reporting. The `hGetChar` computation fails with `isEOFError` if the end of file has been reached. The `hGetLine` computation fails with `isEOFError` if the end of file is encountered when reading the *first* character of the line. If `hGetLine` encounters end-of-file at any other point while reading in a line, it is treated as a line terminator and the (partial) line is returned.

21.9.3   Reading Ahead

Computation `hLookAhead` *hdl* returns the next character from handle *hdl* without removing it from the input buffer, blocking until a character is available.

Error reporting: the `hLookAhead` computation may fail with: `isEOFError` if the end of file has been reached.

21.9.4   Reading the Entire Input

Computation `hGetContents` *hdl* returns the list of characters corresponding to the unread portion of the channel or file managed by *hdl*, which is made semi-closed.

Error reporting: the hGetContents computation may fail with: isEOFError if the end of file has been reached.

21.9.5 Text Output

Computation hPutChar *hdl* *c* writes the character *c* to the file or channel managed by *hdl*. Characters may be buffered if buffering is enabled for *hdl*.

Computation hPutStr *hdl* *s* writes the string *s* to the file or channel managed by *hdl*.

Computation hPrint *hdl* *t* writes the string representation of *t* given by the shows function to the file or channel managed by *hdl* and appends a newline.

Error reporting: the hPutChar, hPutStr and hPrint computations may fail with: isFull-Error if the device is full; or isPermissionError if another system resource limit would be exceeded.

21.10 Examples

Here are some simple examples to illustrate Haskell I/O.

21.10.1 Summing Two Numbers

This program reads and sums two Integers.

```
import IO

main = do
        hSetBuffering stdout NoBuffering
        putStr    "Enter an integer: "
        x1 <- readNum
        putStr    "Enter another integer: "
        x2 <- readNum
        putStr  ("Their sum is " ++ show (x1+x2) ++ "\n")
    where readNum :: IO Integer
            -- Providing a type signature avoids reliance on
            -- the defaulting rule to fix the type of x1,x2
          readNum = readLn
```

21.10.2   Copying Files

A simple program to create a copy of a file, with all lower-case characters translated to upper-case.
This program will not allow a file to be copied to itself. This version uses character-level I/O. Note
that exactly two arguments must be supplied to the program.

```
import IO
import System
import Char( toUpper )

main = do
          [f1,f2] <- getArgs
          h1 <- openFile f1 ReadMode
          h2 <- openFile f2 WriteMode
          copyFile h1 h2
          hClose h1
          hClose h2

copyFile h1 h2 = do
                    eof <- hIsEOF h1
                    if eof then return () else
                        do
                            c <- hGetChar h1
                            hPutChar h2 (toUpper c)
                            copyFile h1 h2
```

An equivalent but much shorter version, using string I/O is:

```
import System
import Char( toUpper )

main = do
          [f1,f2] <- getArgs
          s <- readFile f1
          writeFile f2 (map toUpper s)
```

21.11   Library IO

```
module IO {- export list omitted -} where

-- Just provide an implementation of the system-independent
-- actions that IO exports.
try            :: IO a -> IO (Either IOError a)
try f          = catch (do r <- f
                           return (Right r))
                       (return . Left)
```

```
bracket          :: IO a -> (a -> IO b) -> (a -> IO c) -> IO c
bracket before after m = do
        x  <- before
        rs <- try (m x)
        after x
        case rs of
           Right r -> return r
           Left  e -> ioError e

-- variant of the above where middle computation doesn't want x
bracket_         :: IO a -> (a -> IO b) -> IO c -> IO c
bracket_ before after m = do
        x  <- before
        rs <- try m
        after x
        case rs of
           Right r -> return r
           Left  e -> ioError e
```

JFP **13** (1): 219–222, January 2003. © 2003 Cambridge University Press
DOI: 10.1017/S0956796803002417 Printed in the United Kingdom

Chapter 22

Directory Functions

```
module Directory (
    Permissions( Permissions, readable, writable, executable, searchable ),
    createDirectory, removeDirectory, removeFile,
    renameDirectory, renameFile, getDirectoryContents,
    getCurrentDirectory, setCurrentDirectory,
    doesFileExist, doesDirectoryExist,
    getPermissions, setPermissions,
    getModificationTime ) where

import Time ( ClockTime )

data Permissions = Permissions {
                    readable,   writable,
                    executable, searchable :: Bool
            }

instance Eq   Permissions where ...
instance Ord  Permissions where ...
instance Read Permissions where ...
instance Show Permissions where ...

createDirectory        :: FilePath -> IO ()
removeDirectory        :: FilePath -> IO ()
removeFile             :: FilePath -> IO ()
renameDirectory        :: FilePath -> FilePath -> IO ()
renameFile             :: FilePath -> FilePath -> IO ()
```

```
getDirectoryContents     :: FilePath -> IO [FilePath]
getCurrentDirectory      :: IO FilePath
setCurrentDirectory      :: FilePath -> IO ()

doesFileExist            :: FilePath -> IO Bool
doesDirectoryExist       :: FilePath -> IO Bool

getPermissions           :: FilePath -> IO Permissions
setPermissions           :: FilePath -> Permissions -> IO ()

getModificationTime      :: FilePath -> IO ClockTime
```

These functions operate on directories in the file system.

Any `Directory` operation could raise an `isIllegalOperation`, as described in Section 21.1; all other permissible errors are described below. Note that, in particular, if an implementation does not support an operation it should raise an `isIllegalOperation`. A directory contains a series of entries, each of which is a named reference to a file system object (file, directory etc.). Some entries may be hidden, inaccessible, or have some administrative function (for instance, "." or ".." under POSIX), but all such entries are considered to form part of the directory contents. Entries in sub-directories are not, however, considered to form part of the directory contents. Although there may be file system objects other than files and directories, this library does not distinguish between physical files and other non-directory objects. All such objects should therefore be treated as if they are files.

Each file system object is referenced by a *path*. There is normally at least one absolute path to each file system object. In some operating systems, it may also be possible to have paths which are relative to the current directory.

Computation `createDirectory` *dir* creates a new directory *dir* which is initially empty, or as near to empty as the operating system allows.

Error reporting. The `createDirectory` computation may fail with: `isPermissionError` if the user is not permitted to create the directory; `isAlreadyExistsError` if the directory already exists; or `isDoesNotExistError` if the new directory's parent does not exist.

Computation `removeDirectory` *dir* removes an existing directory *dir*. The implementation may specify additional constraints which must be satisfied before a directory can be removed (for instance, the directory has to be empty, or may not be in use by other processes). It is not legal for an implementation to partially remove a directory unless the entire directory is removed. A conformant implementation need not support directory removal in all situations (for instance, removal of the root directory).

Computation `removeFile` *file* removes the directory entry for an existing file *file*, where *file* is not itself a directory. The implementation may specify additional constraints which must be satisfied before a file can be removed (for instance, the file may not be in use by other processes).

Error reporting. The `removeDirectory` and `removeFile` computations may fail with `isPermissionError` if the user is not permitted to remove the file/directory; or `isDoesNotExistError` if the file/directory does not exist.

Computation `renameDirectory` *old new* changes the name of an existing directory from *old* to *new*. If the *new* directory already exists, it is atomically replaced by the *old* directory. If the *new* directory is neither the *old* directory nor an alias of the *old* directory, it is removed as if by `removeDirectory`. A conformant implementation need not support renaming directories in all situations (for instance, renaming to an existing directory, or across different physical devices), but the constraints must be documented.

Computation `renameFile` *old new* changes the name of an existing file system object from *old* to *new*. If the *new* object already exists, it is atomically replaced by the *old* object. Neither path may refer to an existing directory. A conformant implementation need not support renaming files in all situations (for instance, renaming across different physical devices), but the constraints must be documented.

Error reporting. The `renameDirectory` and `renameFile` computations may fail with: `isPermissionError` if the user is not permitted to rename the file/directory, or if either argument to `renameFile` is a directory; or `isDoesNotExistError` if the file/directory does not exist.

Computation `getDirectoryContents` *dir* returns a list of *all* entries in *dir*. Each entry in the returned list is named relative to the directory *dir*, not as an absolute path.

If the operating system has a notion of current directories, `getCurrentDirectory` returns an absolute path to the current directory of the calling process.

Error reporting. The `getDirectoryContents` and `getCurrentDirectory` computations may fail with: `isPermissionError` if the user is not permitted to access the directory; or `isDoesNotExistError` if the directory does not exist.

If the operating system has a notion of current directories, `setCurrentDirectory` *dir* changes the current directory of the calling process to *dir*.

Error reporting. `setCurrentDirectory` may fail with: `isPermissionError` if the user is not permitted to change directory to that specified; or `isDoesNotExistError` if the directory does not exist.

The `Permissions` type is used to record whether certain operations are permissible on a file/ directory. `getPermissions` and `setPermissions` get and set these permissions, respectively. Permissions apply both to files and directories. For directories, the `executable` field will be `False`, and for files the `searchable` field will be `False`. Note that directories may be searchable without being readable, if permission has been given to use them as part of a path, but not to examine the directory contents.

Note that to change some, but not all permissions, a construct on the following lines must be used.

```
makeReadable f = do
                p <- getPermissions f
                setPermissions f (p {readable = True})
```

The operation `doesDirectoryExist` returns `True` if the argument file exists and is a directory, and `False` otherwise. The operation `doesFileExist` returns `True` if the argument file exists and is not a directory, and `False` otherwise.

The `getModificationTime` operation returns the clock time at which the file/directory was last modified.

Error reporting. `get(set)Permissions`, `doesFile(Directory)Exist` and `getMod-ificationTime` may fail with: `isPermissionError` if the user is not permitted to access the appropriate information; or `isDoesNotExistError` if the file/directory does not exist. The `setPermissions` computation may also fail with: `isPermissionError` if the user is not permitted to change the permission for the specified file or directory; or `isDoesNotExistError` if the file/directory does not exist.

JFP **13** (1): 223–224, January 2003. © 2003 Cambridge University Press
DOI: 10.1017/S095679680300251X Printed in the United Kingdom

Chapter 23

System Functions

```
module System (
    ExitCode(ExitSuccess,ExitFailure),
    getArgs, getProgName, getEnv, system, exitWith, exitFailure
  ) where

data ExitCode = ExitSuccess | ExitFailure Int
                deriving (Eq, Ord, Read, Show)

getArgs               :: IO [String]
getProgName           :: IO String
getEnv                :: String -> IO String
system                :: String -> IO ExitCode
exitWith              :: ExitCode -> IO a
exitFailure           :: IO a
```

This library describes the interaction of the program with the operating system.

Any System operation could raise an isIllegalOperation, as described in Section 21.1; all other permissible errors are described below. Note that, in particular, if an implementation does not support an operation it must raise an isIllegalOperation.

The ExitCode type defines the exit codes that a program can return. ExitSuccess indicates successful termination; and ExitFailure *code* indicates program failure with value *code*. The exact interpretation of *code* is operating-system dependent. In particular, some values of *code* may be prohibited (for instance, 0 on a POSIX-compliant system).

Computation `getArgs` returns a list of the program's command line arguments (not including the program name). Computation `getProgName` returns the name of the program as it was invoked. Computation `getEnv` *var* returns the value of the environment variable *var*. If variable *var* is undefined, the `isDoesNotExistError` exception is raised.

Computation `system` *cmd* returns the exit code produced when the operating system processes the command *cmd*.

Computation `exitWith` *code* terminates the program, returning *code* to the program's caller. Before the program terminates, any open or semi-closed handles are first closed. The caller may interpret the return code as it wishes, but the program should return `ExitSuccess` to mean normal completion, and `ExitFailure` *n* to mean that the program encountered a problem from which it could not recover. The value `exitFailure` is equal to `exitWith` (`ExitFailure` *exitfail*), where *exitfail* is implementation-dependent. `exitWith` bypasses the error handling in the I/O monad and cannot be intercepted by `catch`.

If a program terminates as a result of calling `error` or because its value is otherwise determined to be ⊥, then it is treated identically to the computation `exitFailure`. Otherwise, if any program *p* terminates without calling `exitWith` explicitly, it is treated identically to the computation

```
(p >> exitWith ExitSuccess) 'catch' \ _ -> exitFailure
```

JFP **13** (1): 225–230, January 2003.   © 2003 Cambridge University Press
DOI: 10.1017/S0956796803002612   Printed in the United Kingdom

Chapter 24

Dates and Times

```
module Time (
        ClockTime,
        Month(January,February,March,April,May,June,
             July,August,September,October,November,December),
        Day(Sunday,Monday,Tuesday,Wednesday,Thursday,Friday,Saturday),
        CalendarTime(CalendarTime, ctYear, ctMonth, ctDay, ctHour, ctMin,
                    ctSec, ctPicosec, ctWDay, ctYDay,
                    ctTZName, ctTZ, ctIsDST),
        TimeDiff(TimeDiff, tdYear, tdMonth, tdDay, tdHour,
             tdMin, tdSec, tdPicosec),
        getClockTime, addToClockTime, diffClockTimes,
        toCalendarTime, toUTCTime, toClockTime,
        calendarTimeToString, formatCalendarTime ) where

import Ix(Ix)

data ClockTime = ...                     -- Implementation-dependent
instance Ord  ClockTime where ...
instance Eq   ClockTime where ...

data Month =  January   | February | March    | April
            | May       | June     | July     | August
            | September | October  | November | December
           deriving (Eq, Ord, Enum, Bounded, Ix, Read, Show)

data Day   = Sunday | Monday | Tuesday  | Wednesday | Thursday
            | Friday | Saturday
           deriving (Eq, Ord, Enum, Bounded, Ix, Read, Show)
```

```
data CalendarTime = CalendarTime {
                ctYear                          :: Int,
                ctMonth                         :: Month,
                ctDay, ctHour, ctMin, ctSec     :: Int,
                ctPicosec                       :: Integer,
                ctWDay                          :: Day,
                ctYDay                          :: Int,
                ctTZName                        :: String,
                ctTZ                            :: Int,
                ctIsDST                         :: Bool
        } deriving (Eq, Ord, Read, Show)

data TimeDiff = TimeDiff {
                tdYear, tdMonth, tdDay, tdHour, tdMin, tdSec :: Int,
                tdPicosec                            :: Integer
        } deriving (Eq, Ord, Read, Show) -- Functions on times
getClockTime            :: IO ClockTime

addToClockTime          :: TimeDiff  -> ClockTime -> ClockTime
diffClockTimes          :: ClockTime -> ClockTime -> TimeDiff

toCalendarTime          :: ClockTime    -> IO CalendarTime
toUTCTime               :: ClockTime    -> CalendarTime
toClockTime             :: CalendarTime -> ClockTime
calendarTimeToString :: CalendarTime -> String
formatCalendarTime      :: TimeLocale -> String -> CalendarTime -> String
```

The `Time` library provides standard functionality for clock times, including timezone information. It follows RFC 1129 in its use of Coordinated Universal Time (UTC).

`ClockTime` is an abstract type, used for the system's internal clock time. Clock times may be compared directly or converted to a calendar time `CalendarTime` for I/O or other manipulations. `CalendarTime` is a user-readable and manipulable representation of the internal `ClockTime` type. The numeric fields have the following ranges.

Value	Range	Comments
ctYear	-maxInt ... maxInt	Pre-Gregorian dates are inaccurate
ctDay	1 ... 31	
ctHour	0 ... 23	
ctMin	0 ... 59	
ctSec	0 ... 61	Allows for two Leap Seconds
ctPicosec	$0 ... (10^{12}) - 1$	
ctYDay	0 ... 365	364 in non-Leap years
ctTZ	-89999 ... 89999	Variation from UTC in seconds

The *ctTZName* field is the name of the time zone. The *ctIsDST* field is `True` if Daylight Savings Time would be in effect, and `False` otherwise. The `TimeDiff` type records the difference between two clock times in a user-readable way.

Function `getClockTime` returns the current time in its internal representation. The expression `addToClockTime` *d* *t* adds a time difference *d* and a clock time *t* to yield a new clock time. The difference *d* may be either positive or negative. The expression `diffClockTimes` *t1* *t2* returns the difference between two clock times *t1* and *t2* as a `TimeDiff`.

Function `toCalendarTime` *t* converts *t* to a local time, modified by the timezone and daylight savings time settings in force at the time of conversion. Because of this dependence on the local environment, `toCalendarTime` is in the IO monad.

Function `toUTCTime` *t* converts *t* into a `CalendarTime` in standard UTC format. `toClockTime` *l* converts *l* into the corresponding internal `ClockTime` ignoring the contents of the *ctWDay*, *ctYDay*, *ctTZName*, and *ctIsDST* fields.

Function `calendarTimeToString` formats calendar times using local conventions and a formatting string.

24.1 Library `Time`

```
module Time (
        ClockTime,
        Month(January,February,March,April,May,June,
                July,August,September,October,November,December),
        Day(Sunday,Monday,Tuesday,Wednesday,Thursday,Friday,Saturday),
        CalendarTime(CalendarTime, ctYear, ctMonth, ctDay, ctHour, ctMin,
                ctSec, ctPicosec, ctWDay, ctYDay,
                ctTZName, ctTZ, ctIsDST),
        TimeDiff(TimeDiff, tdYear, tdMonth, tdDay,
                tdHour, tdMin, tdSec, tdPicosec),
        getClockTime, addToClockTime, diffClockTimes,
        toCalendarTime, toUTCTime, toClockTime,
        calendarTimeToString, formatCalendarTime ) where

import Ix(Ix)
import Locale(TimeLocale(..),defaultTimeLocale)
import Char ( intToDigit )

data ClockTime = ...                         -- Implementation-dependent
instance Ord  ClockTime where ...
instance Eq   ClockTime where ...

data Month =  January    | February | March     | April
           |  May        | June     | July       | August
           |  September   | October  | November   | December
            deriving (Eq, Ord, Enum, Bounded, Ix, Read, Show)

data Day   =  Sunday | Monday  | Tuesday  | Wednesday | Thursday
           |  Friday | Saturday
            deriving (Eq, Ord, Enum, Bounded, Ix, Read, Show)
```

```haskell
data CalendarTime = CalendarTime {
                ctYear                       :: Int,
                ctMonth                      :: Month,
                ctDay, ctHour, ctMin, ctSec  :: Int,
                ctPicosec                    :: Integer,
                ctWDay                       :: Day,
                ctYDay                       :: Int,
                ctTZName                     :: String,
                ctTZ                         :: Int,
                ctIsDST                      :: Bool
        } deriving (Eq, Ord, Read, Show)

data TimeDiff = TimeDiff {
                tdYear, tdMonth, tdDay, tdHour, tdMin, tdSec :: Int,
                tdPicosec                                    :: Integer
        } deriving (Eq, Ord, Read, Show)

getClockTime            :: IO ClockTime
getClockTime            = ...                 -- Implementation-dependent

addToClockTime          :: TimeDiff    -> ClockTime -> ClockTime
addToClockTime td ct    = ...                 -- Implementation-dependent

diffClockTimes          :: ClockTime   -> ClockTime -> TimeDiff
diffClockTimes ct1 ct2  = ...                 -- Implementation-dependent

toCalendarTime          :: ClockTime   -> IO CalendarTime
toCalendarTime ct       = ...                 -- Implementation-dependent

toUTCTime               :: ClockTime   -> CalendarTime
toUTCTime ct            = ...                 -- Implementation-dependent

toClockTime             :: CalendarTime -> ClockTime
toClockTime cal         = ...                 -- Implementation-dependent

calendarTimeToString    :: CalendarTime -> String
calendarTimeToString    = formatCalendarTime defaultTimeLocale "%c"
```

```
formatCalendarTime :: TimeLocale -> String -> CalendarTime -> String
formatCalendarTime l fmt ct@(CalendarTime year mon day hour min sec sdec
                                          wday yday tzname _ _) =
        doFmt fmt
  where doFmt ('%':c:cs) = decode c ++ doFmt cs
        doFmt (c:cs) = c : doFmt cs
        doFmt "" = ""

        to12 :: Int -> Int
        to12 h = let h' = h 'mod' 12 in if h' == 0 then 12 else h'

        decode 'A' = fst (wDays l !! fromEnum wday)
        decode 'a' = snd (wDays l !! fromEnum wday)
        decode 'B' = fst (months l !! fromEnum mon)
        decode 'b' = snd (months l !! fromEnum mon)
        decode 'h' = snd (months l !! fromEnum mon)
        decode 'C' = show2 (year 'quot' 100)
        decode 'c' = doFmt (dateTimeFmt l)
        decode 'D' = doFmt "%m/%d/%y"
        decode 'd' = show2 day
        decode 'e' = show2' day
        decode 'H' = show2 hour
        decode 'I' = show2 (to12 hour)
        decode 'j' = show3 yday
        decode 'k' = show2' hour
        decode 'l' = show2' (to12 hour)
        decode 'M' = show2 min
        decode 'm' = show2 (fromEnum mon+1)
        decode 'n' = "\n"
        decode 'p' = (if hour < 12 then fst else snd) (amPm l)
        decode 'R' = doFmt "%H:%M"
        decode 'r' = doFmt (time12Fmt l)
        decode 'T' = doFmt "%H:%M:%S"
        decode 't' = "\t"
        decode 'S' = show2 sec
        decode 's' = ...                    -- Implementation-dependent
        decode 'U' = show2 ((yday + 7 - fromEnum wday) 'div' 7)
        decode 'u' = show (let n = fromEnum wday in
                              if n == 0 then 7 else n)
        decode 'V' =
            let (week, days) =
                    (yday + 7 - if fromEnum wday > 0 then
                                  fromEnum wday - 1 else 6) 'divMod' 7
            in  show2 (if days >= 4 then
                          week+1
                       else if week == 0 then 53 else week)
        decode 'W' =
            show2 ((yday + 7 - if fromEnum wday > 0 then
                                  fromEnum wday - 1 else 6) 'div' 7)
```

```
        decode 'w' = show (fromEnum wday)
        decode 'X' = doFmt (timeFmt l)
        decode 'x' = doFmt (dateFmt l)
        decode 'Y' = show year
        decode 'y' = show2 (year 'rem' 100)
        decode 'Z' = tzname
        decode '%' = "%"
        decode c   = [c]

show2, show2', show3 :: Int -> String
show2 x = [intToDigit (x 'quot' 10), intToDigit (x 'rem' 10)]

show2' x = if x < 10 then [ ' ', intToDigit x] else show2 x

show3 x = intToDigit (x 'quot' 100) : show2 (x 'rem' 100)
```

JFP **13** (1): 231–232, January 2003. © 2003 Cambridge University Press
DOI: 10.1017/S0956796803002715 Printed in the United Kingdom

Chapter 25

Locales

```
module Locale(TimeLocale(..), defaultTimeLocale) where

data TimeLocale = TimeLocale {
        wDays  :: [(String, String)],   -- full and abbreviated week days
        months :: [(String, String)],   -- full and abbreviated months
        amPm   :: (String, String),     -- AM/PM symbols
        dateTimeFmt, dateFmt,           -- formatting strings
          timeFmt, time12Fmt :: String
        } deriving (Eq, Ord, Show)

defaultTimeLocale :: TimeLocale
```

The `Locale` library provides the ability to adapt to local conventions. At present, it supports only time and date information as used by `calendarTimeToString` from the `Time` library.

25.1   Library `Locale`

```
module Locale(TimeLocale(..), defaultTimeLocale) where

data TimeLocale = TimeLocale {
        wDays  :: [(String, String)],   -- full and abbreviated week days
        months :: [(String, String)],   -- full and abbreviated months
        amPm   :: (String, String),     -- AM/PM symbols
        dateTimeFmt, dateFmt,           -- formatting strings
          timeFmt, time12Fmt :: String
        } deriving (Eq, Ord, Show)
```

```
defaultTimeLocale :: TimeLocale
defaultTimeLocale =  TimeLocale {
        wDays  = [("Sunday",    "Sun"),  ("Monday",    "Mon"),
                  ("Tuesday",   "Tue"),  ("Wednesday", "Wed"),
                  ("Thursday",  "Thu"),  ("Friday",    "Fri"),
                  ("Saturday",  "Sat")],

        months = [("January",   "Jan"), ("February",   "Feb"),
                  ("March",     "Mar"), ("April",      "Apr"),
                  ("May",       "May"), ("June",       "Jun"),
                  ("July",      "Jul"), ("August",     "Aug"),
                  ("September", "Sep"), ("October",    "Oct"),
                  ("November",  "Nov"), ("December",   "Dec")],

        amPm = ("AM", "PM"),
        dateTimeFmt = "%a %b %e %H:%M:%S %Z %Y",
        dateFmt = "%m/%d/%y",
        timeFmt = "%H:%M:%S",
        time12Fmt = "%I:%M:%S %p"
        }
```

JFP **13** (1): 233–234, January 2003. © 2003 Cambridge University Press
DOI: 10.1017/S0956796803002818 Printed in the United Kingdom

Chapter 26

CPU Time

```
module CPUTime ( getCPUTime, cpuTimePrecision ) where

getCPUTime        :: IO Integer
cpuTimePrecision  :: Integer
```

Computation `getCPUTime` returns the number of picoseconds of CPU time used by the current program. The precision of this result is given by `cpuTimePrecision`. This is the smallest measurable difference in CPU time that the implementation can record, and is given as an integral number of picoseconds.

JFP **13** (1): 235–240, January 2003. © 2003 Cambridge University Press
DOI: 10.1017/S0956796803002910 Printed in the United Kingdom

Chapter 27

Random Numbers

```
module Random (
        RandomGen(next, split, genRange),
        StdGen, mkStdGen,
        Random( random,    randomR,
                randoms,   randomRs,
                randomIO,  randomRIO ),
        getStdRandom, getStdGen, setStdGen, newStdGen
  ) where

--------------- The RandomGen class ----------------------
class RandomGen g where
  genRange :: g -> (Int, Int)
  next     :: g -> (Int, g)
  split    :: g -> (g, g)

--------------- A standard instance of RandomGen -----------
data StdGen = ...        -- Abstract

instance RandomGen StdGen where ...
instance Read      StdGen where ...
instance Show      StdGen where ...

mkStdGen :: Int -> StdGen
```

```
---------------- The Random class ---------------------------
class Random a where
    randomR :: RandomGen g => (a, a) -> g -> (a, g)
    random  :: RandomGen g => g -> (a, g)

    randomRs :: RandomGen g => (a, a) -> g -> [a]
    randoms  :: RandomGen g => g -> [a]

    randomRIO :: (a,a) -> IO a
    randomIO  :: IO a

instance Random Int      where ...
instance Random Integer  where ...
instance Random Float    where ...
instance Random Double   where ...
instance Random Bool     where ...
instance Random Char     where ...

---------------- The global random generator ----------------
newStdGen      :: IO StdGen
setStdGen      :: StdGen -> IO ()
getStdGen      :: IO StdGen
getStdRandom :: (StdGen -> (a, StdGen)) -> IO a
```

The Random library deals with the common task of pseudo-random number generation. The library makes it possible to generate repeatable results, by starting with a specified initial random number generator; or to get different results on each run by using the system-initialised generator, or by supplying a seed from some other source.

The library is split into two layers:

- A core *random number generator* provides a supply of bits. The class RandomGen provides a common interface to such generators.

- The class Random provides a way to extract particular values from a random number generator. For example, the Float instance of Random allows one to generate random values of type Float.

27.1   The RandomGen class, and the StdGen generator

The class RandomGen provides a common interface to random number generators.

```
class RandomGen g where
  genRange :: g -> (Int,Int)
  next     :: g -> (Int, g)
  split    :: g -> (g, g)

  -- Default method
  genRange g = (minBound,maxBound)
```

- The `genRange` operation yields the range of values returned by the generator. It is required that:

  - If $(a, b) =$ `genRange` g, then $a < b$.
  - `genRange` $\perp \neq \perp$.

  The second condition ensures that `genRange` cannot examine its argument, and hence the value it returns can be determined only by the instance of `RandomGen`. That in turn allows an implementation to make a single call to `genRange` to establish a generator's range, without being concerned that the generator returned by (say) `next` might have a different range to the generator passed to `next`.

- The `next` operation returns an `Int` that is uniformly distributed in the range returned by `genRange` (including both end points), and a new generator.

- The `split` operation allows one to obtain two independent random number generators. This is very useful in functional programs (for example, when passing a random number generator down to recursive calls), but very little work has been done on statistically robust implementations of `split` (Burton and Page [2] and Hellekalek [7]] are the only examples we know of).

The `Random` library provides one instance of `RandomGen`, the abstract data type `StdGen`:

```
data StdGen = ...       -- Abstract

instance RandomGen StdGen where ...
instance Read      StdGen where ...
instance Show      StdGen where ...

mkStdGen :: Int -> StdGen
```

The `StgGen` instance of `RandomGen` has a `genRange` of at least 30 bits.

The result of repeatedly using `next` should be at least as statistically robust as the "Minimal Standard Random Number Generator" described by Park and Miller [12] and Carta [3]. Until more is known about implementations of `split`, all we require is that `split` deliver generators that are (a) not identical and (b) independently robust in the sense just given.

The `Show/Read` instances of `StdGen` provide a primitive way to save the state of a random number generator. It is required that `read (show g) == g`.

In addition, `read` may be used to map an arbitrary string (not necessarily one produced by `show`) onto a value of type `StdGen`. In general, the `read` instance of `StdGen` has the following properties:

- It guarantees to succeed on any string.

- It guarantees to consume only a finite portion of the string.

- Different argument strings are likely to result in different results.

The function `mkStdGen` provides an alternative way of producing an initial generator, by mapping an `Int` into a generator. Again, distinct arguments should be likely to produce distinct generators.

Programmers may, of course, supply their own instances of `RandomGen`.

Implementation warning. A superficially attractive implementation of `split` is

```
instance RandomGen MyGen where
  ...
  split g = (g, variantOf g)
```

Here, `split` returns `g` itself and a new generator derived from `g`. But now consider these two apparently-independent generators:

```
g1 = snd (split g)
g2 = snd (split (fst (split g)))
```

If `split` genuinely delivers independent generators (as specified), then `g1` and `g2` should be independent, but in fact they are both equal to `variantOf` `g`. Implementations of the above form do not meet the specification.

27.2 The Random class

With a source of random number supply in hand, the Random class allows the programmer to extract random values of a variety of types:

```
class Random a where
    randomR :: RandomGen g => (a, a) -> g -> (a, g)
    random  :: RandomGen g => g -> (a, g)

    randomRs :: RandomGen g => (a, a) -> g -> [a]
    randoms  :: RandomGen g => g -> [a]

    randomRIO :: (a,a) -> IO a
    randomIO :: IO a

      -- Default methods
    randoms g = x : randoms g'
                    where
                        (x,g') = random g
    randomRs = ...similar...

    randomIO       = getStdRandom random
    randomRIO range = getStdRandom (randomR range)

instance Random Int      where ...
instance Random Integer  where ...
instance Random Float    where ...
instance Random Double   where ...
instance Random Bool     where ...
instance Random Char     where ...
```

- randomR takes a range (lo, hi) and a random number generator g, and returns a random value uniformly distributed in the closed interval $[lo, hi]$, together with a new generator. It is unspecified what happens if $lo > hi$. For continuous types there is no requirement that the values lo and hi are ever produced, but they may be, depending on the implementation and the interval.

- random does the same as randomR, but does not take a range.

    - For bounded types (instances of Bounded, such as Char), the range is normally the whole type.

    - For fractional types, the range is normally the semi-closed interval $[0, 1)$.

    - For Integer, the range is (arbitrarily) the range of Int.

- The plural versions, randomRs and randoms, produce an infinite list of random values, and do not return a new generator.

- The IO versions, `randomRIO` and `randomIO`, use the global random number generator (see Section 27.3).

27.3   The global random number generator

There is a single, implicit, global random number generator of type `StdGen`, held in some global variable maintained by the IO monad. It is initialised automatically in some system-dependent fashion, for example, by using the time of day, or Linux's kernel random number generator. To get deterministic behaviour, use `setStdGen`.

```
setStdGen    :: StdGen -> IO ()
getStdGen    :: IO StdGen
newStdGen    :: IO StdGen
getStdRandom :: (StdGen -> (a, StdGen)) -> IO a
```

- `getStdGen` and `setStdGen` get and set the global random number generator, respectively.

- `newStdGen` applies `split` to the current global random generator, updates it with one of the results, and returns the other.

- `getStdRandom` uses the supplied function to get a value from the current global random generator, and updates the global generator with the new generator returned by the function. For example, `rollDice` gets a random integer between 1 and 6:

```
rollDice :: IO Int
rollDice = getStdRandom (randomR (1,6))
```

The Web site `http://random.mat.sbg.ac.at/` is a great source of information.

JFP **13** (1): 241–255, January 2003. © 2003 Cambridge University Press
DOI: 10.1017/S0956796803003010 Printed in the United Kingdom

Bibliography

[1] J. Backus. Can programming be liberated from the von Neumann style? A functional style and its algebra of programs. *CACM*, 21(8):613–641, August 1978.

[2] F. W. Burton and R. L. Page. Distributed random number generation. *Journal of Functional Programming*, 2(2), 203–212, April 1992.

[3] D. G. Carta. Two fast implementations of the minimal standard random number generator. *CACM*, 33(1), 87-88, January 1990.

[4] H.B. Curry and R. Feys. *Combinatory Logic*. North-Holland Pub. Co., Amsterdam, 1958.

[5] L. Damas and R. Milner. Principal type schemes for functional programs. In *Proceedings of the 9th ACM Symposium on Principles of Programming Languages*, pages 207–212, Albuquerque, N.M., January 1982.

[6] K-F. Faxén A static semantics for Haskell *Journal of Functional Programming*, 12(4), 295–358, July 2002.

[7] P. Hellekalek. Don't trust parallel Monte Carlo. *ACM Simulation Digest*, 28(1):82–89, July 1998.

[8] J.R. Hindley. The principal type scheme of an object in combinatory logic. *Transactions of the American Mathematical Society*, 146:29–60, December 1969.

[9] P. Hudak, J. Fasel, and J. Peterson. A gentle introduction to Haskell. Technical Report YALEU/DCS/RR-901, Yale University, May 1996.

[10] Mark P. Jones. A system of constructor classes: overloading and implicit higher-order polymorphism. *Journal of Functional Programming*, 5(1), January 1995.

[11] Mark P. Jones. Typing Haskell in Haskell. *Haskell Workshop*, Paris, October 1999.

[12] S. K. Park and K. W. Miller. Random number generators – good ones are hard to find. *CACM*, 31(10), 1192–1201, October 1988.

[13] P. Penfield, Jr. Principal values and branch cuts in complex APL. In *APL '81 Conference Proceedings*, pages 248–256, San Francisco, September 1981.

[14] S.L. Peyton Jones. *The Implementation of Functional Programming Languages*. Prentice-Hall International, Englewood Cliffs, New Jersey, 1987.

[15] Unicode Consortium. *Unicode Character Data and Mappings*. `http://unicode.org`.

[16] P. Wadler and S. Blott. How to make *ad hoc* polymorphism less *ad hoc*. In *Proceedings of the 16th ACM Symposium on Principles of Programming Languages*, pages 60–76, Austin, Texas, January 1989.

Index

Index entries that refer to nonterminals in the Haskell syntax are shown in an *italic* font. Code entities are shown in `typewriter` font. Ordinary index entries are shown in a roman font.

!, 47, 173, 174, 176, 177
!!, 57, 114, 115
$, 57, 105, 110
$!, 105, 110
%, 149, 150
&&, 57, 81, 105, 110
(,), 83
(, ,), 83
( ), *see* trivial type and unit expression
*, 57, 92, 93, 105, 106
**, 57, 93, 105, 107
+, 57, 92, 93, 105, 106, *see also* $n+k$ pattern
++, 57, 114
−, 57, 92, 93, 105, 106, *see also* negation
., 57, 83, 105, 110
/, 57, 92, 93, 105, 107
//, 173, 175–177
/=, 57, 86, 105, 140
:, 57, 82
:+, 153, 154
::, 32
<, 57, 86, 105, 140
<=, 57, 86, 105, 140
=<<, 90, 105, 109
==, 57, 86, 105, 140
>, 57, 86, 105, 140
>=, 57, 86, 105, 140
>>, 57, 90, 99, 105, 109
>>=, 57, 90, 99, 105, 109
@, *see* as-pattern
[ ] (nil), 82
⊥, 19, 224
\\, 179, 180, 185
\, *see* lambda abstraction
\a, 12
\b, 12
\f, 12
\n, 12

\r, 12
\t, 12
\v, 12
\&, 12
\\, 181
^, 57, 93, 94, 105, 109
^^, 57, 93, 94, 105, 109
_, *see* wildcard pattern
| |, 57, 81, 105, 110
˜, *see* irrefutable pattern

abbreviated module, 69
abs, 93, 94, 106
AbsoluteSeek, 213
abstract datatype, 46, 78
accum, 173, 175, 177
accumArray, 173, 175, 177
acos, 93, 107
acosh, 93, 107
addToClockTime, 226, 228
aexp, 18, 22, 24–26, 136
algebraic datatype, 45, 69, 139
all, 118
alt, 27, 136
alts, 27, 136
ambiguous type, 53, 64
and, 118
ANY, 9, 127
any, 9, 127
any, 118
ANYseq, 9, 127
ap, 199, 203
apat, 33, 137
appendFile, 99, 124
AppendMode, 210
application, 21
    function, *see* function application
    operator, *see* operator application
approxRational, 94, 95, 149, 150

243